STUDIES IN FRENCH LITERATURE

XVII

THE ART OF ANATOLE FRANCE

by

DUSHAN BRESKY

The University of Calgary

1969

MOUTON

THE HAGUE · PARIS

LIBRARY OF CONGRESS CATALOG CARD NUMBER: 69-31896

Printed in The Netherlands by Mouton & Co., Printers, The Hague.

To Lou

D. B.

ACKNOWLEDGEMENTS

This work has been published with the help of a grant from the Humanities Research Council of Canada using funds provided by the Canada Council. To these institutions as well as to the reading committee headed by Dr. H. M. Estall I am extending my thanks. I would also like to express my appreciation to The University of Calgary for the research grant which enabled me to revise and considerably extend my 1962 thesis into its present book form. I further gratefully acknowledge the valuable assistance of Dr. Seymour S. Weiner, Mr. Jean Chessex, Dr. Abe Keller, Dr. J. G. Andison, Mr. François d'A. Fleury, Dr. Anthony A. Greaves, Mr. Henri Mydlarski, Mr. Thomas Daigle, Mrs. Margaret Hopwood, Mrs. Hendrika Krol, Mrs. Margaret Brydon and Louise Bresky.

D.B.

TABLE OF CONTENTS

INTRODUCTION

The year Anatole France died, one of his critics characterized the man and his work as a "happy genius".[1] In spite of several personal crises which made his private life far from idyllic, the same epithet could be applied to the history of his creative adventures. He was also a "happy" genius because, for many years of his long literary career, he witnessed in person a steady increase in his literary fame and attained the highest honors any French writer could dream of receiving. Elected to the *Académie Française* in 1896, he became "immortal" long before he completed masterpieces such as *Le Lys rouge, Les Dieux ont soif, Clio* and *La Révolte des Anges.* His international renown reached its peak on the threshold of a new era, after the First World War, when he was awarded the Nobel Prize. But at that time the young French arty set around the surrealist pope Breton saw in him "a living corpse". It was clear that France's star would not shine long. It was obscured by a new haze of experimental art and the sombre clouds of a rather grave moralism (à la Gide, à la Claudel, or à la Montherlant). Soon after his death his literary fame suffered a *baisse.* Perhaps the civilized humanism of this leftish intellectual was not conservative enough for the avant-garde in the twenties: France resurrected only the Graeco-Roman heritage, whereas the true moderns of his later years dreamed of returning much further back. Ch. L. Philippe writes to André Gide: "The days of gentleness and dilettantism are gone, what we need now are the barbars . . . Anatole France is delightful, he knows everything,

[1] Gonzaque Truc, *Anatole France, L'artiste et le penseur* (Paris, Garnier, 1924), p. 147.

he is even erudite; that's why he belongs to the dead race of writers, that's why he marks the end of the XIX century."[2]

Another cause of the rather sudden downgrading of France's life work was a wave of international scholarly criticism from which, so far, the "happy genius" has not fully recovered. Apart from the Christian, especially Catholic, and Marxist doctrinaires, the anti-Francean trend was established by Barry Cerf. This critic accused France of having no purpose in life and of being unable to solve its great problems aesthetically with fire and virile drive.

Where there is no conviction, seriousness, or purpose, fire and virile strength are lacking. And so is explained the effeminate indolence, the lack of drive, of forward movement, of intensity, the nonchalance and indifference of France, which set him apart from the really great writers and make of his works, not things vibrant with life, but collections of ingeniously-wrought gems.[3]

Walter Gottschalk was probably not familiar with Cerf's monograph when his *France, der Dichter und sein Werk* appeared in Germany only one year later, but he reaches similar conclusions. He misses in France's

[2] Cited by André Cuisenier in *L'art de Jules Romains, Jules Romains et l'unanimisme* (Paris, Flammarion [c] 1948), Vol. II, p. 14 (my translation). Reviewing Jean Levaillant's *Essai sur l'évolution intellectuelle d'Anatole France* (see this introduction, n. 16), an anonymous critic offers several practical and general reasons for France's "posthumous bad luck": "First, he was immensely successful during his lifetime, and was probably oversold. Second, he was very much a writer of his time, and that time has not yet revolved. Third, his style, admirably clear as it is, dates badly. But these are details: what really jars is that in substance even more than in style, he was an Olympian; and this manner of thought is profoundly unfashionable. ... A generation which contains Sartre and has invented that curious artefact, human dignity, will not admire a hero of whom the author says: "Il n'aurait pas signé une ligne de la Déclaration des droits de l'homme, à cause de l'excessive et inique séparation qui y est établie entre l'homme et le gorille." ... The present age is Dionysian, not Olympian. We take human existence, human dignity, commitment and a host of other semi-religious concepts very solemnly, and if anyone does not accept our views we take him into the mountains and rend him to pieces. The contemporary gods are chthonic, splanchnic and desperately serious. The approved line in literature and politics is (if one may over-simplify) the Lawrence-Leavis-Lumumba line: all very harsh and above all committed, with a tendency to thrust down into hell anyone who does not accept the Thought of Chairman L. whoever L. may happen to be ... "Olympus Redivivus? Anatole France's Reputation", *The Times Literary Supplement,* Sept. 29, 1966, No. 3, p. 370.

[3] Barry Cerf, *Anatole France The Degeneration of a Great Artist* (New York, Lincoln, MacVeagh, 1926), p. 295.

work "the warm breath of youth, fiery overwhelming spirit, strength and passion".[4] The decline in France's reputation perhaps reached its lowest point in Chevalier's *Ironic Temper* and in Giraud's *Anatole France.* Like Cerf, Chevalier finds that irony is detrimental to art and reproaches France for being unable to achieve a satisfactory synthesis.[5] In Giraud's view, the artist lacks creative originality, sympathy and his prose is poorly composed.[6] Blanck, in his *Anatole France als Stilkünstler in seinen Romanen,* does not rate France's craftsmanship too highly, concluding that France's style has no chance of ever being considered classic.[7] The sum of the opinions of these five critics is that France's Nobel Prize-winning prose has little to say, that it lacks revolutionary drive and pathos, that it avoids the vital issues of life, that France's irony is monotonous, and that whatever he has to say lacks structure, is unoriginal and told in a *Plauderstil.*

The generations of authors who came after France sought other teleological values than he did. They resented France's skepticism and dilettantism and, apparently indifferent to his stylistic perfection and irony, they were unaware of great positive values in France's wisdom and art. Later major critics and biographers, Dargan, Walton, and more recently, Sareil, Bancquart, Jefferson, and Levaillant modified the conclusions of Gottschalk, Cerf, Chevalier and Blanck, but except for Walton,[8] none of them directly reassessed their harsh verdicts.

Today, the political, social and cultural climate, which influences

[4] Walter Gottschalk, "Anatole France der Dichter und sein Werk", *Zeitschrift für die französische Sprache und Literatur,* Vol. 50 (1927), p. 309.

[5] Haakon M. Chevalier, *The Ironic Temper, Anatole France and His Time* (New York, Oxford University Press, 1932), pp. 51-54.

[6] Victor Giraud, *Anatole France* (Paris, Desclée de Brouwer, 1935), p. 223. "Un artiste: c'est, je crois, le premier mot qui vient à l'esprit ou sous la plume, quand, après avoir lu les trente et quelques volumes d'Anatole France, on essaie de traduire l'impression qu'il nous laisse. Un artiste qui n'est point complet, auquel il manque, dans tous les genres où il s'est exercé, la grande originalité créatrice, la puissance de composition et le don de sympathie, mais un artiste qui rachète, en partie, par l'habile exécution du détail, par la grâce élégante et industrieuse de la forme, quelques-unes de ses imperfections ou de ses lacunes."

[7] Robert Blanck, *Anatole France als Stilkünstler in seinen Romanen (Arbeiten zur Romanischen Philologie,* Nr. 7, Münster, 1934), p. 135.

[8] L. B. Walton, *Anatole France and the Greek World* (Durham, Duke University Press, 1950), p. 274. "There were perhaps dilettante aspects of France's immense culture, but Greece was not one of them." (Walton's footnote not retained.) See also Ch. X, p. 221 of this study.

the critic's aesthetic philosophy, has changed again. Despite the heroic self-sacrifice of generations and nations, life does not seem to be much less absurd today than it was in the days of Candide, of Gamelin or of M. Bergeret. The causes which appeared worthy of *engagement* to the contemporaries of Malraux, Hemingway and Sartre, often contributed to the starvation or hopeless suffering of whole continents and races. Intolerance, fanaticism, ignorance, ruthlessness flourish now as ever in man's individual as well as his collective life. The remedies offered by politicians, economists, priests and psychologists are probably as effective as they were in the days of Dreyfus, Lenin, or Hitler. Man remains corrupt and whatever original sins he may have committed are daily matched or surpassed by posterity. Yet, not being disposed to commit suicide, he has to keep living and find a wisdom which will either change life or enable him to accept and possibly even enjoy it.

Surrounded by a Babylon just as full as ever of charlatans and maniacs in politics, in economics, in culture, the contemporary critic judges various moral lessons, creeds, and aesthetic doctrines with more suspicion and even cynicism than intellectuals in the thirties displayed. He has learned that revolutions often make things worse. Saturated, if not nauseated by the monotonous messages of crusading authors, he may find that their works are hardly ever "ingeniously wrought gems". The fascinating puzzles and the rebus-like obscurities of hermetic art have become conventional. Having experienced various political and aesthetic ideologies, various forms of artistic anarchy and ephemeral experiments ranging from surrealism to pop art, from dadaism to the present-day *alittérature*, or from *unanimisme* to the poetic trance produced by the euphoria of mescaline, the contemporary critic has lost many of his illusions. Perhaps now he is ready to re-evaluate the aesthetic verdicts of the Bretonian apostles, of socialist realism, of the *engagé* critics; perhaps he is ready to find a few merits in tradition. The critic tired of mushrooming artistic doctrines is ready to re-examine the artistic sins of the Pyrrhonian Socialist who twice spurned revolution and chose Epicure as his master and Apollo, Dionysios and the Muses as his gods. The contemporary reader may discover new values in the art of the old skeptic who found life as tragic and as absurd as any of the *engagé* authors, but unlike them, chose to glorify its joy and beauty rather than bow to its nausea and anxiety.

Many critics and literary historians have discovered in France's work values other than those which were judged so coolly by the scholars mentioned above. Michaut thinks France is mainly inspired by "pessimisme jouisseur" or "sombre optimisme" and by the hedonistic quest for "désir" and "volupté".[9] Des Hons believes that the key to France's work is an extensive stylistic and contentual *imitatio* of Racine.[10] Sareil defines the nature of Voltairianism in France's tone, disposition and thought.[11] Alvida Ahlstrom[12] and L. B. Walton, who outline respectively the scope of France's *imitatio* of medieval and Greek art, would at least partly agree with Des Hons, and so would Woolsey.[13] In Masson's view, France is above all an aesthete and a seeker of beauty.[14] Guehenno characterizes him as "the last wise man".[15] The author of the most recent major study devoted to France's intellectual evolution, Jean Levaillant, shows France especially as a modernizer who "made of humanism something quite different than an ossified belief in universal values: he made it an existentialism of reason". His brand of humanism is an "antidote to the crusading romanticism of our era which tends to accept man's death and misery as a path leading toward the fulfillment of modern salvation myths".[16] H. L. Stewart maintains that most of France's artistic charm emanates from his deep-rooted "Parisianism",[17] whereas Bancquart sees him primarily as a

[9] G. Michaut, *Anatole France* (Paris, Fontemoing, 1913), pp. 300, 303.
[10] Gabriel Des Hons, *Anatole France et Racine, ou la clé de l'art francien* (Paris Colin, 1927). See also pp. 211-12 of this study.
[11] Jean Sareil, *Anatole France et Voltaire* (Paris, Minard, Genève, Droz, 1961), pp. 431-32.
[12] Alvida Ahlstrom, *Le Moyen Age dans l'Œuvre l'Anatole France* (Paris, Editions Les Belles Lettres, 1930).
[13] E. Wolsey, *Greek and Latin Influence in the Work of Anatole France.* (Thesis Cornell University, 1932).
[14] G. A. Masson, *Anatole France: Son œuvre* (Paris, Nouvelle Revue Critique, 1923).
[15] Jean Guehenno, "Anatole France ou le dernier sage", *Grande Revue,* April 14, 1924.
[16] Jean Levaillant, *Essai sur l'évolution intellectuelle d'Anatole France* (Paris, Colin, 1965), pp. 830, 831. (My translation).
[17] Herbert L. Stewart, *Anatole France the Parisian* (New York, Dodd, Mead, 1927).

journalist and "chroniqueur". She discovers in France's work traces of his personal polemics and concludes that these conflicts lend continuity to his art, and, in fact, are the chief motifs of his art.[18] Others, like Fernand Gregh, see in France's style and formal perfection sufficient guarantee that France will be ranked forever among the classics of French literature.[19] All of France's critics have found enough evidence in the twenty-five volumes of France's collected works and many articles to substantiate their diverse critical opinions. It would be difficult to judge which of these critics really had found the key to France's art. Paul Stapfer realized the danger of basing an aesthetic interpretation of France's work chiefly on one or two major aesthetic features, as, for example, the author's wit or style. To discover the real beauty of his prose one should read it several times, as only after the second or third reading is the reader astonished by the rare flavor of France's philosophical wisdom and by the variety and solidity of the author's erudition.[20] He finds the art of France far too complex to unlock with a single key: "L'art de M. Anatole France est formé de trop de qualités diverses, composant un ensemble très délicatement nuancé, . . ."[21]

[18] Marie-Claire Bancquart, *Anatole France polémiste* (Paris, Nizet, 1962), p. 10 and pp. 613, 617. The same scholar also touches on the fluctuation of opinions on France and on the hesitation of critics to assess his role in the literary history (*ibid.*, p. 9). "Après avoir été, de son vivant, proclamé le plus grand écrivain français, Anatole France est devenu après sa mort la proie des critiques, du mépris, des attaques. Bien souvent, on dépeignit l'homme en négligé, sans éviter les indiscrétions ni les bassesses. Ainsi se créa autour de France une légende d'autant moins estimable qu'elle concernait seulement sa vie et sa personalité. Aux environs de 1930 parurent les premiers ouvrages dans lesquels l'œuvre de France était considérée en elle-même. Mais la mode n'était point alors à la forme d'art et de pensée que représentait l'écrivain. Vers 1936, seulement, on s'avisa que France avait combattu les mystiques de la force et le racisme; il semble moins démodé, moins lointain, quoique nul mouvement politique n'ait pu se le rattacher sans quelque méprise. Sous l'occupation, le silence se fit sur le libéralisme de France.

Trente-cinq ans après sa mort, Anatole France n'a toujours pas conquis une place bien définie." See also pp. 235-36 of this study.

[19] Fernand Gregh, "Le Style", *Les Annales politiques et littéraires,* July-December 1924, p. 421.

[20] P. Stapfer, "L'Union de l'Atticisme et de l'humour", *Humour et Humoristes* (Paris, Fischbacher, 1911), pp. 159-160. (See also the article by the same critic "L'Art et la matière chez Anatole France", *Bibliothèque Universelle et Revue Suisse,* Vol. XXIII, p. 225.

[21] *Ibid.* p. 162.

This study accepts this premise of diversity in France's art. Its main goal is to identify and analyze the essential aesthetic qualities and techniques of France's subtle prose, to fill some of the gaps in the scholarly literature on his art, and to undertake a new critical synthesis of aesthetic values in his work. To reach such a goal, one has to define and assess the essential characteristics of the author's art, and arrange them conveniently, emphasizing those less examined by previous critics.

France has a traditional concept of art. He believes that aesthetic values appeal naturally to imagination and instinct: "L'art . . . est instinctif. C'est peu pour lui de connaître; il faut qu'il sente. La science ne peut être son moyen, puisque la vérité n'est pas son but. Le roman est une espèce de poème familier qui parle au sentiment et à l'imagination."[22] Similar criteria are applied in this analysis of France's art. Aesthetic enjoyment is a distinct sensation, which, through the reader's imagination, strikes his innate faculties, his senses, intellect, curiosity, sense of humor, spirit. The general cause of aesthetic enjoyment is surprise produced by a disturbance of the *status quo*, an incongruity which usually originates in a contrast evident or latent. Naturally, no such incongruity is an aesthetic element *per se*: rhymed prose, paradox, humor, violence, conflicts, are merely appropriate artistic raw material. Only in a vital and felicitous union of style and matter, only if presented in symbols of experience which neither science nor religion offer, can they transcend their original substance and become art.

It is comparatively simple to unravel the individual fibers of a vast literary work, but it is not so easy to establish their relative significance in an objective manner nor to arrange them in an acceptable scholarly order. The main difficulty is that rarely are any of the specific aesthetic features to be found in their pure form. For example, humor may be a result of stylistic skill, but very often it is not so. An erotic subject may be idyllic, tragic or *risqué*. A conflict can be farcical, tragic or heroic. To avoid the danger of repetition or confusion, which could result from two different aesthetic elements having one ingredient in common, the critic has to subordinate his method to the simplest practical premises.

Anatole France is a typical *homme de lettres* from the old school: a

[22] Anatole France "André Cornélis". *Temps,* February 6, 1887 not included in the *Œuvres complètes* (Cited from Bancquart, *op. cit.,* pp. 138-139).

sound craftsman familiar with all the aspects and tricks of the literary *métier*, and a broadly erudite and witty sage as well. Although all his works bear the unmistakable seal of his irony, his skepticism, his delight in conflict, his pagan hedonism, and his cult of beauty, it would be an exaggeration to say that any of these characteristics is omnipresent. What shapes every page, every line, every fragment of his prose, what indeed is omnipresent, is his style. It lends either clear or hazy contours to every detail of the *Wahrheit* which the poet has transformed into the *Dichtung*. Therefore it seems practical to analyse France's style first, and to examine other creative techniques only after making clear to what extent they are affected by France's style. However, certain exceptions must be made in the interest of economy. For example, lyrical subjects will be treated along with the lyrical accents provided by rhythmical and musical prose. On the other hand, *gauloiseries* will be treated with erotic subjects rather than with the analysis of humor or even of style. France's farce will be discussed along with his irony. The simultaneous treatment of different but related features within the same chapter is also inspired by the effort to illustrate their structural integration. For instance, certain Francean conflicts grow from his taste for paradox; the dividing line between a lyrical topic and a lyricism produced by style is rather problematic. The structural integration is also illustrated by abundant cross references and footnotes.

This study does not intend to add anything to France's biography or to the history of his work; it limits itself to an analysis of the most characteristic aesthetic features and techniques of France's art. Although not exhaustive, such an evaluation should provide a sufficiently broad basis for valid conclusions.

I

THE BIOGRAPHICAL, PHILOSOPHICAL AND AESTHETIC SOURCES OF FRANCE'S ART

Great art grows from life and experience. When the critic finds little or no organic unity between reality and that art, he may be inclined to seek pretence and artificiality in it. Like Jean Christophe's Uncle Gottfried, he may suspect that the ambitious artist wants to say something vital without really having much to say. Discrepancies between life and art may reveal aesthetic weaknesses, whereas a harmonious integration of life and art may corroborate the overall aesthetic interpretation. From the broad experience of his own life, the writer draws inspiration for his art, and this experience may have many immaterial aspects. A quiet bourgeois observer like Thomas Mann may have much more to say about life than an heroic pilot with moral fire and a literary flair. A bookish experience may excite in a creative author more *furor poeticus* than a gored abdomen suffered by a writer-toreador in a bull-fight. Petrarch, Du Bellay, Ronsard, Rabelais, Racine and many others cannot be accused of artistic anemia and lack of vigor merely because they assimilated and imitated the ancient literary heritage. A literary pilgrimage to the sources of our culture may be as profitable as, for example, Malraux' discovery of archeological treasures in oriental jungles and his subsequent arrest for their unauthorized sale to Parisian art lovers. Seeing the *Wahrheit* from this point of view, one may say that the diverse techniques and features of France's prose analyzed in this study are neither inorganic, aesthetic elements nor a result of France's contrived rationalizations; most of them are organically rooted in his rich life as well as in his broad humanist experience and thought.

France believes that the dearest gift nature gave him is ability to dream.[1] Dreaming is the miraculous vehicle which transports him to the realm of poetry or even to the supernatural. Had he a more practical disposition, perhaps Greek poetry would not have bewitched him to the extent he indicates in *Le Livre de mon ami*.[2] Yet his lyrical reveries are not unpredictable flashes of aimless illumination occasionally experienced by any sensitive dilettante, they are constant expressions of his creative genius. His inborn sense of poetry, raised to a higher power by classical erudition and by his familiarity with all tricks and techniques of his literary métier, is the main source of lyrical accents and of poetic visions in his work. France's admiration of Racine and his thorough knowledge of the tragedian's work, as well as that of the other great French poets, must also have contributed to his taste for lyricism.

France's hunger for poetry and for the unusual can be illustrated by a passage from *M. Bergeret à Paris*. This autobiographical hero, trying to find an apartment in Paris after his divorce and his appointment at the Sorbonne, expresses his grudge (which in this case is without doubt France's own) against the drab regularity and conventional standardization typical of bourgeois urban living. Like France, a lover of the charmingly unusual, M. Bergeret resents many features of a modern civilization pervaded with monotony and banality. The small dining rooms, built one above the other, are lit always at the same hour, and the living rooms, each equipped with a piano, do not make the tenants' living particularly pleasant. The design of such houses reveals the inhabitants' daily routine. One can imagine their private life as clearly as if the walls were made of glass, "et ces gens, qui dînent l'un sous l'autre, se couchent l'un sous l'autre, . . . composent . . . un spectacle d'un comique humiliant".[3] Following this criticism, the elderly scholar asks his sister to consider as their future apartment a dilapidated habitation which for thirty years had served as a storage space for a chemical factory and which the owner does not intend to repair, preferring to rent it as a shop. "Les fenêtres sont à tabatière.

[1] The critical works which most convincingly reveal the organic link between France's eventful life, full of struggles and intense contemplations, and between his art, are the cited studies by Dargan, Bancquart and Levaillant.

[2] *Œuvres complètes illustrées d'Anatole France,* 25 volumes (Paris, Calmann-Lévy 1925-1935), III, pp. 335 and 317-318; subsequently referred to as *O.C.*

[3] *O.C.,* XII, p. 306.

Mais on voit de ces fenêtres un mur de lierre, un puits moussu, et une statue de Flore, sans tête et qui sourit encore".[4] Here is M. Bergeret-France, the socialist, who believes in progress including the modernization of the style of living; yet, if he cannot live in an aristocratic villa drowned in the emerald poetry of a park, he at least wants to have his unique corner overgrown with ivy.[5] He wants a charming courtyard where time is not a tool of death but of poetry. He wants to be inspired by the headless but smiling Flora, which neither time nor the vandalism of his fellow citizens can destroy.

From his very childhood France manifests a curious interest in the mysterious, the dreamlike and the supernatural. Evoking France's vision of a charming feminine ghost described in *Le Livre de mon ami*, J. L. May even speaks about the author's "second sight". "He certainly is an ironist and a mocker; but he is a poet and a visionary as well." To illustrate this gift the biographer recalls "a strange little story which, with its suggestion of the mysterious and supernatural, is singularly reminiscent of Edgar Allan Poe, ..."[6] France's critics although they cannot deny May's direct knowledge of France's personal qualities or his poetical disposition, may doubt May's "proof" of the author's "second sight". The significance of the episode cited by May might be overestimated.[7] It rather seems that France's interest in the supernatural springs from his curiosity and from his belief in the aesthetic value of supernatural topics and from his delight in ridicule of creeds based on a belief in supernatural phenomena about which man knows nothing. Despite his love of lyricism, his intensely rational constitution is far from being visionary in a mystical or occult sense as implied by May. France's skepticism naturally restrains his childish faith and boyish "second sight". His supernatural heroes are not demons which make one's blood curdle as do the metamorphoses of Doctor Jekyl; except for a few rare cases, such phenomena are almost always parodied. France's taste for the mysterious and unusual thrived along

[4] *Ibid.*, p. 307.
[5] E. P. Dargan, *Anatole France 1844-1896* (New York, Oxford University Press, 1937), p. 558. "... the problem was posed when Barrès issued his challenge as to how this luxurious living comported with the doctrines of the Left."
[6] J. L. May, *Anatole France, The Man and His Work* (London, John Lane, 1924), p. 9.
[7] *O.C.*, III, pp. 331-335.

with his respect for literature in the milieu of his father's bookshop, where from his earliest childhood France explored the contents of its dusty shelves and eavesdropped on the conversations of its colorful clientele. Dargan points out that the customers of the "dernier libraire à chaises" became models for the typical Francean heroes. In the paternal bookshop France may have acquired a taste for the learned and bizarre controversies of the bibliomaniacs, novelists, and historians who patronized his father's business.[8] And of course a very fertile soil for the growth of François Thibault's interest in all sorts of *bizarreries* was not only his father's bookshop but the whole left-bank milieu, with its *bouquinistes* and curio or antique shops, where he used to browse with his friends, Etienne Charavay and Fontanet-Cazeaux, and dream of establishing his own museum.[9]

France seemed to have realized his youthful dream as soon as his income permitted him to do so. His collections, accumulated with such a passion, supplied enough material for a richly illustrated biographical monograph. The photographs in Pierre Calmette's *La Grande passion d'Anatole France* show a fantastic collection of Italian marble fireplaces, canopied beds, carved Renaissance chests, hundreds of paintings in rich frames, statuettes, bas-reliefs, antique chairs in various styles, decorative rococo urns, gilded altars, chandeliers, an ancient hand press, oriental tapestry, ceramics, old clocks, and colorful kitchenware.[10] Looking at all these cherished treasures of art and craft which

[8] Among France's biographers, Dargan (*op. cit.*, pp. 41-42, 81, 91) gathered the most evidence about the formation of France's taste for the supernatural and fantastic phenomena: "The later Gospels, especially *Petit Pierre,* are well populated with monsters. Unknown beings, quite different from ordinary men or animals, floated around in the darkness; and 'marine monsters pursued me in my sleep'. So he was led into a kind of double existence, which became quite super-natural at night-time. Deformed and twisted folk pranced round his couch; his imagination armed them with such domestic utensils as syringes and brooms. ... Thus his tantalizing dreamlife was an 'unknown, sombre and silent world, the very notion of which made me experience all the delight of fear'. From the age of five he indulged in the supernatural and had a lively curiosity about *diableries.* ... The same cult of terror for terror's sake is visible in the *Livre de mon ami.* ... From early times, Pierre was fond of maniacs, saints, and gods, these first effigies of humanity." (Dargan's footnotes omitted.)

[9] *Ibid.*, pp. 45, 286.

[10] Pierre Calmette, *La grande passion d'Anatole France* (Paris, Seheur, 1929), pp. 81, 83.

covered France's walls and filled his living space, one wonders how this lover of Greek simplicity could live in such a museum, the exhibits of which he gradually moved from M. Daressy's shop[11] into his various residences. At first sight one might be inclined to say that in his private life, unlike in his art, his grand collecting passion defeated his love of classical simplicity. But, giving a second thought to this seeming contradiction, one realizes a striking similarity between these harmoniously overdecorated interiors, where each item must stimulate the aesthetic sense of the refined inhabitant or guest, and his prose, composed of all sorts of bizarre scenes, obscure historical references, libertine anecdotes, lyrical intermezzoes, unexpected contrasts, aphorisms or paradoxes, sparkling like brilliant crystal chandeliers or subdued like the dull sheen of old bronze. Indeed, like the mansion, La Béchellerie, his prose is a literary museum of all sorts of *objets d'art* and bizarre decorations; in one word, a monumental *contaminatio*. France's collecting passion leaves no doubt about his love of the unusual and about his inborn delight in seeking and finding exciting *bizarreries*. His considerable knowledge of the visual arts, antiques and of lesser-known aspects of ancient and medieval history, added much glitter to his prose. Like his heroes, Bergeret or Bonnard, France is a critical connoisseur not only of ancient but also of medieval and 18th century culture and history, as Jean Sareil, Loring Walton, Pierce Woolsey, Alvida Ahlstrom and Léon Carias, so thoroughly proved in their studies.[12]

His youthful sympathy for the ancient world, first awakened through his reading of the great ancient authors at Stanislas, increased as he grew older. His frequent trips to Italy and Greece enabled him to maintain a vivid contact with whatever of the ancient heritage may still have been smouldering on Italian soil. His nostalgic desire to resurrect the lasting wisdom, the serene joy of bygone eras is the main impulse of his Epicurean paganism. This outlook and the classical erudition suggest to him not only the typical literary conflicts between

[11] Dargan, *op. cit.*, p. 45.

[12] Walton, *op cit.*; Pierce Woolsey, *Greek and Latin influence in the work of Anatole France* (Doctoral dissertation, Cornell University, Ithaca, N.Y., 1932), Alvida Ohlstrom, *Le Moyen Age dans l'Œuvre d'Anatole France* (Paris, Editions Les Belles Lettres, 1930); Jean Sareil, *op cit.*; Léon Carias, "Quelques Sources d'Anatole France", *La Grande Revue,* December 25, 1912, pp. 725-37.

the Judeo-Christian world and paganism, but are also the foundation of his hedonistic concept of love. Perhaps the same hedonism and his own intimate life may account for the scope and nature of the erotic topics in his work. The autobiographical passages offer sufficient evidence of his erotic curiosity, dating back to his early boyhood. Perhaps his frivolous, Voltairean grandmother was the first to plant the seed of the boy's libertine taste. Typically enough, the object of his first romantic love was an actress. He fell "passionately" in love with Isabelle Constant, the actress he met when he was only fourteen.[13] His turbulent matrimonial life, his divorce, his affair with Madame de Caillavet, who was on the verge of suicide in the days of France's liaison with actress Jeanne Brindeau, his romance with Mrs. Gagey-MacAdoo who actually took her life because of the master's coolness, his affair with Madame de Caillavet's chamber maid, Emma Laprévotte, various other adventures and finally his late marriage to Emma, betray sufficiently the intensity of his erotic instinct.[14] There is no doubt that the women he loved and the peripeties of his intimate adventures inspired many pages in his work, but his general approach to love is above all oriented by his pagan naturalism uninhibited by the idea of original sin and by his typically French taste for frivolity à la Montesquieu or Voltaire. With these authors and their period France has much more in common than a philosophy of love. With some justice he is called "M. Voltaire" by the critics. He has the same taste for satire, skeptical reasoning, irreverence, caustic wit, and the same *esprit* which harmonizes with his Epicurean religion of joy.

France himself and his biographers offer various testimonies of his inborn sense of humor and especially of his irrepressible irony. Seeing his life from the perspective of an old, wise man, France comments on this precious gift which made his life pleasant even when circumstances

[13] Dargan, *op. cit.*, p. 106. "His longing for Isabelle was followed by a series of disappointments." Jean Suffel, *Anatole France par lui-même* (Paris, Ed. du Seuil, 1954), p. 14, says: "Quant aux déceptions amoureuses, il en eut plus d'une. On peut citer Élise Rauline, rencontrée en Avranchin, qui se fit religieuse; Isabelle Combrouse, fille du numismate, qui lui préféra un certain de Launay; l'actrice Élise Devoyod, qui se moqua de ses déclarations; Marie Charavay et Marie Nottet, qui se récusèrent ... Mécomptes sentimentaux ... mécomptes professionels."

[14] Suffel, *op. cit.*, pp. 185-187, 189.

made him bitter.[15] Will Durant says in the *Adventures in Genius* "... he had the broad laughter of Rabelais, the kindly humor of Montaigne, the subtle satire of Voltaire".[16] May calls him "the most genial mocker of our day.".[17] Discussing the autobiographical characters in France's work, Herbert L. Stewart says: "We get again and again the same features of critical temperament, – a tone of detached mockery.[18] Cerf, Chevalier's forerunner, sees in France's irony the factor which greatly contributes to what he calls in the title of his critical study "the degeneration of the great artist": "I am going to try to show now that he has been misled by undue indulgence of a gift which he possesses in unusual degree. I refer to his ironic manner."[19] One may question Durant's parallel between the broad laughter of Rabelais and France's sense of humor; one may see in France's sense of humor a smaller artistic curse than Cerf. Yet in spite of their diverse appraisals of France's humor, none of these critics doubts that France was a born wit. His wit lights up his satire and the same wit, allied with France's craftsmanship, sets off the whole stylistic firework.

His humor does not grow merely out of the cheerful disposition of a merry joker who knows how to make people chuckle and excite superficial optimism. It often strikes tragic understones. Seeing the comical side of things presupposes a considerable personal detachment. To be fully amused by the absurdity and ridiculousness of events, one has to be neutral and judge them *sine ira et studio*. And, to get a really penetrating view, the spectator has to be above them and see them *sub specie aeternitatis*.[20] But such an enlightened, objective observer is not only amused by the ridiculous futility of human life; he is aware of its inherent tragedy. At the same time, he must realize the evanescence of his own amusement and his own perspective. No deep humor can see

[15] *O.C.*, XXIII, 413; "Peut-être serais-je tombé malade de chagrin dans cet affreux collège si un don, que j'ai gardé toute ma vie, ne m'avait sauvé, le don de voir le comique des choses. Mes professeurs Crotty, Brard, et Beaussier m'ont, par leurs ridicules et leurs vices, donné la comédie. Ils me furent des Molières sans le savoir; ils m'ont sauvé de l'ennui mortel. ..."

[16] Will Durant, *The Adventures in Genius* (New York, Simon and Schuster, 1931) p. 254.

[17] May, *op. cit.*, p. 8.

[18] Stewart, *op. cit.*, p. 66.

[19] Cerf. *op. cit.*, p. 226.

[20] Dargan, *op. cit.*, p. 132.

the full scope of the comical side of things without intense melancholy, without a half-ironical, half-sad smile at the author's own spectatorship. He cannot be carried away by the superficial gaiety of things. Haakon M. Chevalier points out this temperamental dualism of France's personality by quoting France's personal friend, Nicolas Ségur, and by referring to other critics who state the same.[21] France's hero, Brotteaux des Ilettes, is a literary incarnation of this temperamental dualism: facing death in the furor of the Revolution, Brotteaux sees the comical side of patriotic fanaticism until the very end. His skepticism makes him aware of his tragedy and of the tragic nature of the whole human existence, but it does not make him lose his sense of humor. He meditates with melancholy about man's fate, reading and translating Lucretius Carus. His lines, "*Sic ubi non erimus* . . . Quand nous aurons cessé de vivre, rien ne pourra nous émouvoir, non pas même le ciel, la terre et la mer confondant leurs débris . . .",[22] become a *leitmotif* of *Les Dieux ont soif*, giving a perspective of eternity to France's cutting satire. Like Brotteaux, France is deeply attached to life, yet he smiles sadly at the inevitability of its fateful end.

> Plus je songe à la vie humaine, plus je crois qu'il faut lui donner pour témoins et pour juges l'Ironie et la Pitié . . . L'Ironie et la Pitié sont deux bonnes conseillères; l'une en souriant nous rend la vie aimable; l'autre qui pleure nous la rend sacrée. L'Ironie que j'invoque n'est point cruelle. Elle ne raille ni l'amour ni la beauté.[23]

Irony is not only France's way to joy, irony is joy itself. In his essay on Rabelais France comments on Rabelais' and Montaigne's limits of non-conformism and, as one can expect, he agrees with the frequently quoted aphorism that paying by one's death for one's loyalty to an idea means putting quite a high price on one's conjectures. The desire for martyrdom indicates a disturbed set of values. What is even worse, martyrs lack irony and that is a fault which cannot be pardoned, ". . . car sans l'ironie le monde serait comme une forêt sans oiseaux; l'ironie, c'est la gaieté de la réflexion et la joie de la sagesse."[24] Life would not be worth living. Without irony France's pagan teleology

[21] Chevalier, *op. cit.*, p. 17.
[22] *O.C.*, XX, p. 242. See also this study, p. 221.
[23] *O.C.*, IX, p. 450.
[24] *O.C.*, VII, p. 43.

would lose its human dimensions and possibly approach Zarathustra's heroic longing with all its consequences.

One cannot call France's creed a philosophy. Possibly one could say he has a practical philosophy but it would be more precise to call it wisdom. His wisdom is free of any dogmatism, doctrinal discipline, or the gravity inherent in philosophical systems, and therefore is capable of reconciling various fateful conflicts of life. Practically all the conflicts, contrasts, paradoxes, and solutions expressed by the major themes in his work, originate in his cult of beauty. France resents pure philosophy. This antipathy dates back to his student years, when he became superficially familiar with some elements of philosophy at the Collège Stanislas. Unlike the learned polyhistor, Faust, the young François Thibault did not need many years of ardent toil to conclude that the lessons conventional philosophy can teach man will not make him wiser. "Sans être très intelligent, je trouvai la philosophie qu'on m'avait enseignée tant sotte, tant inepte, tant absurde, tant niaise, que je ne crus rien des vérités qu'elle établit et qu'il faut professer et pratiquer . . ."[25] France became more thoroughly familiar with philosophy in the course of his literary career, but he never substantially modified his youthful lack of confidence in the noble science. His constant resentment of philosophical systems is not only implied by the nature of his life work, but is clearly spelled out in both his biographical and his critical writings. In his comment in *Le Petit Pierre* on one of the Cartesian fallacies, France generalizes on all architects of philosophical systems:

Si Descartes a voulu, contre toute apparence, que les animaux fussent des machines, il faut l'en excuser, puisque sa philosophie l'y obligeait et qu'un philosophe soumettra toujours la nature qui lui est étrangère à son système qui est sorti de lui.[26]

France attributed the temporary acceptance of all philosophical systems to the intellectual genius of their authors rather than to the brilliance of the systems themselves.[27] Like Voltaire, France has a particular aversion to metaphysics.[28] He regards the contemplative method of

[25] *O.C.*, XXIII, p. 427.
[26] *O.C.*, XXIII, pp. 206-207.
[27] *O.C.*, VII, p. 384.
[28] *O.C.*, XXIII, p. 9.

metaphysical thinkers, like any kind of thinking, nothing else than a play on words which cannot lead to any worthwhile conclusion. We think in words and all a metaphysician has available to conceive and to formulate his system is merely the improved utterances of monkeys and dogs.[29] In France's eyes the learned treatises of metaphysicians are just as amusing as fiction and about as truthful.[30] France didn't think that philosophy based on the premises supplied by science was much closer to any worthwhile truth than metaphysics. The philosopher has no scientific grounds on which to build his theories, but rather just a heap of incoherent fragments of truths, half-truths, and errors. No magic philosophical synthesis can shape such fragments into an indestructible monument of truth. In spite of the many tributes Anatole France pays to different scientists and to science in general in other places in his work, he keeps pointing out that the scientific information on man, life, and the universe is incomplete and doubtful. It is true that if the premises and conclusions of science were complete and correct they would reveal truth. But constant progress proves that scientific methods have not yet provided solid grounds for irrefutable conclusions.[31] Although the sciences, religion, witchcraft, and superstitions are now more clearly divided than they used to be, elements of their former alliance still survive.[32] Besides, scientists' intellectual horizons are limited. In the opening of his causerie entitled "Sur le scepticisme", France makes, half jokingly, half seriously, one of his typically controversial statements eulogizing the charms of leisurely contemplation unaffected by the sterile scientific approach. A loafer usually discovers more than scientists in their laboratories and offices. Besides, scholars are more ignorant than most of us.[33] There is no

[29] *O.C.*, IX, pp. 430-431.

[30] *Ibid.*, p. 448.

[31] *O.C.*, I, p. 249.

[32] *O.C.*, X, pp. 393-394; "Je ne vous reprocherai point d'opposer les sciences aux religions. ... que sont les religions, je vous prie, que sont-elles, sinon de très vieilles sciences, des astrologies, des arithmétiques, des météorologies, des médecines usées, déformées, obscurcies, ... Notre science produira aussi des superstitions. ... Des religions naissent sous nos yeux. Le spiritisme élabore en ce moment ses dogmes et sa morale. Il a ... ses conciles, ses pères ..."

[33] *O.C.*, VI, 446; "Alors, comme je n'étudiais rien, j'apprenais beaucoup. En effet, c'est en se promenant qu'on fait les belles découvertes intellectuelles et morales. Au contraire ce qu'on trouve dans un laboratoire ... est en général

truth, and if there were, no one could understand it.[34] In a way it is more comfortable to keep one's ignorance. Man is blind and imprisoned in the dark room of life. Those who grope around trying to find out more about the dark room will bump against the walls and hurt themselves, while those who stay quietly in the center will remain safe.[35] It is even silly to try to understand oneself: the Socratic *to gnothi s'auton* is nonsense. We will never know ourselves or anyone else. Our intelligence may enable us to create a universe, but will we understand it? Never.[36] Experience taught France that whatever man does usually has a flaw. And in a speculation as complex as that of a philosophical system, errors are inevitable.[37] In addition, every system has an extremely short life. None of them so far has been proved by the realities of life.[38] Although the artist owes some of the premises of his *Weltanschauung* to Comte, on the whole he considers Comte's system an obsolete religion, which sees life as a geometrical construction and which is inspired by tyrannical love.[39] Other authors of philosophical systems do not contribute much more to human wisdom: the systems such as those formulated by Kant and Hegel do not differ basically from the *réussite* in a game of solitaire.[40]

Like Renan, France doubts, but he keeps seeking answers to the questions: What is the universe? What is life? Who is man and which forces created him? In spite of his caution in taking for an absolute

---

fort peu de chose et il est à remarquer que les savants de profession sont plus ignorants que la plupart des autres hommes."

[34] *Ibid.*, pp. 194-195.

[35] *O.C.*, IX, p. 431.

[36] *Ibid.*, p. 429.

[37] *O.C.*, VI, p. 326.

[38] *O.C.*, VII, p. 8.

[39] *O.C.*, IX, pp. 447-448.

[40] *Ibid.*, p. 437. Levaillant points out that France's philosophical and idealogical independence is one of the sources of his originality. "France refuse toute doctrine, et ne se fait pas faute, bien au contraire, de juger. L'ataraxie n'est pas son fort. Ce scepticisme, qu'il emprunte d'abord aux anciens, il lui a donné une valeur et un sens nouveaux, ..." (*Op. cit.*, p. VII). The same scholar concludes that precisely France's resentment of any system is a factor which may secure his immortality as a writer: "Du moins, cette absence de système, mais aussi cette affirmation d'une permanence essentielle, lui assurent la survie." (*Ibid.*, p. 832.)

truth any discovery of science, he absorbs some of its doctrines. Perhaps the universe is a vast space filled with very dynamic processes. There is nothing perfect in this anonymous creation full of destructive revolutions and dying.[41] Change is the first condition of life, yet what we see may be illusory. It is possible that life is a pathological thing. M. Bergeret formulates it as one of the vulgar forces of the universe and terms it a leprosy.[42] He even finds it somewhat consoling that this kind of corruption called organic life cannot exist on Saturn, Jupiter, Uranus, and Neptune. He hopes that organic life is an evil limited to our planet, because it would be despair to think that one eats and is eaten everywhere in the endless skies. But Anatole France is not sure that it is the worst possible world. It would be too flattering to attribute to it any kind of excellence. It is probable that life and evil rule also on Mars where the general conditions resemble those on earth.[43] In this cosmic setting man is just an animal, subject to laws of evolution and to final, inevitable degeneration like all other living species. Basing his vision of human destiny on Darwin's and Spencer's theories, France foresees tragic poetry in the extinction of an imbecilic, degenerated man, vegetating under the anemic rays of the dying sun.[44]

All these unexpected and depressing views shocked and still shock the average reader, even in the era which laid the foundations for scientific materialism, because the same era continued to cherish

[41] *O.C.*, IX, p. 397.

[42] *O.C.*, XI, p. 38.

[43] *O.C.*, XII, pp. 388-389.

[44] *O.C.*, IX, pp. 405-406; "L'Espèce humaine n'est pas susceptible d'un progrès indéfini. . . . Il fut un temps où notre planète ne convenait pas à l'homme : elle était trop chaude et trop humide. Il viendra un temps où elle ne lui conviendra plus: elle sera trop froide et trop sèche. Quand le soleil s'éteindra, ce qui ne peut manquer, les hommes auront disparu depuis longtemps. Les derniers seront aussi dénués et stupides qu'étaient les premiers. Ils auront oublié tous les arts et toutes les sciences. . . . Ces derniers hommes, . . . ne connaîtront rien de nous, rien de notre génie, rien de notre amour, et pourtant ils seront nos enfants. . . . Un faible reste de royale intelligence, hésitant dans leur crâne épaissi, leur conservera quelque temps encore l'empire sur les ours. . . . Femmes, enfants, vieillards, engourdis pêle-mêle, verront par les fentes de leurs cavernes monter tristement sur leur tête un soleil sombre. . . . Un jour, le dernier d'entre eux exhalera sans haine et sans amour dans le ciel ennemi le dernier souffle humain. Et la terre continuera de rouler, emportant à travers les espaces silencieux les cendres de l'Humanité, les poèmes d'Homère et les augustes débris des marbres grecs, attachés à ses flancs glacés."

bourgeois liberal optimism rooted in conservative nationalism and religion. Such ideas are the very source of what Dargan calls "the imp of the perverse of Anatole France".[45] Taking such views into account, Lanson sums up France's "philosophy" as follows: "Sa philosophie est ce qu'il peut y avoir de plus désolant pour une âme humaine; et elle nous désole, en effet, quand elle nous surprend. Elle emplit notre âme d'amertume et de cendre."[46] And Marxist ideologists, whose political programs found grace in France's eyes, could rarely find support for their views in France's ideas and writings. All France's typical heroes, such as M. Bonnard, Doctor Trublet, M. Bergeret, Abbé Coignard, M. Boni, or secondary heroes such as Choulette, d'Astarac, Brotteaux, and Tudesco, draw their surprisingly controversial views, paradoxes, contradictions-in-terms and most of their shocking statements from the huge reservoir of France's skepticism. This inborn speculative disposition prompts him to challenge or parody the weak points of whatever he may observe or contemplate. This flair for discrepancies and hidden fears of life is not only typical of his artistic invention but perhaps the mainspring of his literary conflicts; it stimulates the reader's cynicism by shaking up his confidence in the moral progress of man and in ideals. To many a reader it may seem that life without such values is not worth living. Resenting the grim materialistic prognosis of life, which after all is not a result of France's own original contemplation, but rather the last word of science in France's day, Ferdinand Brunetière accuses France of being a nihilist. France admits that he may have played with the idea of systematic skepticism, but explains why he never accepted it as his poetic basis.

J'ai regardé, je l'avoue, plus d'une fois du côté du scepticisme absolu. Mais je n'y suis jamais entré; j'ai eu peur de poser le pied sur cette base qui engloutit tout ce qu'on y met. J'ai eu peur de ces deux mots d'une stérilité formidable: "Je doute." ... Si l'on doute il faut se taire; ... Et puisque je n'avais pas le courage du silence ..., j'ai cru. J'ai cru ... à la relativité des choses et à la succession des phénomènes.[47]

Such faith in the Comtean "relativity of things" and "succession of

[45] E. P. Dargan, "Anatole France and the Imp of the Perverse", *The Dial*, February 8, 1919.

[46] Gustave Lanson, "La Vie et l'œuvre". *Les Annales Politiques et littéraires*, Vol. LXXXIII (July-December 1924), p. 420.

[47] *O.C.*, VII, p. 9.

phenomena" does not contradict Lanson's conclusion. But to this faith we have to add several significant teleological beliefs which Lanson seems to exclude from his general summary of France's philosophy. Buddhist pity is one of them. His reading of the *Histoire des religions de l'Inde* by L. M. Milloue, and Jean Lahore's the *Histoire de la littérature hindoue* inspired France's warmest tribute to this Oriental wisdom. Buddhism attracts France precisely because it is not a religion in the western sense. It has neither cosmogony, gods, nor rigid cult. It is most tolerant toward science. Sumangala, the liberal leader of the southern Buddhists, counts Darwin and Littré among their saints. Like the great Occidental skeptic, Schopenhauer, Anatole France is inspired by the wisdom of Çakya-Mouni. Buddha's elementary lesson of pity[48] is among the fundamentals of France's wisdom, but he refuses Buddha's resignation. The traditionalist France, an admirer of Greek culture, is imbued with its spirit of curiosity, its thirst for knowledge and beauty. In this heart flickers a subdued, gay, and quite vital flame of Promethean revolt against the limitations imposed on man by the gods. He does not belong to the breed of passive observers; he is rather the Faustian "edle Glied, . . . wer immer strebend sich bemüht". France realizes that Buddhist quietism does not quite suit the active European race. However, Buddha can be one of our dearest advisors. "Çakya-Mouni n'est pas venu pour nous; il ne nous sauvera pas."[49]

Humanitarian socialism rather than Marxism is another of the active teleological values in France's wisdom. Jacob Axelrad, in *Anatole France, a Life Without Illusions*, somewhat contradicts the subtitle of his work in describing France's meeting with George Bernard Shaw at the London banquet of the Fabian Society in 1913. Axelrad draws a parallel between the two writers:

> The Fabians were there to honor him, the Socialist. Bernard Shaw, a younger man than he, . . . was chairman. . . . both were preoccupied with the stupidities of life; both pilloried the pretensions of property, the cruelties of its dominion, and the vanities of men. Both were Socialists, bent on the regeneration of a hopeless world. And both were hopeful, nevertheless.[50]

[48] *O.C.*, VII, pp. 364-366.
[49] *Ibid.*, p. 368.
[50] Jacob Axelrad, *Anatole France, a Life Without Illusion (1844-1924)* (New York, Harper, 1924), p. 390.

In spite of the inevitable fate man and the earth are facing, France sees several admirable factors in life which make it worth living. One of them is man's Promethean spirit of revolt against his own imperfections inflicted upon him by the Creator.

In his essay, *La Vertu en France*, France talks about the possible existence of angel-like beings who, invisible to man, observe him as Sir John Lubbock observes ants and their life. One of them might say: "Voilà de méchants petits animaux. Ils se rendent justice puisqu'ils se mangent les uns les autres."[51] But soon he notices that man suffers. He discovers man's *grandeur*. He realizes that man, who is born weak, suffering and starving, who is doomed by nature to struggling with his fellow man and to devouring him, often rises above the wickedness of the divine scheme. The angel can even see some symptoms of human solidarity: men help and console one another, they have invented industries and the arts to face with dignity the evils implied in creation.

> Leur dieu avait créé la maladie; ils ont créé le médecin et ils s'emploient de leur mieux à réparer la nature. La nature a fait le mal, ... C'est eux qui font le bien ... La Terre est mauvaise: elle est insensible. Mais l'homme est bon parce qu'il souffre. Il a tout tiré de sa douleur, même son génie.[52]

Mr. Bergeret, France's loyal spokesman, observes man from a closer distance. He also comments on man with some hope, though without the angel's enthusiasm. Man is far from being good by nature and only painfully tries to subdue his barbaric atavism and to introduce a shaky justice. The cruel law of the stronger will continue to rule in human society and man will not cease to tear his fellow man to pieces.

> ... je crois aussi que les hommes sont moins féroces quand ils sont moins misérables, que les progrès ... déterminent ... quelque adoucissement dans les mœurs, et je tiens d'un botaniste que l'aubépine transportée d'un terrain sec en un sol gras y change ses épines en fleurs.[53]

Paradoxically, man's progress and general refinement is a result of evil. Evil is actually more beneficial to man than the intolerant supreme good – God. This is at least the fundamental idea of one of France's most mature works, *La Révolte des anges*. The Promethean Lucifer,

[51] *O.C.*, VI, p. 298.
[52] *Ibid.*, p. 298-99.
[53] *O.C.*, XII, p. 444.

the torch-bearer, is humbler and wiser than the ferocious Demiurge-Ialdabaoth, the Judeo-Christian God. Satan no longer aspires to revolt against the divine ruler. If his possible revolt succeeded, he, the fallen angel, would become a tyrant like Ialdabaoth. Lucifer's war would lead to another war and his possible victory to a new defeat. Lucifer is too wise to embark on such a vain action. In any case, man's victory lies within himself. Man has to defeat his own ignorance and his own fear of the tyranny of the despotic Demiurge, the ancient enemy of the Muses, in his own heart. But this is not all; he has to listen to the friendly demons, Dionysios and Apollo, and to the Muses.[54] The two divine charioteers show man the path of spontaneous joy and sublime beauty. France's Satan is a selfless anarchist with aesthetic tastes. The finale of *La Révolte des anges*[55] has to be considered as an integral part of France's hedonistic confession expressed in *La Vie en Fleur*, his last major work: "J'ai toujours cru que la seule chose raisonnable est de chercher plaisir."[56]

One of his biographers, Michel Corday, cites many touching examples of France's endeavour not only to find pleasure for himself but also for his fellow man. "Anatole France ne savait pas résister au plaisir de faire plaisir. C'est bien une des clefs de sa vie."[57] Epicurus, not Darwin and Spencer, Pyrrho, or Buddha, planted the most striking seeds in France's garden of wisdom. The goal of life, which is woven of so many uncertainties and contradictions, is joy, above all spiritual, intellectual, and sensual joy, and man instinctively seeks all forms of it.

France's search for pleasure intensifies his lack of confidence in the sciences because they frequently interfere with the materialization of this ultimate value. When it comes to a conflict between joy and the glory of scientific revelations France does not hesitate over which side to take.[58] But from the discrepancy between the aim of science to reveal unknown truths and between man's desire to find as much joy as

[54] *O.C.*, XXII, p. 322.
[55] See pp. 192-194.
[56] *O.C.*, XXIII, p. 480.
[57] Michel Corday, *Anatole France d'après ses confidences et ses souvenirs* (Paris, Flammarion, 1927), p. 27.
[58] *O.C.*, IX, 532; "Elle [la science] développe le cerveau qui est l'organe inutile que nous avons en commun avec les bêtes, elle nous détourne de la jouissance, dont nous avons un besoin instinctif."

possible, France does not draw any romantic conclusions à la Rousseau or Tolstoy. He does not preach a return to nature: after all, nature is worse than man; nor does he recommend passive resistance to technological progress. The fact that science makes many false steps, or the fact that there are charlatans among scientists and scholars, does not diminish the merits of scientific goals. The curious mind of Occidental man is one of his finest qualities and the sciences, with all their errors, ignorance, half-knowledge, and quackery, were the finest tokens given to our culture in its ancient cradle. France might occasionally ridicule the results of scientific achievements but the Promethean aims of true science are sacrosanct. The most distilled form of joy is beauty. Beauty is France's supreme guide, the richest source of joy.[59]

The joyful or sorrowful perception of beauty is not a simple agreeable stimulation but a complex feeling which springs from many sources and which is bipolar. Joy and suffering, as contrary as they may seem to be, are merely opposite poles of the same feeling. Without its antipole, joy could not be the same joy, it could not be at all. The nature of most spiritual, moral, emotional, intellectual and physical values is bipolar; life, which is full of related surprising contrasts, is a dualistic order. The source of suffering and pain is evil and so joy and evil are fatefully linked. Evil is indispensable. If it did not exist, good and joy would not exist either. One cannot imagine virtue without vice, love without hatred, and beauty without ugliness. Destroy a vice and a virtue perishes with it. We owe much to evil and to suffering. Love and suffering are the two ever-welling sources of beauty and aesthetic pity.[60]

Man's loving and suffering taught him heroism and noble self-

[59] *O.C.*, VI, 327. "Le sentiment du beau me conduit. Qui donc est sûr d'avoir trouvé un meilleur guide." See also G. A. Masson, *Anatole France: Son œuvre* (Paris, Nouvelle Revue Critique, 1923), pp. 32-33. "Quelle idole nouvelle installera-t-il dans le temple d'où il a chassé tous les dieux? Ce sera la notion de bonté, et celle de beauté. Et sans doute, il ne construira pas une métaphysique sur ces mouvantes données, mais il nous les proposera comme de suffisants 'buts de vie'. Nous lisons déjà, dans la *Vie Littéraire,* cette profession de foi: ... 'Pour ma part, s'il me fallait choisir entre la beauté et la vérité, je n'hésiterais pas, c'est la beauté que je garderais, certain qu'elle porte en elle une vérité plus haute et plus profonde que la vérité elle-même. J'oserai dire qu'il n'y a de vrai au monde que le beau.' "

[60] *O.C.*, IX, pp. 435, 419.

sacrifice for his fellow man. The contradiction between France's skepticism and his love of life may have been a lesson in practical philosophy to Albert Camus. His grave Sisyphean heroes are like France's Bergeret, Coignard, Brotteaux, or Nicias, who learn to love their absurd stones. Camus' characters, like France himself, also love life, not only for the joy it gives them but also for its tragic absurdity: loving this tragic absurdity lends an heroic dignity to life. For France, suffering and pain are integral parts of any joy.

> "Elle est tout entière douloureuse la vie ..., et il n'est pas trêve à nos souffrances." Ainsi parle la nourrice de Phèdre et les soupirs de sa poitrine n'ont point été démentis. Et pourtant, ajoute la vieille Crétoise, nous aimons cette vie, parce que la suite n'est que ténèbres sur lesquelles on a semé les fables. "On aime aussi la vie, la douloureuse vie, parce qu'on aime la douleur. Et comment ne l'aimerait-on pas? Elle ressemble à la joie et parfois se confond avec elle." [61]

Profoundly aware of this irrevocable human destiny, France does not accuse life and its invisible architect with the egotistic pathos of some Romantics, or with the sorrowful nihilism of Pirandello, the intransigent bitterness of Cocteau or the stoic gravity of Camus. He does not accuse it at all, but regards the beauties and crudities of Creation with tender melancholy and a resigned smile. He loves life for its joy and suffering and for the charming and sad beauty which he seeks and finds in it. Perhaps like Mozart writing his *Sinfonia concertante*, he both weeps and smiles, contemplating life's gaiety and its fateful end.

The critic considering the view that France's irony and skepticism border on sterility and nihilism must be aware that France also preaches the tears and pity, courage and self-sacrifice, which make an absurd life profoundly beautiful. It is beautiful because the evil inherent in nature is stronger than man and his stubborn fight against it is lost in advance. It is surprisingly beautiful because man not only manages an ironical smile but even finds poetry in the face of nature's cruelty. And it is triumphantly beautiful because man, against all expectation, contrives to rise above the cosmic forces which handicap him so mercilessly. The human quest for sublime beauty, the gay ironic

[61] *O.C.*, XXIII, p. 558.

smile, the tears of pity, the absurd and amazing determination to fight lost battles against evils inflicted upon man by his Creator, are all integral parts of France's hedonism.

It is not surprising that the paradoxes, conflicts, tragic or absurd contrasts of this hedonism inspire his literary creation. What makes this especially probable is the similarity between France's hedonistic goal of life and what he considers the primary function of art: "La science a le droit d'exiger de nous un esprit appliqué, une pensée attentive. L'art n'a pas ce droit. Il est, par nature, inutile et charmant. Sa fonction est de plaire; il n'en a point d'autre."[62] France believes that the only reasonable thing in life is to seek pleasure and the only function of art is to please, i.e., to cause pleasure and contribute thus to the fulfillment of the goal of life. Such a teleology of art, or course, is nothing revolutionary in the late nineteenth century. It does not differ in any way from the aesthetic code of the great *arbiter elegantiarum* of French classicism, Boileau.[63] Whether or not an aesthetic pleasure can be justified rationally is irrelevant. Besides, it is impossible to define precisely what pleases us. "Les choses . . . les plus belles . . . sont précisement celles qui demeurent toujours vagues pour nous et en partie mystérieuses. La beauté, la vertu, le génie garderont à jamais leur secret."[64] But it is typical of France that, although he believes that beauty is indefinable, he should attempt to define it. ". . . le beau dépend de nous; il est la forme sensible de tout ce que nous aimons."[65] Of course, such a *definitio lata* is vague enough not to contradict the first statement. Besides, definable or not, the secret of beauty can be understood instinctively by children whose *naiveté* sharpens their aesthetic receptivity. If man could define beauty without using vague abstractions and dynamically changing notions and without using metaphors fully comprehensible only to those with an intense aesthetic instinct, if man could provide thus a reliable aesthetic formula, art and its beauty would be degraded to a craft or perhaps changed into a science. Like science, art also tries to penetrate the unknown, but, while the scientist wants to conquer it, the poet wants

[62] *O.C.*, VI, p. 519.
[63] Nicolas Boileau, *L'Art poétique* (Paris, Larousse, 1934), Ch. I, v. 103. v. 103. "N'offrez rien au lecteur que ce qui peut lui plaire."
[64] *O.C.*, VII, p. 13.
[65] *O.C.*, VI, p. 304.

to be charmed by that part of the unknown which is unconquerable.[66] Beauty is assessed subjectively by our instincts and inborn qualities and therefore it is a relative value. The source of aesthetic enjoyment can be "any perceptible form of all that we love". This may imply real or artistically stylized persons, things, dreams, qualities and relations, which in some way desirably stimulate any among man's instincts and inborn qualities. And if we are not fond of some of them, for example violence, we are nonetheless stimulated by them. A harmonious symphony of such features may become a work of art and possibly can be called a thing of beauty. Man's longing for indefinable beauty is the main source of his aesthetic joy.[67] Although there is something inexplicable and mysterious in beauty, there are on the other hand various indispensable ingredients in beauty and art which can be defined. Several generations of critics, preoccupied with the definition of art, tried to outline its principles. When it came to practical aesthetics, the progressive France was certainly not a pioneer. On the contrary, he was conservative and traditional.[68] He found legitimate most of the classical aesthetic postulates and gladly accepted tested artistic experience without risking the failure of experimentation. In the classical doctrine, art blends the inexplicable with the definable. The foundation of literary art is the solid, conservative craft of writing. For France, clarity is one of the first virtues of any *homme de lettres*. Speaking about Maupassant, France says that he has the three great qualities of a French writer "... d'abord clarté, puis encore la clarté et enfin la clarté. Il a l'esprit de mesure et d'ordre qui est celui de

[66] *O.C.*, VI, p. 100; "N'est-ce pas plutôt un heureux instinct qui pousse le poète dans les pays lointans et dans les âges reculés? Il y trouve le mystère et l'étrangeté, dont il a tant besoin, car il n'y a de poésie que dans le désir de l'impossible ou dans le regret de l'irréparable."

[67] *O.C.*, XXIII, p. 482; "Tous mes désirs étaient de beauté et je reconnus que cet amour de la beauté, que peu d'hommes ressentent et dont j'étais transporté, est une source jaillissante de plaisir et de joie."

[68] Dargan, *op. cit.*, p. 592 " ... as Thibaudet says, although his thought progressed toward the Left his style clearly belonged to the Right'." Levaillant who, in his context, lends the term "style" a much broader range than Thibaudet, naturally does not agree with this opinion (*op. cit.*, p. 827): "Dira-t-on, avec Thibaudet, que ces idées 'de gauche' s'expriment dans un style 'de droite'? Certainement pas. France se méfie trop des ivresses de l'instinct pour ne pas vouloir donner d'abord une leçon d'ordre et d'unité: la forme de son œuvre contient sa signification."

notre race."[69] Clarity is especially desirable for one reason: without it, art loses its charming ease and simplicity. "The more I live the more I feel that there is no beauty except that which is simple", France says in the already cited answer to Charles Morice. The joy the art lover draws from art should not cost him the slightest fatigue.[70] France's request for clarity and simplicity again echoes many a line of *L'Art poétique*.[71] Simplicity is usually a result of considerable discipline, economy, and meticulous craftsmanship, which judges its own products and suppresses all that does not comply with the laws of literary craft. It is an inventive assimilation of certain literary traditions. France especially emphasizes conciseness and ease. In his essay, "Demain", he deplores the literary overproduction which results not only from the commercial interests of the publishers but also from the lack of discipline on the part of the young writers.[72] France's complaint is typical of a literary veteran of any era. What France claims was claimed by many generations of critics, including Boileau.[73]

[69] *O.C.*, VI, p. 58.

[70] *O.C.*, VI, p. 519; "Plus je vis, plus je sens qu'il n'y a de beau que ce qui est facile. Les plaisirs que l'art procure ne doivent jamais coûter la moindre fatigue."

[71] Boileau, *op. cit.*, Chant I, vv. 27-28, 45, 66, 123-128, 151-154, 269.

[72] *O.C.*, VI, 511-512; "On publie deux ou trois romans par jour. ... Le XVIIIe siècle n'en a pas laissé dix, et c'est un des beaux siècles de la fiction en prose. Nous avons trop de romans, et de trop gros. ... Les contes les plus aimables ne sont-ils pas les plus courts? .... Il faut être léger pour voler à travers les âges. Le vrai génie français est prompt et concis. Il était incomparable dans la nouvelle. Je voudrais qu'on fît encore la belle nouvelle française; je voudrais qu'on fût élégant et facile, rapide aussi. ....

On peut beaucoup dire en un petit nombre de pages. Un roman devrait se lire d'une haleine. J'admire que ceux qu'on fait aujourd'hui aient tous également trois cent cinquante pages. Cela convient à l'éditeur. Mais cela n'est pas toujours au sujet. ... L'examen des tendances de la jeunesse intellectuelle nous entraînerait beaucoup trop loin. Vous constatez que ces tendances sont très divergentes. En effet, il est de plus en plus difficile de distinguer des groupes nettement définis. Il n'y a plus d'écoles, plus de traditions, plus de discipline. Il était sans doute nécessaire d'arriver à cet excès d'individualisme. Vous me demandez si c'est un bien ou un mal d'y être arrivé. Je vous répondrai que l'excès est toujours un mal."

[73] Boileau, *op. cit.*, Chant I, vv. 59-60, 65;

Fuyez de ces auteurs l'abondance stérile,
Et ne vous chargez point d'un détail inutile
. . . .
Qui ne sait se borner ne sut jamais écrire.

Literary discipline also implies a voluntary submission to certain traditional social and aesthetic conventions. As for the originality of art, France is quite skeptical. In his view, originality represents a very small portion of any aesthetic achievement even in the case of the greatest authors. The material from which an artist creates – words, genres, and the ideas themselves – all this has been whispered to him from every side.[74] Like their forerunners, modern authors cannot ignore all that was created by previous generations. M. Dubois, of *La Vie en fleur*, whose views so impressed the young Nozière, says: "En poésie, en art, en philosophie, il faut revenir aux anciens. Pourquoi? Parce que rien ne se peut plus faire de beau, de bien, de sage."[75] Such a view is in perfect harmony with the classical doctrine. Modern authors must imitate like Homer, like Horace and Virgil, like Petrarch and Ronsard, like Rabelais and Montaigne, like Racine, Molière, and Shakespeare, like Goethe and Voltaire.

Bon goût, another postulate of French classicism, is also stressed by France, who resents the vulgarity he feels is so characteristic of naturalistic literature. The lack of taste, that is, the inability to perceive beauty, is disastrous for an artist and probably is the mysterious sin mentioned in the Scriptures which never shall be pardoned. The poor chief of the naturalists, Zola, is its miserable victim. For this and other shortcomings Zola deserves profound pity in the eyes of France.[76]

But clarity, ease, simplicity, good taste, avoidance of any vulgarity and ingenious imitation cannot produce a work of art without another important factor – surprise. Without surprising effects the reader's stimulation may vanish. Various surprising features in a work of art are the most reliable means of maintaining or increasing the reader's interest. "A mon sens, le poète ou le conteur, pour être tout à fait galant homme, évitera de causer la moindre peine, de créer la moindre difficulté à son lecteur. Pour faire sagement il n'exigera point l'attention; il la surprendra."[77] Every constituent of France's art may become, in the proper moment, a vehicle of surprise: unusually rich subject matter, the form in which it is presented, his structural anarchy with

[74] *O.C.*, VI, p. 512.
[75] *O.C.*, XXIII, p. 436.
[76] *O.C.*, VI, pp. 213-214. See also p. 165 of this study.
[77] *O.C.*, VI, p. 519.

its surprising digressions, his unpredictable wit, his lyricism. He knows profoundly that whoever wants to avoid being monotonous or boring must have a rich if not inexhaustible stock of surprise and must be able to serve it to the readers skilfully.

Even this aesthetic lesson is nothing new. It belongs among the traditional postulates of the literary métier. In many ways, France's novels and short stories are direct successors of the Graeco-Gallo-Roman epos. They are full of unexpected anecdotes, obscure references, aphorisms, paradoxes, literary embroidery of all kinds, divine and devilish actions, saints, mythological heroes and heroines, assonances, rhymed and rhythmical passages. France imitates practically to the letter the classical advice of the aesthetic counsellor to so many generations of French writers.[78] He follows nearly every rule of the classical recipe, though not without some very unorthodox modifications, such as his adaptations of many medieval and Judeo-Christian supernatural elements which Boileau banished from the classical epos.

The comparison of the main tenets of the classical doctrine with France's practical aesthetics sufficiently justifies the conclusion that France's literary techniques are deeply rooted in the classical tradition.[79] The many literary trends which originated in Western Europe during France's lifetime influenced his art only slightly. It is paradoxical that France, an outspoken *homme de gauche* and an indefatigable satirist of the conservative bourgeoisie, military circles, clergymen, capitalistic Jews and the aristocracy, remains, in terms of his literary techniques,

[78] Comparing the epos with the tragedy, Boileau says, (*op. cit.,* Chant III, v.v. 173-74 and 180-85):

> Le poète s'égaye en mille inventions,
> Orne, élève, embellit, agrandit toutes choses,
> . . . .
> Que Neptune en courroux, s'élevant sur la mer,
> D'un mot calme les flots, mette la paix dans l'air
> Délivre les vaisseaux, des syrtes les arrache,
> C'est là ce qui surprend, frappe, saisit, attache.
> Sans tous ces ornements le vers tombe en langueur, . . .

[79] Stapfer (*op. cit.,* p. 226) emphasizes Frances classical erudition and its contribution to his artistic inspiration: "La vieille culture hellénique de M. Anatole France: voilà le fond, la base ferme et solide, le roc patiemment et lentement creusé où s'appuie et s'élève tout l'édifice de son beau talent, substance et forme, art et matière, style et philosophie, atticisme du penseur et de l'écrivain."

among the most conservative artists of his era. Neither contemporary science nor political doctrines helped him to solve his fundamental teleological problems. It is true that politically he lined up with socialism, but he found his truth in the Greek cult of joy and beauty and in art. To his satisfaction, this cult was transplanted and bloomed gloriously in the fertile soil of French culture. Its forms and aesthetic principles were clearly repeated by the classical doctrine of the seventeenth century, a doctrine which became the very marrow of the French literary tradition. France not only respectfully adhered to this classical heritage so dear to him, but in his own way enriched it.

II

FRANCE'S ART OF EXPRESSION

Any author who values beauty must be profoundly conscious of style. France, "the Atticist", admires and imitates elegant, classical simplicity, but in striving for it, he has learned that, in art, simplicity is not at all a simple achievement. It is even difficult to define it,[1] as it is usually an illusion. France compares a good style to the sun ray.

Un bon style, enfin, est comme ce rayon de lumière ... qui doit sa clarté pure à l'union intime des sept couleurs dont il est composé. Le style simple est semblable à la clarté blanche. Il est complexe, mais il n'y paraît pas ... dans le langage, la simplicité belle et désirable n'est qu'une apparence et ... elle résulte uniquement du bon ordre et de l'économie souveraine des parties du discours.[2]

Restricting the notion of simplicity and opposing it not to "complexity" but to "ingeniousness", Cerf condemns France's paradox, saying: "France is defining his own simplicity, which is not simplicity at all. It is the opposite of simplicity; it is ingeniousness; it is dust in the reader's eyes."[3] The same scholar also accuses France's "laudatory critics" for characterizing his style as "classic simplicity", whereas it would be more proper to speak about "classic lucidity" which is not "synonymous with simplicity".[4] Although from the point of view of scholarly accuracy Cerf's remark is pertinent, one may point that hardly any contemporary replica either of Homer or of Cicero would be judged by modern critics as "classically" simple. Besides, Racine and Voltaire (for example) are also among France's classical ancestors.

[1] *O.C.*, IX, p. 442.
[2] *Ibid.*, p. 445.
[3] Cerf, *op. cit.*, pp. 213-14.
[4] *Ibid.*, p. 205-207.

Cerf himself retracts a part of his previous comment when saying:

> France is right when he says that there are styles which seem simple but none that are really simple. The classic style is, in truth, neither simple nor natural in the sense in which these words are commonly used to-day. It is a work of art, artificial. But the artist is able to create the impression of a simple, natural style . . .[5]

Admitting that no classic style is so simple and that, in any case, it only creates the impression of being simple, Cerf seems to imply that, like France's style, any classic style, too is "dust in the reader's eyes". Perhaps it would be more accurate to say that, far from being a faithful imitation of the Ancients, France's illusory stylistic simplicity reflects much of their influences as well as that of French classical traditions.

France learned the finest points of stylistic art as an editor in Lemerre's publishing house. "C'est par les travaux de l'éditeur qu'il apprit le métier d'écrivain", says his biographer, Jacques Suffel,[6] but he was not entirely inexperienced when he accepted this post. We may assume that the seeds of France's exceptional stylistic skill were sown by some of the pedants who instructed him at Collège Stanislas. Undoubtedly they were among the first to educate him in lucidity and elegance. The alliance between France's taste for poetry and his expert craftsmanship illustrates the ancient saying that *poeta nascitur orator fit*, for he is both a born poet and a witty and eloquent rhetor who never stops inventing verbal surprise. J. J. Brousson records one of France's practical remarks on the Voltairean approach to adjectives:

> . . . je soigne mes adjectifs. Je me range au sentiment de Voltaire. Rappellez-vous sa boutade si plaisante, si judicieuse: " 'Quoique l'adjectif s'accorde avec le substantif, en genre, en nombre et en cas, néanmoins. [sic] L'adjectif et le substantif ne se conviennent pas toujours.' A quoi bon les multiplier pour dire la même chose. Si vous les prodiguez, contrariez-les. Vous surprendrez ainsi votre lecteur."[7]

France refers here to one of his frequent stylistic elements, the oxymoron, and the remark stresses the importance he attributes to surprise.

A skilful writer has to be able to charm or to astound his reader by

[5] *Ibid.*, p. 220.
[6] Suffel, *op. cit.*, p. 14.
[7] Jean-Jacques Brousson, *Anatole France en pantouflès* (Paris, Crès, 1917), p. 62.

two contradictory expressions, but occasionally a single word must be enough to achieve it. Scattered in France's prose are various unexpected lexical elements which range from comical to tragic, from vulgar to sublime. Thus the author's semantic skill incessantly animates his narration. Adjectives such as *tudesque*,[8] *spagirique*,[9] a term coined by Paracelsus for *alchimiste*, *insulaire*[10] instead of *anglais*, the invented noun *chatnoiresque*,[11] or the obscure bibliophile term *bipontique*[12] surprise by their bizarre quality, pseudo-scholarly or even snobbish tone. On the other hand, a low colloquialism, or a parody of the quasi-legal jargon of the police, equally enhances the reader's interest in the subject matter. Crainquebille's "mort aux vaches", the policeman's "Voulez-nous que je vous f.... une contravention",[13] and some passages of his report, such as "Ordre de circuler auquel il refusa d'obtempérer ... je l'avertis que j'allais verbaliser ...",[14] produce an illusion of an authentic *couleur locale.*

The epilogue to M. Bergeret's marriage and to his love for his wife culminates in a single vulgarity which one does not expect from a cultivated scholar, even when he intends to get a divorce. "Je ne vous ai jamais aimé, ... Vous êtes laide, vous êtes ridicule, et le reste. Et l'on sait dans toute la ville que vous n'êtes qu'un foutriquet ... oui, un foutriquet ..."[15] The emphatic confirmation of the insult lends to the sarcastic matrimonial confession a grotesque tinge which, however, does not obscure the tragic undertone.

A contrast is produced by the humanistic insults the mob hurls at Gamelin and other condemned Jacobins on their way to the guillotine: "Cannibales, anthropophages, vampires!"[16] The reader cannot but be surprised when France unexpectedly calls Christ "thaumaturge galiléen",[17] the women attending confession "péronelles de pénitentes",[18]

[8] *O.C.*, II, p. 7.
[9] *O.C.*, VIII, p. 166.
[10] *O.C.*, II, p. 8.
[11] *O.C.*, VI, p. 526.
[12] *O.C.*, VIII, p. 19.
[13] *O.C.*, XIV, p. 17.
[14] *Ibid.*
[15] *O.C.*, XI, p. 452.
[16] *O.C.*, XX, p. 304.
[17] *O.C.*, V, p. 238.
[18] *O.C.*, V, p. 334.

when he refers to the lechery of Zola's heroes as "satyriasis".[19] France does not hesitate occasionally to descend to a low literary level. He may entertain the reader by the gallic roguishness of playful vulgarities such as: "... un prince ... pénétra jusqu'au lit où dormait la princesse. C'était un principicule allemand qui avait une jolie moustache et des hanches orbiculaires",[20] or by putting into the mouth of the distinguished duchess a locker-room term: "Boulingrin, ... vous puez le pissat de chat."[21] An obscure *acte gratuit*, the third motto of the eighth book of *L'Ile des Pingouins*, belongs in a category of aesthetic triviality all its own. "Bqsfttfusftpvtusbjufb mbvupsjufeftspjtfueftfnqfsfv ... ojpo. VOUFNPJOXFSJEJRVF."[22] To the conservative reader this bit of utopian nonsense may even seem to be an innocent harbinger of contemporary experimental techniques. In any case, aside from its visual effect, its meaning, if any, is known only to the author. France, who is fond of mythological and medieval terms, knows how to create the illusion of the historical setting or of the social atmosphere he dramatizes. The description of Proconsul Gallio's residence in Corinth epitomizes the elegant style of living of the Roman upper class in the days of Claudius. The ancient *couleur locale* is inherent in the diction.

Sa *villa*, construite au temps d'*Auguste*, agrandie et embellie depuis lors par les *pro-consuls* qui s'étaient succédé dans le gouvernement de la *province*, s'élevait sur les dernières pentes *occidentales* de l'*Acrocorinthe*, dont le *sommet chevelu* portait le *temple de Vénus* et *les bosquets des hiérodules*. C'était une maison assez vaste qu'entouraient des jardins plantés d'arbres touffus, arrosés d'eaux vives, ornés de *statues*, d'*exèdres*, de *gymnases*, de *bains*, de *bibliothèques*, et d'autels *consacrés aux dieux*. ... Dans le ciel rose le soleil se levait humide et *candide*. Les *ondulations douces* des collines de l'*Isthme* cachaient le *rivage saronique*, le *Stade*, le *sanctuaire des jeux*, le port oriental de *Kerkhrées*. Mais on voyait, entre les *flancs fauves* des monts *Géraniens* et le rose *Hélicon* à la double cime, dormir la *mer bleue des Alcyons*.[23]

The accumulation of geographical proper names and Hellenisms and

[19] *O.C.*, VI, p. 328 see also this study, p. 165.
[20] *O.C.*, XIX, p. 239.
[21] *Ibid.*, p. 229.
[22] *O.C.*, XVIII, p. 397.
[23] *O.C.*, XIII, p. 379. (The italics in this and the subsequent quotations in this chapter are mine unless indicated otherwise.)

words of Greek or Latin origin enables the reader to visualize Gallio's mansion without ever having seen the blue sea of Alcyons. However, in this case the density of Latin and Greek words is excessive and draws too much attention to the style. Additional editorial streamlining of *les flancs fauves des monts Géraniens* might have increased the lyrical charm of the passage.

Blanck extensively illustrates France's stylistic parody of Biblical diction with the florid statements of Paphnuce, the hero of *Thaïs*. The literary caricature of this militant enemy of Hellenism amuses the reader not only by Paphnuce's fanatical actions and thoughts but also by his expression. The monk's mind is so pervaded with Biblical texts that whatever he says echoes their primitive and exalted diction:

Puisse-t-elle fleurir par mes soins comme un rosier balsamique dans ta Jérusalem céleste.

Le bon Seigneur Dieu, lui dit-il, vivait dans le ciel comme un Pharaon sous les tentes de son harem et sous les arbres de ses jardin. [Sic]

... sache que, pas plus que les lis des champs, il ne travaille ni ne file.[24]

In "Amycus et Célestin", the satyr and the friar take each other by surprise and Brother Célestin immediately wants to exorcize the peace-loving faun. In imitating archaic diction, France intensifies the serene lyrical climate of the ancient setting.

– Bon *ermite*, lui dit-il, ne m'*exorcise* pas. Ce jour est pour moi comme pour toi un jour de fête. Il ne serait pas *charitable* de me *contrister* dans le temps *pascal*. Si tu veux, nous cheminerons ensemble. ...
– Bon vieillard, tu es plus savant que moi et tu vois l'invisible. Mais je connais mieux que toi *les bois* et *les fontaines*. J'apporterai au *dieu* des feuillages et des fleurs. Je sais les *berges* où le *cresson* entr'ouvre ses *corymbes lilas*, *les prés* où le coucou fleurit en *grappes* jaunes. Je devine à son *odeur légère* le *gui du pommier sauvage*. Déjà, une *neige de fleurs* couronne les *buissons d'épine noire*.[25]

The italicized words form two contrasting groups which represent the two opposing cults. The first series parodies monastic asceticism, fear of the devil, and Christian suffering. The terms in the second part suggest the vital, mysterious forces and the pagan joy of rebirth in nature.

[24] Blanck, *op. cit.*, p. 117. Blanck's references not based on Calman-Lévy edition were not retained.
[25] *O.C.*, V, 244-45.

Many words acquire an unexpected meaning if used in an unconventional context, others surprise by their singularity.

Dargan points out that France is forever seeking the *mot juste* and generally finds it. The critic illustrates France's skill with the following examples: "Hamilcar, *prince somnolent* de la cité des livres . . .; M. Brunetière est un critique guerrier, d'une *intrépidité rare* . . .; Les immortels doivent plus qu'on ne croit à leurs adorateurs: ils leur doivent *la vie.*"[26] The vicious Bluebeard is characterized as "ce bon seigneur abbatu par une constante adversité domestique"[27] or the modern Arab's ethical code as a chivalrous puerility: ". . . l'Arabe actuel ressemble assez par sa puérilité chevaleresque à nos seigneurs du XIVe siècle."[28] France parodies the unctuously elegant and subtle semantics of a humanist cleric in Abbé Lantaigne's long letter to the Archbishop. In this epistle, the abbé denounces the alleged pastoral flaws of M. Guitrel, his rival for the bishopric:

Et là, penché sur les buffets, les consoles, les tables il [abbé Guitrel] examine avec un intérêt profond et une *assiduité laborieuse* les friandises amassées dans les assiettes et dans les plats. Puis, s'arrêtant à l'endroit où sont dressées ces sortes de gâteaux *qu'on m'a dit se nommer éclairs et babas,* il touche du bout du doigt une de ces pâtisseries, puis une autre, et il fait envelopper ces *bagatelles de bouche* dans une feuille de papier . . . on se demandera si le professeur d'éloquence du grand séminaire ne *laisse* point *chez la pâtissière* quelque part de *sa dignité* . . . monsieur Guitrel est peu excusable d'*avoir donné* par sa mauvaise tenue une *apparence de vérité à la calomnie.*[29]

The last insinuation is a typical example of M. Lantaigne's art of "innocent" slandering. While dissociating himself from the calumny the happy finder of an ideal *mot juste* corroborates all suspicions without using a single ambiguity. The last *tour* astonishes by the degree of hypocritical bias compatible with a relative truth.

France's prose is enriched by various stylistic and rhetorical features which writers have cultivated and the readers have relished for generations. The goal of most of them is comparable to the goal of the oxymoron, to surprise or to amuse the reader. The oxymoron is one of

[26] Dargan, *op. cit.*, p. 590. (Dargan's italics.)
[27] *O.C.*, XIX, p. 14.
[28] *O.C.*, X, p. 387.
[29] *O.C.*, XI, pp. 30-31.

the simplest figures of speech, consisting generally of two elements, a noun and an adjective, or two co-ordinated adjectives. This use of contradictory words in the same phrase is quite characteristic of France's indulgence in controversy. Both Blanck and Dargan comment on this technique. The latter says:

His desire to startle by unexpected correlations is thus transferred from thought to phrase, to figure, and to epithet. Nowhere is the device more apparent than in A. F.'s choice of seemingly incongruous adjectives, which, as M. Maurois has indicated, is a part of his habitual 'alternance des thèmes dissonants'. A gesture will be 'placide et menaçant'; a château will be 'alchimique et délabré'; ... Or there may be a warfare between adjective and noun: 'une gloire crapuleuse'; 'la douceur ... cruelle! This kind of thing, declares Maurois, is France's 'folie reglée'.[30]

Maurois seems to judge this technique too harshly. It would seem also fair to distinguish between France's early and more mature works. In this respect, it seems that Blanck is more objective, attributing to France sufficient refinement of taste to prevent him from making a fetish of any single literary device. "Er versteht es nicht nur das richtige Maß zu finden, seine Antithesen ... erscheinen uns natürlich, wirkungsvoll, nicht gesucht, bizarr oder farblos. Sie beleben seine Sprache und vermeiden Eintönigkeit."[31]

Sometimes France's oxymorons are paradoxical; sometimes their incongruity is illusory and based only on a deviation from general use. In the latter case the oxymoron, dramatizing merely a contrast in meaning but not a real contradiction, resembles the antithesis in the narrower sense. Terms such as "Euripide était tout ensemble athée et mystique";[32] or "un grand et effroyable saint"[33] are paradoxical. However, the last example could also be considered a hyperbole, especially in the case of a non-Christian holy man whose sainthood could stem from theological merits other than those expressed in the Gospel. The following are a few examples of the kind of oxymoron in

[30] Dargan, *op. cit.*, p. 587. (Dargan's footnotes not retained.)

[31] Blanck, *op. cit.*, p. 109. (Like several other critics Blanck classifies the Francean antonym as an antithesis, not taking into account that the oxymoron expresses a contradiction, or at least Maurois' "thèmes dissonants", whereas the antithesis may be limited merely to expressing a contrast.)

[32] *O.C.*, VI, p. 456.

[33] *O.C.*, VII, p. 142.

which the conflicting ideas are not completely incompatible: "Les doux hérétiques"[34] – although a heretic is usually stubborn or pig-headed he certainly can be both kind and mild. "Les beaux vices, des vices nobles, impérieux, très hauts"[35] – the vice of Doña Maria or Thérèse Martin-Bellème could be called beautiful and noble, at least from their points of view. "L'heureuse perversité"[36] – a perversity can often contribute to the happiness of the perverted person. "Un beau crime"[37] – a conspiracy against a cruel law, for instance, might be heroically beautiful. "Anachorète moderne"[38] – modern man could imitate the Anchorites' style of living. "Paul était alors le plus célèbre des fakirs chrétiens"[39] – a detached non-Christian observer could easily call a Christian monk a fakir, although it normally is a term reserved for Moslem monks. But in spite of these possibilities all these examples yield the same effect as a pure oxymoron, perhaps because, in the first moment, the reader resents the associations of heresy and gentleness, or of vice and beauty, etc.

Plain antithesis rarely implies any contradiction. In France's work it is perhaps one of the most frequent techniques of direct characterization. To dramatize Bismarck's chief ability, namely the art of commanding, France uses a strong, simple antithesis: "Il est soldat comme ses aieux; mais c'est, comme eux, pour commander, non pour obéir."[40] France uses the antithetical qualities of another man to bring out those of Worms-Clavelin: "Ils n'avaient pas une idée commune et ne s'entendaient sur rien; Frémont aimait la contradiction, Worms-Clavelin la supportait; Frémont était abondant et violent en paroles, Worms-Clavelin cédait à la violence et parlait peu."[41] Such an antithesis sharpens the prefect's political profile. The relative density of this figure in France's younger works often makes too evident his striving for stylistic effect. In *Jocaste*, a mere description of the ravings of the dying Mr. Haviland did not provide sufficient contrast; another

[34] *O.C.*, VI, p. 477.
[35] *O.C.*, XIX, p. 328.
[36] *O.C.*, VI, p. 488.
[37] *O.C.*, IX, p. 459.
[38] *O.C.*, II, p. 251.
[39] *O.C.*, VI, p. 465.
[40] *O.C.*, VI, pp. 125-126.
[41] *O.C.*, XI, p. 339.

antithesis was needed to sharpen the distinction between his tenderness and fury:

Il soupirait le nom d'Hélène avec une douceur plaintive, et aussitôt poussait des glapissements aigus et des ricanements sinistres, et le contraste était si brusque qu'on ne pouvait concevoir de telles alternatives de tendresse et d'ironie furieuse, même dans un cerveau déjà décomposé.[42]

To characterize Mr. Haviland's peculiar kind of generosity, France arranges three contrasts climactically, expressing the last in the form of a paradox.

Après avoir donné des diamants à sa femme, il la torturait naïvement pendant deux heures pour un compte de trois francs qu'elle ne savait pas rendre. Il faisant des largesses d'une façon étroite; la prodigalité avait chez lui un air d'avarice.[43]

In his more mature works France disciplines his stylistic verve and better attains what he preaches, namely to conceal his art. In evaluating the function of antithesis in France's art, Blanck finds that the countless antitheses in France's work do not contribute to his originality because antitheses can be found in the work of all authors. Yet he admits that even quite conventional antitheses lend vitality and expressiveness to France's diction. Among other examples he cites the following passages from *Thaïs*, to prove his statements.

Les hymnes qu'ils chantaient avec le peuple exprimaient les délices de la souffrance et mêlaient dans un deuil triomphal, tant d'allégresse à tant de douleur que Thaïs, en les écoutant, sentait les voluptés de la vie et les affres de la mort couler à la fois dans ses sens renouvelés.

... et Thaïs, oppressée par l'étreinte du moine, sa chair délicate froissée contre le rude cilice, sentait courir en elle les frissons de l'horreur et de la volupté.

Le lis de la vertu a fleuri sur le fumier de ta corruption.[44]

The first sequence of antitheses does not indicate the "classical" artistic moderation and the contrasts are somewhat stereotyped. On the other hand, the second and the third are more restrained and inventive. Aesthetically speaking, the less direct antitheses are more unexpected and, naturally, yield more astonishment: "... mais en dépit du cuistre,

[42] *O.C.*, II, p. 69.
[43] *Ibid.*, p. 35.
[44] Blanck, *op. cit.*, p. 110. (Blanck's references not retained.)

j'avais vu Cléopâtre";[45] "... cette belle voix d'ange... qui répétait 'Cochon!' 'Cochon!' "[46] Like these two examples, many Francean antitheses strike a comical note – they may be farcical or emphasize the irony of fate – but, on the whole, antithesis is not typical of France's humor. His wit and his mischief manifest themselves more often in other rhetorical conceits such as dazzling periphrases, euphemisms and understatements. With circumspect diplomacy and tact they charm by the contrast between the unpleasant reality and its equivocal expression. Therefore, they are typical companions of touchy erotic topics or terms banned by convention: " 'Fermez les yeux and prenez ce petit remède'; et aussitôt l'innocente faisait, au gré des fripons qui voulaient d'elle ce qu'il était bien naturel d'en vouloir, car elle était jolie."[47] France not only gets away from the term, but also ambiguously puns, increasing our amusement. In the same category of somewhat *risqué* periphrase belongs: "Le zèle de la religion l'échauffait à ce point qu'il recommanda à sa fille d'immoler même ce qu'elle avait de plus cher, si ce sacrifice devait tourner à l'avantage de Mahom";[48] the description of Jacques Tournebroche's first erotic experience, "Un soir, ... elle m'apprit ce que je ne savais pas encore et qu'elle savait depuis longtemps";[49] the guiding principle of Elodie's erotic philosophy: "Elle envisageait sans terreur l'idée de s'unir à son ami par des liens secrets et de prendre l'auteur de la nature pour seul témoin de leur foi mutuelle."[50] The theme of love and death must project the unreserved and profound devotion by most intimate, yet tragically noble, words such as Rose Thévenin's sincere confession to Brotteaux in the jail: "Et si ce que je vais vous dire peut vous rattacher à la vie, croyez-le: je serai pour vous ... tout ce que vous voudrez que je sois."[51]

Understatement is another aspect of periphrase, but instead of evading an objectionable term or situation, it exaggeratedly minimizes it, as in the following: "Cette jeune demoiselle perdit son innocence,

[45] *O.C.*, VII, p. 508.
[46] *O.C.*, V, p. 330.
[47] *O.C.*, XIX, p. 141.
[48] *O.C.*, X, p. 473.
[49] *O.C.*, VIII, p. 29.
[50] *O.C.*, XX, p. 36. See also this study p. 54.
[51] *Ibid.*, p. 246. See also this study pp. 160-61, n. 8.

sans, autant dire, s'en apercevoir."[52] In the next example, a hyperbole and the understatement which immediately follows increase, through contrast, the effect of the two figures of speech. "Elle le trompa avec tous les gentilhommes des environs. Elle y mettait tant d'adresse qu'elle le trompait dans son château et jusque sous ses yeux sans qu'il s'en aperçût. La pauvre Barbe-Bleue se doutait bien de quelque chose, mais il ne savait pas de quoi."[53] An understatement and a litotes are united in the following statement: "On le disait égoiste et parcimonieux. Je crois qu' . . . il ne recherchait pas les occasions de faire des largesses."[54] Abbé Coignard, after having knocked down M. Guéritaude with a bottle of wine and having mortally "tripped" his footman, comments: "Je crois, en effet . . . que j'ai été quelque peu homicide."[55] The description of Homer's suicide found in "Le Chanteur de Kymé" is a poetically tragic periphrase: "Et le vieil Homère s'avança sur le haut promontoire jusqu'à ce que la terre, qui l'avait porté si longtemps, manquât sous ses pas."[56]

Euphemism is a figure of speech somewhat similar to the periphrase and the understatement. To soften the profanity of Komm l'Atrébate's physiological bravado, France writes: "Reconnaissant, debout sur son socle de marbre, la déesse Rome, . . . il accomplit devant elle, avec une intention injurieuse, la plus ignoble des fonctions naturelles."[57] M. Bergeret uses an ironical euphemism in referring to the commercial competition of midway merchants who hope to encourage both patriotism and profits by advertising "Véritable bière Jeanne d'Arc. – Café de la Pucelle." The scholar points out that one has to admire "ce concours de citoyens réunis pour honorer la libératrice d'Orléans".[58] In the last two cases the ironical euphemism approaches the *mot juste.* Instead of saying "coquin" or "fripon", France uses ironically milder terms: "M. Joursavault vint lui dénoncer *les impies* qui, la veille, avaient mis de l'encre dans les bénitiers."[59] Euphemism may be allied

[52] *O.C.*, XIX, p. 204.
[53] *Ibid.*, p. 139.
[54] *O.C.*, XXIII, p. 339.
[55] *O.C.*, VIII, p. 176.
[56] *O.C.*, XIII, p. 23.
[57] *O.C.*, XIII, p. 52.
[58] *O.C.*, XI, p. 100.
[59] *O.C.*, V, p. 358.

with ambiguity implying varying degrees of eroticism or license: a word used most often in a moral sense may be given a frivolous connotation "... il lui dit tout ce qui pouvait ... calmer sa peine, et il la consola. Car elle avait une âme douce et qui voulait être consolée."[60] Summing up Elodie's approval of what modern marriage counsellors would refer to as premarital sexual relationships, France uses a longer periphrase composed of a litotes and two extended ironic euphemisms: "Elle envisageait sans terreur l'idée de s'unir à son ami par des liens secrets et de prendre l'auteur de la nature pour seul témoin de leur foi mutuelle."[61]

Hyperbole creates surprise through an opposite form of distortion. Usually, it is an ironic exaggeration, as in the following: "M. Dubois était grammairien d'une force qui faisait peur. Pour le sens et les rapports des termes, rien n'égalait sa justice sévère."[62] The exaggeration is sometimes ironical (that is, contrary, or at least a step toward the contrary, to what is meant) or sometimes farcical. The following farcical hyperbole, describing one of Bluebeard's mothers-in-law, is France's contribution to the standard joke: "En réalité elle n'avait rien et devait jusqu'à ses fausses dents."[63] In "La Chemise", M. Chaudesaigue's ironically lofty hyperbole, allied with a series of metaphors, paradoxes, antitheses and a climax, resembles Panurge's ironic eloquence:

> Le vice est l'unique distraction qu'on puisse goûter en ce monde; le vice est le coloris de l'existence, le sel de l'âme, l'étincelle de l'esprit. Que dis-je, le vice est la seule originalité, la seule puissance créatrice de l'homme; il est l'essai d'une organisation de la nature contre la nature, de l'intronisation du règne humain au-dessus du règne animal, d'une création anonyme, d'un monde conscient dans l'inconscience universelle; le vice est le seul bien propre à l'homme, son réel patrimoine, sa vraie vertu au sense propre du mot, ...[64]

M. Montragoux' pathos is comically overstated as follows: "... en tirant du fond de ses entrailles des soupirs à renverser un chêne."[65]

[60] *O.C.*, XIX, p. 199.
[61] *O.C.*, XX, p. 36.
[62] *O.C.*, XXIII, p. 449.
[63] *O.C.*, XIX, p. 147.
[64] *O.C.*, XIX, p. 327.
[65] *Ibid.*, p. 149.

There is a spark of mischievous ambiguity in such exaggeration. In "Le Chanteur de Kymé", France parodies the "Homeric" hyperbole "Je sais encore six fois soixante chansons très belles", which, without wasting a second, he respectfully rectifies with a tolerant twinkle: "De cette manière il faisait entendre qu'il en savait beaucoup. Mais il n'en connaissait pas le nombre."[66]

Like Rabelais, Molière or Voltaire, France is fond of the climactic arrangement as a means of surprise. Often the gradual accumulation of emphasis or of meaning achieves effects similar to comical pleonasm and hyperbole. The gradation usually parodies the florid, redundant eloquence of France's characters and the final rhetorical peak is almost always a qualified exaggeration. The opening of Maître Lemerle's plea for Crainquebille is charged with this rhetorical device:

Il [Matra] est parfois *fatigué, excédé, surmené.* Dans ces conditions il peut avoir été la victime d'une sorte d'hallucination de l'ouïe. Et, quand il vient vous dire, messieurs, que le docteur David Matthieu, *officier de la Légion d'honneur, médecin en chef de l'hôpital Ambroise-Paré, un prince de la science et un homme du monde*, a crié: "Mort aux vaches!" nous sommes bien forcés de reconnaître que Matra est en proie à *la maladie de l'obsession* et, si le terme n'est pas trop fort, au *délire de la persécution.*[67]

Les Sept Femmes de la Barbe-Bleue belongs among the rich sources of climax:

Le pape fulmina contre lui la bulle *Maleficus pastor*, dans laquelle le vénérable pontife était traité de *désobéissant, d'hérètique ou fleurant d'hérésie, de concubinaire, d'incestueux, de corrupteur de peuple, de vieille femme et d'olibrius.*

Foudroyé par le vicaire de Jésus-Christ, *abreuvé* d'amertume, *accablé* de douleur, le saint homme Nicolas *descendit* sans regret de son siège illustre et *quitta, pour n'y plus revenir* la ville de Trinqueballe, témoin durant trente années de ses *vertus pontificales* et de ses *travaux apostoliques.*[68]

In the latter quotation, the climactic effect is heightened by the *mots justes*, metaphors and by antitheses. The following passage is a combination of climax and oxymoron: "Ce savant... a vécu parmi les

[66] *O.C.*, XIII, p. 18.
[67] *O.C.*, XIV, pp. 28-29.
[68] *O.C.*, XIX, p. 211.

moines ignares, paresseux, dégradés, heureux."[69] Here maximum surprise is produced by the least expected climactic adjective. After having characterized Flaubert's attitude towards life and his temperamental *habitus* with a French comparative of the Greek superlative, *tragikotatos*, France adds, in a climatic series of ironic hyperboles, that this life pose would probably become even more acute if Flaubert could see the operatic version of his *Salammbô*. His imaginary reaction to this musical masterpiece is summed up in the following climax, a double anaphora, a frequent stylistic ingredient in any gradation, and in a blend of hyperboles and metaphors:

Tragikotatos, il le serait aujourd'hui plus que jamais, s'il voyait sa *Salammbô* mise en opéra. A ce spectacle horrible, quel éclair sortirait de ses yeux! quelle écume de sa bouche! quel cri de sa poitrine! Ce serait pour lui le calice amer, le sceptre de roseau et la couronne d'épines, ce serait les mains clouées et le flanc ouvert. . . .[70]

Satirizing the division of the nation during the Dreyfus case in the *Ile des Pingouins*, France ends a climax with a gauloiserie:

Il n'y avait que mille ou douze cents pyrotins dans la vaste république; on croyait en voir partout. On craignait en trouver en promenades, dans les assemblées, dans les réunions, dans les salons mondains, à la table de famille, dans le lit conjugal.[71]

The Rabelaisian enumeration belongs in the same family of figures of speech. It achieves its amusing effect without the climax by the grotesque chain of bizarre culinary techniques.

. . . il le reçut des mains d'un habile tonnelier, le parfuma de genièvre, de thym et de romarin. La seigneur Garum n'a pas son pareil pour saigner la chair, la désosser, la découper curieusement, studieusement, amoureusement, et l'impregner des esprits salins qui la conservent et l'embaument. Il est sans rival pour assaisoner, concentrer, réduire, écumer, tamiser, écanter la saumure.[72]

This passage is followed by a short climactic anaphora: "Goûtez de son pétit salé, mon père, et vous vous en lècherez les doigts; goûtez de son petit salé, Nicolas, et vous m'en direz des nouvelles." Also mixed

[69] *O.C.*, VII, p. 132.
[70] *O.C.*, VII, p. 286-287.
[71] *O.C.*, XVIII, p. 276.
[72] *O.C.*, XIX, p. 177.

with anaphora and antithesis and elements of hyperbole is France's satirical account of M. Drumont's anti-Semitism.

M. Edouard Drumont voit des juifs où personne n'en voit. Il en voit parmi les chrétiens, il en voit parmi les prêtres catholiques. Pour lui, Marat était juif, Napoléon était juif, Gambetta était juif. "La guerre de 1870, dit-il, est une guerre juive." C'est aux juifs qu'on doit les affaires de Tunisie et du Tonkin. C'est pour eux seuls que M. Disraëli a fait la guerre de l'Afghanistan. Il voit la main des juifs dans la crise industrielle et dans le progrès du socialisme. Il est hanté.[73]

Enumeration is a typical technique applied in literary embroideries. The following cited from "Le Miracle du Grand Saint Nicolas" reads like a catalogue sent to wealthy patrons by a plush antique dealer. France, a collector himself, undoubtedly was familiar with this kind of commercial literature, and it amused him to parody it.

Seligman, Issachar et Meyer enlevèrent les châsses d'or ornées de pierreries, d'émaux et de cabochons, les reliquaires en forme de coupe, de lanterne, de nef, de tour, les autels portatifs en albâtre encadré d'or et d'argent, les coffrets émaillés par les habiles ouvriers de Limoges et du Rhin, les croix d'autel, les évangéliaires recouverts d'ivoire sculpté et de camées antiques, les peignes liturgiques ornés de festons de pampres, les diptyques consulaires, les pyxides, les chanceliers, les candélabres, les lampes, dont ils soufflaient la sainte lumière et versaient l'huile bénite sur les dalles: les lustres semblables à de gigantesques couronnes, les chapelets aux grains d'ambre et de perles, les colombes eucharistiques, les ciboires, les calices, les patènes, les baisers de paix, les navettes à encens, les burettes, les ex-voto sans nombre, pieds, mains, bras, jambes, yeux, bouches, entrailles, cœurs en argent, et le nez du roi Sidoe et le sein de la reine Blandine, et le chef en or massif de monseigneur saint Cromadaire premier apôtre de Vervignole et bênoit patron de Trinqueballe.[74]

The brocade-like texture of the passage glitters with this bizarre, liturgical inventory, whose redundancy is emphasized by a grotesque litany, full of primitive rhymes and assonances and various accords (e.g. enlevèrent – reliquaires – évangéliaires recouverts – consulaires – lumière; encadré – émaillés – camées – ornés; antiques – liturgiques – dyptiques; accords: Issachar – chasse d'or; orné – en forme – portatifs; lanterne – en albâtre).

Pleonasm, is related to the climax and to enumeration. Its effect is generally comical:

[73] *La Vie littéraire,* cinquième série, p. 11.
[74] *O.C.*, XIX, p. 201.

– Je déplore, je répudie, je condamne, je réprouve, je déteste, j'exècre, j'abomine mes erreurs passées, présentes et futures, dit-il; je me soumets à l'Eglise pleinement et entièrement, totalement et généralement, purement et simplement, et n'ai de croyance que sa croyance, de foi que sa foi, de connaissance que sa connaissance; je ne vois, n'entends ni ne sens que par elle. Elle me dirait que cette mouche qui vient de se poser sur le nez du diacre Modernus est un chameau, qu'incontinent, sans dispute, contestation ni murmure, sans résistance, hésitation ni doute, je croirais, je déclarerais, je proclamerais, je confesserais, dans les tortures et jusqu'à la mort, que c'est un chameau qui s'est posé sur le nez du diacre Modernus.[75]

In this passage, the first pleonastic series, which begins with the weakest "je déplore" and ends with the strongest "j'abomine", is arranged climactically, whereas the second series of redundant adverbs creates the illusion of a *decrescendo*, "pleinement . . . simplement". Among other stylistic stimulations are the monotonous rudimentary anaphorae, "je . . . , je . . . , je . . .", and the primitive rhyming, "pleinement et entièrement", etc., or "je croirais . . . je déclarerais", etc.

The various fragments of text analyzed in the previous passage to illustrate climax were also rich in metaphors; for example, "Le pape fulmina", "foudroyé par le vicaire de Jésus Christ", "Le vice est . . . le sel de l'âme, l'étincelle de l'esprit", "calice amer . . . couronne d'épine", "le flanc ouvert".

One of the many descriptive statements in Coleridge's long definition of imagination characterizes it as a power "which reveals itself in the balance or reconcilement of opposite or discordant qualities, of sameness with difference, of the idea with the image . . ."[76] In other words, imagination is the power which may discover surprising similarities between two different phenomena and express the unexpected parallel in a simile or a metaphor. One may see in such figures a barometer of the author's imaginative power. Metaphors permeate France's prose but do not over-saturate it. Many of them are relatively conventional and their aesthetic value is limited: ". . . et pour la seconde fois dans un tour de cadran, il rougit de son père";[77] "géographie de l'inconnu"[78] for "métaphysique". Others are more original

[75] *Ibid.*
[76] Cited from Herbert Read's "The Definition of Art", *A Modern Book of Esthetics,* ed. Melvin Rader (New York, Holt, 1953), p. 37.
[77] *O.C.*, III, p. 44.
[78] *O.C.*, VI, p. 327.

and unexpected: "le désir de se mêler aux dieux";[79] "il redouta les flèches du fils de Léto";[80] "l'essaim des désirs flotte autour de ta ceinture."[81]

The image in the simile is always digressive and contrasting and may inject any kind of new topical element: comical, erotic, poetic, bizarre, tragic. A satirical simile may be raised to a higher power by a striking antithesis: "... il respire l'odeur des cadavres comme un parfum aphrodisiaque."[82] An unexpected satirical simile lends fresh life to a trite and vulgar refusal: "je m'en fiche comme le Roi de sa première maîtresse".[83] The eternal play of sea waves on the beach is evoked to describe an abstract disposition: "M. Jérôme Coignard était ... d'une mansuétude exemplaire et il avait coutume de dire qu'il devait cette douceur aux vicissitudes de la vie, la fortune l'ayant traité à la façon des cailloux que la mer polit dans son flux et dans son reflux."[84] By the following metaphorical *salto*, "En esthétique, c'est à dire dans les nuages",[85] punning France converts a pedantic term into an image and the lofty image becomes the fact. The last two examples support Blanck's conclusion that most comparisons in France's novels are inspired by nature. Here is just one in Blanck's rich collection of such similes: "... j'ai vu les riches emportés par le vice de luxure qui, semblable à un fleuve à la barbe limoneuse, les poussait dans le gouffre amer."[86] Other frequent sources of Francean imagery are the Bible and Greco-Roman mythology.[87]

France's prose is also pervaded with many less common figures of speech and with puns. Notably in his mature works, these are generally well integrated in the narrative. The following examples may help to illustrate the range of rhetoric devices current in France's prose. Allegory – "Etranglé par justice";[88] Hellenism – "Quels chants sais-tu

[79] *O.C.*, XIII, p. 23.
[80] *Ibid.*, p. 5.
[81] *Ibid.*, p. 16.
[82] *O.C.*, VII, p. 36.
[83] *O.C.*, VIII, p. 165.
[84] *Ibid.*, p. 174.
[85] *O.C.*, VII, p. 385.
[86] Blanck, *op. cit.*, p. 117, (Blanck's references not retained).
[87] Several metaphors and similes in biblical style were cited earlier in the comments on antithesis, p. 51.
[88] *O.C.*, XIX, p. 128.

dire?"[89] or "Si comme tu dis, et comme il me semble, tu es un joueur de lyre."[90] Prosopopeia, i.e., personification, "elle soufflait sur les brindilles de bois sec jusqu'à ce qu'un Dieu les enveloppât de flammes"[91] or "le chœur des lois augustes."[92] Litotes, "Pour être véridique, nous dirons que, sans doute, en sa claire jeunesse ... Marguerite la dentelière n'avait pas égalé sainte Lucie en pureté, sainte Agathe en constance et sainte Catherine en sagesse."[93] The sentence, "Trop généreuse pour se garder (1), trop intelligente pour se perdre (2), sage dans ses folies (3), le goût d'aimer ne lui avait jamais fait oublier les convenances sociales (4)",[94] contains brachylogy (1, 2, 3), paradox (3), and litotes (4). The two related figures of speech, metonymy and synecdoche, are quite current in France's narration. Referring to amorous adventure France speaks about "le lit de Cassandre";[95] "la lance d'Achille"[96] indicates courage, or "le casque de Bélisaire"[97] begging; "chausser les bas violets"[98] means in its context to become a bishop. In "Le Miracle du Grand Saint Nicolas" France explains with a humanist precision his own gallic rhetoric: "Elle appelait, ... la respectable dame Basine vieille bique, et même, prenant la partie pour le tout, cul de bique."[99] More than the low joke amuses: the pedantic reference to the synecdoche hints that the rude insult to the respectable lady is actually an understatement – a *pars pro toto.* A synecdoche in which France poetizes the vigorous spirit of the inhabitants of Attica also contains an unexpected antithesis and a metaphor: "tout un peuple de matelots nourri d'ail et de chansons."[100]

In France's prose there are the two types of pun. One is based on the same sound of two different words, "... divertissez-vous et faites bonne chère",[101] or the ambiguous description of the nuances of love

[89] *O.C.*, XIII, p. 18.
[90] *Ibid.*, p. 16.
[91] *Ibid.*, p. 8.
[92] *O.C.*, VI, p. 297.
[93] *O.C.*, XIX, p. 21.
[94] *O.C.*, XX, p. 36.
[95] *O.C.*, XXIII, p. 62.
[96] *Ibid.*
[97] *O.C.*, III, p. 134.
[98] *O.C.*, XI, p. 60.
[99] *O.C.*, XIX, p. 185.
[100] *O.C.*, VI, p. 457.
[101] *O.C.*, XIX, p. 154.

which the pious bishop, Nicolas, had for his "niece": "Sans doute, il l'aimait en Dieu, mais distinctement; il se plaisait en elle; il aimait à l'aimer."[102] The other gives a different application to a single word to create a comical effect: "C'était un principicule allemand ... et dont, aussitôt réveillée, elle [la Belle-au-Bois-Dormant] tomba, ou plutôt se leva amoureuse."[103] Or: "Vous savez que vous ne savez pas l'étrusque, mon cher confrère. C'est en cela que vous êtes un savant honorable."[104] France uses puns sparingly and unobtrusively. Although conventional tools of the literary métier, these figures of speech, because they are used so inventively, account for much of France's stylistic perfection. They are a source of dramatic, lyrical, comical and libertine accents, they change the mood of the narrative, they make the expression more plastic. His ingenious rhetoric banishes the danger of monotony. Rarely is it artistically pernicious. The too lavish use of antitheses and metaphors brings, especially in a few passages of his earlier works, a certain undesirable artificiality. Occasionally, excessive doses of poetic archaisms in France's visions of ancient settings overdecorate his descriptive passages. Cerf, who questions France's paradoxical concept of simplicity, designates similar flaws in the author's style, also somewhat paradoxically, as "the monotone of grace".[105] But the same critic is aware of the pitfalls of an overly indifferent and even contemptuous approach to style. "The antipathy to 'mere style', a result of the excesses of the last few generations before our own, has naturally, but very unfortunately, brought about a demand for writing which has no style at all."[106]

Such a comment on the trend toward a drab stylistic functionalism, expressed by France's severe critic, partly justifies the opinion that, in spite of admitted weaknesses especially in earlier works, France's rich stock and expert use of the tested rhetorical forms[107] most often lend an unusual elegance and an enviable ease to his art of expression.

[102] *O.C.*, XIX, p. 198.
[103] *O.C.*, XIX, p. 239.
[104] *O.C.*, IX, p. 117.
[105] Cerf, *op. cit.*, p. 225.
[106] *Ibid.*, p. 106.
[107] Irony, ambiguity and paradox, whose functions often exceed that of a figure of speech, and euphony and alliteration will be treated in subsequent chapters.

III

THE ART OF ARRANGEMENT

The all-importance of arrangement in art is one of France's main aesthetic creeds.[1] "Of course a good 'arrangement' is concealed so as to give the appearance of nature itself", points out Barry Cerf,[2] commenting on France's idea of arrangement. Believing that "style is but an indispensable handmaid" and hinting that artists should take only the necessary minimum of liberties in transforming "life" into the art, the same critic makes the accusation that France " 'arranges' life in accordance with his own whimsies". In France's literary arrangements "that gift of design which might lend fitting form to the vision" has no role and these arrangements manifest no "imagination which is architectonic". His skill of arrangement is above all the "art of moulding plastic phrases into ravishing shapes, of pouring liquid syllables into golden matrices".[3] There is certainly very little left to chance in France's diction and syntax and the resented "plastic" phrase is precisely what gives linear elegance and streamlined yet varied contour to France's subject matter. Walton sees in the harmonious integration of France's lexical invention and of his sober syntax the very source of his Atticism.

Words instead of colors were the medium. They were used with an unerring sense of their suggestive as well as of their direct value, so that unwanted suggestions were eliminated and unnatural uses dictated by syntactical formalism were avoided. Sentences were his brush strokes, moving sometimes so lightly they scarcely touched the canvas and, again, leaving sinuous, graceful lines of color, always delicate, searching out the

[1] *O.C.,* VII, p. 357. "... l'art consiste dans l'arrangement et même il ne consiste qu'en cela."
[2] Cerf, *op. cit.,* p. 280.
[3] *Ibid.,* pp. 225, 285.

revealing relief. The whole was harmonized into an ensemble which took on the rhythm and the proportions of a painting in which it seems as if nothing could be otherwise. Everywhere we sense balance and restraint at work, under rather than overstatement . . . No wonder that its poised, even, discreet flow made his generation talk of Atticism.[4]

This is far from the prose which Blanck calls "Plauderstil", far from the style Cerf describes "Alexandrian", "unsinewed, effeminate" and "Romantic" – a "monotone of grace".[5] The two scholars' appraisal of France's style deviates considerably from the general trend of criticism which tends to seek the roots of France's "Atticism" in his Parnassianism and his undeniable debt to French classicism.

The complexity of France's style can be best illustrated by a formal *explication* of a typical sample of his prose. The following excerpt from "La Légende des Saintes Oliverie et Liberette" parodies the missionary activities of the royal prince Bertauld and the theological conflict in which he was engaged. The comical conflict is intensified aesthetically by the satire of miracles and by a *gauloiserie.*

Or, Bertauld, fils de Théodule, roi d'Ecosse, ayant reçu le saint (1a) baptême, vivait dans le palais de son père, moins en prince qu'en ermite (2). Enfermé dans sa chambre, il y passait tout le jour à réciter des prières et à méditer sur les saintes (1b) Ecritures (3), et il brûlait du désir d'imiter les travaux des apôtres (4). Ayant appris, par une voie miraculeuse (5), les abominations (6) du pays Porcin, il les détesta (7) et résolut de les faire cesser (8).

Il traversa la mer dans une barque sans voile ni gouvernail, conduite par un cygne (9). Heureusement parvenu dans le pays Porcin, il allait par les villages, les bourgs et les châteaux, annonçant la bonne (1c) nouvelle.

– Le Dieu que je vous enseigne, disait-il, est le seul véritable. Il est unique en trois personnes, et son fils est né d'une vierge (10).

Mais ces hommes grossiers (1d) lui répondaient:

– Jeune étranger, c'est une grande simplicité de ta part de croire qu'il n'y a qu'un Dieu. Car les dieux sont innombrables. Ils habitent les bois, les montagnes et les fleuves. Il y a aussi des dieux plus amis qui prennent place au foyer des hommes pieux (1e). D'autres, enfin, se tiennent dans les étables et dans les écuries, et la race des dieux emplit l'univers (11).

[4] Loring B. Walton, "A Manuscript Fragment of *Thaïs:* its stylistic and other Revelations", *Publications of the Modern Languages Association of America,* Vol. LXXI, No. 5, p. 921.

[5] Cerf, *op. cit.,* pp. 258-261, 204-206, 225.

Mais ce que tu dis d'une vierge divine n'est pas sans vérité. Nous connaissons une vierge au triple visage (12), et nous lui chantons des cantiques et nous lui disons: "Salut, douce! Salut, terrible (13)! Elle se nomme Diane, et son pied d'argent effleure, sous les pâles clartés de la lune, le thym des montagnes (14). Elle n'a pas dédaigné de recevoir dans son lit d'hyacinthes fleuries (15) des bergers et des chasseurs comme nous (16). Pourtant elle est toujours vierge (17).[6]

The arrangement of the passage is striking for its economy and dramatic pace typical of a fairy tale. Each sentence is perfectly clear; a small child could read it. The longest sentence has thirty-two words, the shortest two, but most phrases range from twelve to twenty words. Yet technically, the narrative is quite intricate; it contains: several ironical epithets (1, a – e); a grotesque antithesis (2); rhymes and assonances: *baptême – père – prière, réciter – méditer – imiter, vivait – palais – brûlait*, etc. which, while parodying the royal ascetic's monastic life, suggest the litanies he may have sung and their cadence (3); ironical hyperbole (4); sublime irony, which, with an almost journalistic objectivity, refers to the miracle as if it were a standard form of medieval communication, perhaps equivalent to press or television today (5); *mot juste* also combined with ironical overstatements which parody the religious intolerance of the first missionaries, in whose eyes any other cult than Christianity was an abominable idolatry (6, 7); another spark of sublime irony implied in the latent "justification" of Bertauld's militant religious intolerance (8); a grotesque parody of the miracle, ironically told as an undeniable historical event (9); a satirical résumé of the Christian doctrine (10). Without hesitation, France contrasts one trait of Bertauld's gospel, the Holy Virgin, with the bizarre goddess of the local pagan cult to be destroyed (12). Other stylistic effects are: another series of comical rhymes, such as: *véritables – innombrables – étables, dieux – pieux*, etc. which evoke vaguely but unmistakably the rhyming and assonances of medieval legends (11); comical anaphora and contrast which at the same time parody the litanies: "Salut, Reine des cieux. Salut, Souveraine des Anges. Salut, tige féconde, salut, porte du ciel! . . ." Or: "Salut, Mère de miséricorde, Mère de Dieu et Mère du pardon, . . ." (13); lyricism produced both by subject matter and sonorous diction evocative of

[6] *O.C.*, V, pp. 250-251 (the numbers in parentheses are mine).

ancient poetry–a "pagan" poetic counterpoint of the legend-like rhyming (14); an archaic *epitheton ornans* suitable for the love-bed of gods (15); a *gauloiserie* expressed in the form of an archaic litotes (16); a new miraculous paradox and another echo of the blasphemous similarity between "primitive" pagan and "refined" Christian cults (17). Stylistically climactic features of this excerpt seem to be the condensed version of the Christian tidings expressed by an aphoristic paradox (10), the contrast between the holy mother and the divine mistress of the Porcin shepherds (12, 16), with subtle poetic accents (3, 14). Essentially three basic techniques lead to these effects: syntactic abbreviations, which in no way simplify the content but rather grasp and dramatize its unexpected incongruities, France's quest for contrasts, and his poetic technique.[7] Such procedures are not simple at all, but they lead to simplicity. All the care and sophistication dissolve in the polished text. Calling the style of a thorough craftsman effeminate seems unjust. No one would call effeminate a marble sculpture merely because it has received the high polish it deserves. Yet it might be more "virile" to work in granite or bronze, or to be a lumberjack who works with an axe rather than a chisel. The style France developed to say what he had to say is hardly effeminate; it is a style of an *homme – homme de lettres.*

Walton and Dargan, who compared France's approved manuscripts with the preparatory drafts, describe his relentless striving for stylistic perfection. The former comments on his tendency to avoid the relative pronoun "qui" and "que" whenever he could.[8] The latter critic portrays France equipped with scissors and sharp wit to give his phrase the desired edge.

A sneer at virtue may be born if we contort a whole phrase, thus: 'La dame de Théroulde était riche et de bonne renommée.' A stupid remark, badly in need of the scissors, which elucidate: 'Comme la dame de Théroulde était riche, on la disait de bonne renommée.'[9]

A typical result of this technique in the longer passage cited above is the definition of the only true God, single in three persons and father of a son born of a virgin. Such a stylistic gem characterizes

[7] Only the first two techniques are subjects of this chapter.
[8] Walton, the cited article p. 911.
[9] Dargan, *op. cit.*, p. 587.

France's art of summing up a metaphysical or practical problem or an intricate situation in the condensed form of an aphorism. Perhaps his zealous identification with the Latin genius and heritage in French culture and his thorough humanistic training taught him the art of witty generalization on any subject in the form of brilliant maxims. It was not difficult for France to glean from his own prose enough aphorisms for *Le Jardin d'Epicure*, a collection similar to those of La Rochefoucauld, Pascal, La Bruyère, Montesquieu, and others.

Integrated in his fiction, especially in his more mature works, the aphorism is like a fine engraving framed in striking gold and suspended in a distinguished place in the room – it dominates. The thematic scope of the aphorism is endless. Most of them, playing the same role in France's prose as they play in *Candide* or in *Lettres persanes*, are philosophical and moral observations on the nature of things, on man's dispositions, and on metaphysical problems:

Rien n'est qui ne soit naturel.[10]

Au fond nous ne reprochons jamais aux gens que de ne pas sentir et de ne pas penser comme nous.[11]

L'humilité, assez rare chez les doctes, l'est encore plus chez les ignares.[12]

L'ignorance est la condition nécessaire, je ne dis pas du bonheur, mais de l'existence même. Si nous savions tout, nous ne pourrions pas supporter la vie une heure.[13]

Le mal est nécessaire. S'il n'existait pas, le bien n'existerait non plus. Le mal est l'unique raison d'être du bien. Que serait le courage loin du péril et la pitié sans douleur? [14]

France's facetious remarks on love or women also are frequently expressed in the form of a maxim:

Nous mettons l'infini dans l'amour. Ce n'est pas la faute des femmes.[15]

Le christianisme a beaucoup fait pour l'amour en en faisant un péché.[16]

Many aphorisms may be just an outburst of France's whimsy. In the earlier works his immoderate use of mediocre aphorisms in some

[10] *O.C.*, XIX, p. 241.
[11] *O.C.*, VI, p. 29.
[12] *O.C.*, IX, p. 436.
[13] *Ibid.*, p. 409.
[14] *Ibid.*, p. 434.
[15] *Ibid.*, p. 413.
[16] *Ibid.*, p. 399.

passages compromises the aesthetic merits of this technique. In *Jocaste*, for example, France offers the reader a whole bouquet of irreverent rather than witty aphorisms: "La vertu est un produit, comme le phosphore et le vitriol.... L'héroïsme et la sainteté sont l'effet d'une congestion du cerveau.... La paralysie générale fait seule les grands hommes.... Les dieux sont des adjectifs."[17] The cluster of satirical aphorisms on Flaubert's regrets that he did not live in the era of Agamemnon and the Trojan war[18] is much better integrated in France's literary causerie. Each of the first five sentences is an aphoristic generalization and each becomes a logical precedent of the immediately following statement yet each can stand independently. All of them efficiently persuade the reader that Flaubert's hunger for Homeric heroism is a comical aspiration and that our "degeneration" and our forms of boredom are, after all, not so hopeless.

> Car enfin toute époque est banale pour ceux qui y vivent; en quelque temps qu'on naisse, on ne peut échapper à l'impression de vulgarité qui se dégage des choses au milieu desquelles on s'attarde. Le train de la vie a toujours été fort monotone, et les hommes se sont de tout temps ennuyés les uns des autres. Les barbares, dont l'existence était plus simple que la nôtre, s'ennuyaient encore plus que nous. Ils tuaient et pillaient pour se distraire. Nous avons présentement des cercles, des dîners, des livres, des journaux et des théâtres qui nous amusent un peu.[19]

France's stylistic economy dictates a relatively short sentence. But he never hesitates to use a florid sentence of Proustian length whenever the more complex nature of his subject matter requires it. Although it seems paradoxical, even these periods can be designated as stylistic short-cuts, because they usually condense a complex logical whole into one lucid, syntactically unified statement. In this respect the critic of *Le Temps* is not affected by the trends observable in the contemporary press. Our era, fond of "simplicity", worships brevity. It tends to simplify, often forgetting that the stylistically simplified fact or idea may become an over-simplification. This taste may have contributed to the modern cult of the short sentence and to the view that considerable length in a sentence is detrimental to clarity. This

[17] *O.C.*, II, p. 31.
[18] *O.C.*, VI, p. 353.
[19] *Ibid.*, p. 354.

cult may have had some influence on the younger generation of authors. The reader of Camus's *La Peste* may remember the caricature of the literary Sisyphus, Grand, whose dream it was to write a literary *chef d'œuvre* and who spent all his spare time polishing its first sentence. Although not particularly long, Grand's opening sentence is a polished caricature of a euphonious *phrase bien tournée.* Camus parodies it, yet he seems to be well aware of its aesthetic value. Modification of the sentence even becomes one of the *leitmotifs* of the work: "Par une belle matinée au mois de mai, une élégante amazone parcourait, sur une superbe jument alezane, les allées fleuries du Bois de Boulogne."[20] Rhythm, rhymes, euphonies, careful structure, unusual expressions attract the reader. There are many similar sentences in France's work, such as the opening sentence of *Abeille:*

> Ce matin-là, qui était celui du premier dimanche après Pâques, la duchesse sortit du château sur son grand alezan, ayant à sa gauche Georges de Blanchelande, qui montait un cheval jayet dont la tête était noire avec une étoile au front, et, à sa droite, Abeille, qui gouvernait avec des rênes roses son cheval à la robe isabelle.[21]

Such a florid statement, which, in one sonorous period, sums up with sublime irony the whole pomp of the ducal entourage, ostentatiously heading toward the humble asylum of an old hermit during a glorious spring morning after Easter, and which at the same time describes the great alezan of the duchess, the star on the forehead of George's jet horse, the pink bridle and cream colored isabelline coat on Abeille's horse, is a literary achievement as memorable as any glittering sentence buried in Cicero's rhetorical monuments, venerated by more than sixty generations of learned humanists. Each word sparkles. Each clause of this perfectly clear narration is elegant. The whole sentence has grace and yet it is a subtle parody. We know that the author laughs at all this because he gently overstates the fairy-tale diction and the equine excellence of the superb animals from the ducal stable. The style gives spurs to his irony or, better, gives it wings. The calculated contrast of this long sentence with the laconic one which follows, "Ils allaient entendre la messe à l'Ermitage", heightens the effect.

[20] Albert Camus, *La Peste,* (Paris, Gallimard) p. 88.
[21] *O.C.*, IV, p. 245.

In the framework of his eloquent apology for stealing M. d'Astarac's white wine in the early morning hours, Abbé Coignard says that if St. Peter had had a thimbleful of Moselle he would not have betrayed Jesus before the cock's second crowing. Further developing his hypothesis, he continues his invective against St. Peter and, at the same time, against his vicar.

A la honte éternelle des pharisiens et des gens de justice, un grossier marinier du lac de Tibériade, devenu par sa lâcheté épaisse la risée des filles de cuisine qui se chauffaient avec lui, dans la cour du grand prêtre, un rustre et un couard, qui renonça son maître et sa foi devant des maritornes bien moins jolies, sans doute, que la femme de chambre de madame la baillive de Séez, porte au front la triple couronne, au doigt l'anneau pontifical, est établi au-dessus des princes-évêques, des rois et de l'Empereur, est investi du droit de lier et de délier; le plus respectable homme, la plus honnête dame n'entreront au ciel que s'il leur en donne l'accès.[22]

The main aesthetic aim of the sentence is probably to parody the rhetoric verve of an eloquent scholar inspired by more than a thimbleful of Moselle. Such an long-winded diatribe may not appeal to every reader but patient students of the humanities may enjoy its stylistic sinuosity.

France excels when it comes to a résumé of an intricate situation, problem or complex goal. In one lucid sentence, with the economy of a classical *rhetor*, he brings out all the piquant details of a political scandal. The same sentence indirectly reveals the rottenness of the whole political system.

Tout à coup, par un malheureux hasard, par un de ces sinistres survenus d'une manière sourde et perfide comme les voies d'eau qui se déclarent soudain dans les bateaux fatigués, sans raison politique ni morale, en pleine honorabilité, le vieux serviteur de la démocratie, le fils de ses œuvres, que M. le préfet Worms-Clavelin, la veille encore, aux comices, donnait en exemple à tout le département, l'homme d'ordre et de progrès, le défenseur et de la société laique, l'ami intime des anciens ministres et des anciens présidents, le sénateur Laprat-Teulet, le non-lieu, fut envoyé en prison avec une fournée de parlementaires.[23]

The chief source of stimulation, of course, is the subject matter, the

[22] *O.C.*, VIII, p. 145.
[23] *O.C.*, XI, p. 376. Levaillant (*op. cit.*, pp. 488-489) sums up the historical events which may have inspired France's satire.

unexpected arrest of a venerable senator, Laprat-Teulet, a faithful political ally of big business, whose trial and threatened arrest for shady dealings several years before was quashed by a circumspect administrative decision, *non-lieu*.[24] So the focal point of the surprise, which France saves until the very end, is the word *prison*. But its effect would have been minimal, had it not been for subordinate surprises produced by the ironic implications, the climactic enumeration of the senator's virtues and associations, their anticlimactic confrontation with prison and the comical nickname, *le non-lieu*. One can imagine a newspaper story which would report a similar political scandal in short sentences, arranging the facts differently, omitting some details and avoiding all irony. The truth of the news alone would surprise acutely but its surprise, not being artistically "conserved", would vanish in a few days if not hours.

In spite of their length, similar florid syntactic monuments do not seem to contradict in any way the earlier evaluation of France's technique as a modern version of Attic style. Besides, they are rare and so lucid that they cause more amusement than discomfort to the reader. The occasional verbosity of France's heroes, such as M. Coignard, Abbé Lantaigne, or M. Bergeret, is characteristic of their ponderous humanistic wit.

Both the cited passage from *La Légende des Saintes Oliverie et Liberette*, the aphorisms and the examples of the florid sentence, also show to what extent France's art is permeated by contrasts. *Prince* contrasts with *ermite* as well as with *hommes grossiers*. The Holy Virgin contrasts with the pagan goddess, and the miraculous virginity of both deities contrasts with common sense. Other contrasts, just to recall a few, are: *ignorance – bonheur; l'amour – péché; la duchesse – ermitage; grossier marinier – triple couronne; ami intime des anciens présidents* and *le non-lieu – prison*. The contrasting pairs are never stereotyped opposites. They rather strike an off-beat discord. France knows that contrast essential to any change belongs to the normal course of things. So, to surprise, he must say something more unexpected than that night follows day. Although there must be a certain antithetical symmetry between the juxtaposed features, the

[24] *Ibid.*, p. 374.

resulting contrast must be relatively original or at least fresh, and have a certain dramatic or lyrical power. The possibilities of such extended antitheses are infinite. They can occur not only between opposite homogeneous factors but also between heterogeneous ones. Blue can contrast not only with yellow but also with red and various shades of blue, or it can contrast with entirely different factors, such as sound or texture or an idea. The concrete can be contrasted with the abstract; the tangible with the intangible. The unlimited scope and omnipresence of contrast as an aesthetic feature make its systematization impractical. Yet this does not mean that some of its roles cannot be recognized and illustrated. Without contrast, neither farcical nor tragic distortions nor the ironical implications could exist. Ambiguity, paradox, contradiction, all conflicts, *bizarrerie*, the supernatural and utopian elements, – all these features stimulate by some obvious or latent discrepancy. Contrast has a primary function in many figures of speech. Many striking character and ideological contrasts are integral parts of France's conflicts. But the contrasts, for example, between the slovenly Paphnuce and both the beautiful Thaïs and the elegant hedonist Nicias, between the latter's practical philosophy and Paphnuce's mystical phantasmagories are not based only on style and thus they are deeper, cumulative, and in the end more powerful than if they were. The syntactic contrasts have a different function in France's art: they extend the narrator's scale of accents, and undertones, which bring out the contours of his subjects. The series of sharp contrasts in the opening passage of *Les Dieux ont soif* inject into the solemn twilight of the Saint-Paul church the anxiety of political terror and fear of popular justice.

... Gamelin ... s'était rendu ... à l'ancienne église qui depuis trois ans servait de siège à l'assemblée générale. ... l'on avait inscrit au-dessus de la porte ... "Liberté, Égalité, Fraternité ou la Mort." ... Les voûtes qui avait entendu les clercs de la congrégation de Saint-Paul chanter en rochet les offices divins, voyaient maintenant les patriotes en bonnet rouge assemblés pour élire les magistrats. ... Les Saints avaient été tirés de leurs niches et remplacés par les bustes de Brutus, de Jean-Jacques.[25]

The reader's curiosity is provoked by this sudden conversion of the

[25] *O.C.*, XX, pp. 3, 4.

church into the revolutionary headquarters. What a contrast between the votive and the political functions of the temple! And how symptomatic of the generally contrasting changes which took place all over France! And what an alternative of the new freedom and brotherhood, which imply tolerance! Instead of solemn ceremonies of the ancient cult, there is radical politicking; instead of the humble examples of Christian faith and charity, there is the ancient freedom fighter indulging in terrorist methods side by side with the neurotic father of Romantic ideology. Such pessimistic contrasts strike a graver note in reflecting the tense atmosphere of the time and man's perennial folly. An entirely different effect is achieved in the same novel by the following accumulation of contrasts dramatizing the difference between Brotteaux's sunny past and stormy present and the comical contrasts between his colorful careers in the new order of things.

Au bon temps, Maurice Brotteaux se nommait monsieur des Ilettes et donnait, dans son hôtel ... des soupers fins que la belle madame de Rochemaure, épouse d'une procureur, illuminait de ses yeux, femme accomplie, dont la fidélité honorable ne se démentit point tant que la Révolution laissa à Maurice Brotteaux des Ilettes ses offices, ses rentes, son hôtel, ses terres, son nom. La Révolution les lui enleva. Il gagna sa vie à peindre des portraits ... à faire des crêpes et des beignets sur le quai de la Mégisserie, à composer des discours pour les représentants du peuple et à donner des leçons de danse aux jeunes citoyennes. Présentement, dans son grenier, où l'on se coulait par une échelle et où l'on ne pouvait se tenir debout, Maurice Brotteaux, riche d'un pot de colle, d'un paquet de ficelles, d'une boîte d'aquarelle et de quelques rognures de papier, fabriquait des pantins. ... Au milieu des troubles publics et dans la grande infortune dont il était lui-même accablé, il gardait une âme sereine, lisant pour se recréer son Lucrèce, ...[26]

Contrasting with the general climate of fear is the hero's serenity. The same Brotteaux, an atheist and a gentleman who used to live in a palace, offers his poor attic dwelling as an asylum to a persecuted Barnabite monk[27] and to the prostitute Athénaïs who cried "Vive le Roi"[28] and is sought by revolutionary justice. The absurd "crimes" of this contrasting trio arrested at the same time and their dispropor-

[26] *Ibid.*, p.12.
[27] *Ibid.*, p. 158.
[28] *Ibid.*, p. 189.

tionate penalty – death – show the sentenced political criminals and their judges in contrasting moral perspective. Such contrasts are significant details of the tragic irony of fate expressed by the whole work.

The short story, "Le Chanteur de Kymé", in itself can illustrate the aesthetic versatility of this technique. Its brief text contains many kinds of contrast, from grotesque to lyrical and even tragic. Homer, tutoring the young generation of bards, gives them two heterogeneous items of advice delivered in one breath.

Quand vous vous tiendrez assis dans les assemblés, ramenez votre tunique sur vos cuisses et que votre maintien exprime la grâce et la pudeur.

Il leur disait encore: – Ne crachez pas dans les fleuves, parce que les fleuves sont sacrés.[29]

Elsewhere in the story, France stimulates by a lyrical contrast between the already cited metaphors: "Jeune fille, l'essaim des désirs flotte autour de ta ceinture.... Et moi, vieillard, je loue ta beauté comme un oiseau nocturne qui pousse un cri méprisé...."[30] The cowherd's fight, which contrastingly interrupts Homer's solemn performance, is further contrasted with the bard's curse, his lyrical exodus, and his poetic death.[31]

The idyllic setting of French country life is casually contrasted with murder in *Le Petit Pierre.* The Nozières' servant girl, Mélanie, recalls the presence of the Russian cossacks in France in 1815. She tells the little boy about their forceful manners and vigorous temperament mixed with profound melancholy and tenderheartedness, and then remembers in a most contrasting context how her cousin killed one of them.

– Et très méchants, les Cosaques?

– Oh! oui ... Quand ils avaient bu de l'eau-de-vie, il ne fallait pas les contrarier; car alors ils devenaient furieux, et frappaient tout autour d'eux, sans regarder à l'âge ni au sexe. A jeun, bien souvent, ils pleuraient du regret d'avoir quitté leur pays et certains d'entre eux jouaient sur une petite guitare des airs si tristes que le cœur se fendait à les entendre. Mon cousin Niclausse en tua un et le jeta dans un puits. Mais personne n'en

[29] *O.C.*, XIII, p. 12.
[30] *Ibid.*, p. 16.
[31] *Ibid.*, pp. 22-23, see also this study, pp. 154-55.

sut rien ... Nous en logions une douzaine à la ferme. Ils puisaient de l'eau, portaient du bois et gardaient les enfants.[32]

If the same murder were brought up in Mélanie's stream of consciousness earlier, for instance in connection with the Russians' determined method of courting French women, the dramatic effect would be much less striking. But the words, "mon cousin Niclausse en tua un et le jeta dans un puits", dropped out of the blue into a romanticized reminiscence of the sad, singing Slavs, certainly take the reader by surprise. Nothing in the text up to this moment indicates that Mélanie's own cousin will be a murderer on this occasion. His action becomes somewhat grotesque when confronted with the sentimental tribulations of the Russian horsemen following their victory over the French tyrant. The whole tragic absurdity of human life emerges from such an incongruity.

The caricatures of the virtuous uncle Hyacinthe and his dear friend Huguet, whose decisions were inspired by rather practical considerations, base their humour largely on a series of comical contrasts:

Huguet fit le *commerce* des vins et *frauda* l'octroi, ce qui lui valut cinq mille francs environ de *bénéfice* et six mois de *prison*. "Ce n'est pas la plus mauvaise affaire que j'aie faite", disait Huguet après réflexion. Ce *cynisme* révoltait le héros de Craonne qui avait des principes, professait *la morale du vicaire savoyard* agrandie du sentiment de l'honneur, et enseignait à Huguet, quand ils *buvaient* ensemble, les *règles du devoir* et l'autorité des lois. *Suivre la droite voie* ou la reprendre après *l'avoir quittée; l'innocence ou repentir*, telle était la devise du vieux soldat. Huguet, en l'écoutant, le regardait avec admiration et pleurait dans son verre. Le voyant ainsi réhabilité par le repentir, Hyacinthe fonda avec lui une société pour la distribution des imprimés dans la ville de Paris, qui ne réussit pas.[33]

Ironical expressions, "révoltait", "le héros de Craonne", and the farcical absurdity, "société pour la distribution des imprimés", add to the final satirical contrast between the beginning of an honest business and its immediate failure. The accumulation of contrasts in the previous passage is organic and brings up the profiles of the two comical heroes. But the same technique may become a stylistic affectation. A page in *Le Chat maigre* indicates how an excess of comical

[32] *O.C.*, XXIII, p. 242.
[33] *O.C.*, XXIII, p. 183. (Italics mine.)

contrasts may be an aesthetic liability. It describes the door in Labanne's studio and is calculated to strike a comical note. Topical contrasts are even emphasized by typographical contrasts.

La porte était couverte d'inscriptions tracées diversement par des mains différentes. ...

La plus haute, gravée à la pointe d'un canif en lettres capitales, disait:

LA FEMME EST PLUS AMÈRE QUE LA MORT.

La seconde, moulée au crayon Conte, en ronde, disait:

Les académiciens sont des bourgeois. Cabanel est un coiffeur.

La troisième, tracée à la mine de plomb, en cursive, disait:

Gloire aux corps féminins qui, sur le mode antique,
Chantent l'hymne sacré de la beauté plastique!

PAUL DION

La quatrième, tracée à la craie, d'une main inhabile, disait:

J'ai rapporté du linge blanc. Lundi je prendrai le sale chez le concierge.

La cinquième, marquée au moyen d'une épingle à cheveux qui avait légèrement égratigné la peinture, disait:

Labanne est un rat. Je me fiche de lui.

MARIA.[34]

Such buffoonery is not likely to add much to the general aesthetic value of the work in which it is integrated. It inevitably becomes a long digression unless its content acquires a more significant role than that of a literary prop. Perhaps the more tolerant reader might read a few incoherent messages without objection, if they were used more sparingly. This passage, published in 1879 and written earlier, is an example of France's youthful stylistic sins. But France's apprenticeship was not too long. In the works written during and after the mid-eighties, he disciplined his literary techniques, including that of integrating dramatic contrast.

Antithesis and direct contrast are in the fiber of Francean structure. The variety and density of contrasting arrangements is increased by extensive digressions. A craftsman and critic of France's calibre cannot

[34] *O.C.*, II, pp. 185-186.

help but be aware that digression can be fatal; that it may destroy the desirable harmony of general composition; that it may slow down the dramatic pace of any genre, reducing a witty essay to a *causerie* and epic prose to rambling chit-chat. But he also knows that such literary heresy has hidden merits. He knows that even cultivated readers frequently prefer a *causerie* to an essay or amusing trivia to a polished sermon. The art of suave digression may offer much charm to the reader who desires something new and unexpected. The wide success of many digressive literary masterpieces seems to indicate that readers of all backgrounds enjoy a witty remark, a well-told anecdote, a bizarre allusion, a controversial comment, or a grotesque description which has nothing or little to do with the main topic, provided that such a heterogeneous theme is organically integrated. On the whole, France's concept of composition stems, like the rest of his aesthetic views, from tradition. His everyday contact with literature taught him that many of the great writers of long, versified or prosaic works were apparently indifferent to tight composition: Homer, Virgil, Horace, Rabelais, Cervantes, LaFontaine, Voltaire, Fielding, Goethe, Dickens, Tolstoy, Gogol, Proust, all frequently disregard the unity of action to digress. Even *The Divine Comedy*, admired for its poetry, its universal symbolism, its numerical structure and its prosodic integrity as a literary cathedral, does not fulfil the ideal of an absolute unity of action to the same extent as the ancient or classical tragedies, or even the minor modern *chefs d'œuvre*, such as Stevenson's *Treasure Island* or Prevost's *Manon Lescaut*. Intellectually agile authors resent the yoke of the Catonian *rem tene*. No literary critic can be too dogmatic about any recognized principle, even about the canons of composition. Without constant violations of aesthetic "principles", art would become stagnant and many delightful passages would end in the author's waste-paper basket. Were digression too rigorously damned, the reader would never savor the anecdote, full of satire, irony, farce, *gauloiserie*, and paradoxes, related by Saint Gal to prove the validity of the Penguins' baptism.[35] Without such digressions, France's work would lose much of its typical flavor; without them, France would not be France.

[35] *O.C.*, XVIII, 41-42." – Le sacrement du baptême, répondit saint Patrick, est nul quand il est donné à des oiseaux, comme le sacrement du mariage est nul quand il est donné à un eunuque.

Although it would be unwise to consider digression an artistic virtue, one can see a certain aesthetic value in it. Often it introduces the least expected yet most entertaining subject matter, taking the reader by surprise. Moreover, a richer thematic texture breaks the monotony and enables the author to alternate the tone and mood more frequently than in a rigidly treated single theme. Changing a grave tone into a humorous one might relieve the reader; the reverse might increase his tension. A contrasting variety of interpolated themes naturally provides a wider range of aesthetic features. Imitating a technique typical of Voltaire and Montesquieu, France makes abundant use of a relative, participial, or causal clause to reveal a detail partially related to one feature of the content, but generally irrelevant, topically contrasting, and therefore digressive. The tone of the clause may be comical, ironical, skeptical, or lyrical; it may introduce a bizarre detail or, frequently, it may in passing unmask the absurdity of the main statement or even completely deny it. It may strike an unexpected tragic note in the midst of farce, or simply enhance the farce with a spark of irrelevant buffoonery. Describing Bluebeard's fourth wife, France mentions in one sentence the military episode which cost her father his ear. The remark, passed apropos of M. Montragoux's courtship, creates a grotesque effect. "... mais il fut lui-même choisi pour époux par demoiselle Blanche de Gibeaumex, fille d'un officier de cavalerie qui n'avait qu'une oreille; il disait avoir perdu l'autre au service du roi. Elle avait beaucoup d'esprit, dont elle se servit à tromper son mari."[36] The digressive clause, "qui n'avait qu'une

---

Mais Saint Gal:

– Quel rapport prétendez-vous établir entre le baptême d'un oiseau et le mariage d'un eunuque? Il n'y en a point. Le mariage est, si j'ose dire, un sacrement conditionnel, éventuel. Le prêtre bénit par avance un acte; ... si l'acte n'est pas consommé, la bénédiction demeure sans effet. ... J'ai connu sur la terre, ... un homme riche nommé Sadoc qui, vivant en concubinage avec une femme, la rendit mère de neuf enfants. Sur ses vieux jours, cédant à mes objurgations, il consentit à l'épouser et je bénis leur union. Malheureusement le grand âge de Sadoc l'empêcha de consommer le mariage. Peu de temps après, il perdit tous ses biens et Germaine (tel était le nom de cette femme), ne se sentant point en état de supporter l'indigence, demanda l'annulation d'un mariage qui n'avait point de réalité. Le pape accueillit sa demande, car elle était juste. Voilà pour le mariage. Mais le baptême est conféré sans restrictions. ... Il n'y a point de doute: c'est un sacrement que les Pingouins ont reçu."

[36] *O.C.*, XIX, p. 139; see also this study, p. 166.

oreille", leads to digressive anecdote and only then does France return to the character sketch of Blanche.

Such a digressive aside may inject humorous incongruity into a tragic action. Dramatizing Chevalier's suicide, France describes the reactions of de Ligny and Félicie when the actress's old lover bursts in upon them: "Tout à coup elle sauta du lit avec une telle vivacité d'instinct et un mouvement si rapide de jeune animal que Ligny, bien qu'il fût peu littéraire, songea à la chatte métamorphosée en femme."[37] The irrelevant remark on de Ligny's literary erudition strikes a satirical note in a tense melodramatic situation. Such digressive clauses often add desirable flexibility to the blade of France's irony. The typical characteristics of such a stylistic feature are its relative redundancy and/or its unexpectedness. Without it, the central thought would lose spice. In the essay, "Sur le scepticisme", the digressive reference to the calf leather bindings of metaphysical works, which a learned Pyrrhonist had thoroughly studied and disbelieved, subtly discredits the significance of the philosophical contemplations in the ornately bound volumes. "Il avait lu tout ce qu'on peut trouver sur les parapets de théologie, de morale et de métaphysique relié en veau, avec des tranches rouges."[38] France often links a digressive generalization with the description of a specific event. "Jean le Diacre rapporte que, saint Grégoire ayant pleuré à la pensée que l'empereur Trajan était damné, Dieu, qui se plaît à accorder ce qu'on n'ose lui demander, exempta l'âme de Trajan des peines éternelles."[39] The ironic maxim on God's policy is related only vaguely to one of his specific decisions, namely Trajan's eternal damnation.

M. Lantaigne's comment on the beauty and antiquity of the diocese is pure rhetorical padding, to conceal the cutting edge of his denunciation of Abbé Guitrel.

Mais comme cette affaire ... intéresse le gouvernement de ce diocèse, qui compte parmi les plus antiques et les plus belles provinces de la Gaule chrétienne, je me fais un devoir de soumettre à l'équité vigilante de Votre Eminence les faits qu'elle est appelée à juger dans la plénitude de son autorité ..."[40]

[37] *O.C.*, XIII, pp. 187-188.
[38] *O.C.*, VI, p. 447.
[39] *Ibid.*
[40] *O.C.*, XI, pp. 23-24.

The digressive clause frequently injects the controversial element. From the point of view of aesthetic surprise, it is most effective when it denies or questions the content of the main statement, as in the following example: "Si nous en croyons ce paisible conducteur de nos âmes, on ne peut échapper à la bonté divine et nous irons tous en paradis, à moins qu'il n'y ait pas de paradis, ce qui est bien probable."[41] Abbé Coignard comically invalidates M. d'Astarac's theory, while ostensibly accepting it as a possibility, by his reference to the eccentric's mental condition. "Nous ne connaissons, j'en conviens, qu'une petite partie de l'univers, et il se peut, comme le dit monsieur d'Astarac, qui d'ailleurs est fou, que ce monde ne soit qu'une goutte de boue."[42] The same kind of brief digression may suggest a poetical or lyrical mood. In "Le Chanteur de Kymé", France imitates the Homeric epical breadth. A young girl, giving Homer directions, digresses poetically: "Il n'est pas possible d'y arriver du côté de la mer, parce qu'elle [la maison] est située sur ce haut promontoire qui s'avance au milieu des flots et qui n'est visité que par les alcyons."[43] Sometimes the digressive relative clauses are decorative. Although they have little bearing on the main topic, they add a touch of *bizarrerie*, as in the following sentence: "Mon père servit un quartier de volaille à l'abbé, qui, tirant de sa poche un morceau de pain, un flacon de vin et un couteau dont le manche de cuivre représentait le feu roi en empereur romain sur une colonne antique, commença de souper."[44] A single participial clause may smoothly integrate a short anecdote. "Rehabilitating" Bluebeard, France argues with Charles Perrault who accuses the famed murderer of feigning an important trip in order to spy on his new wife. France "reveals" the details which prove beyond any doubt that the "affaire de conséquence" was not a ruse but an historical event dictated by legitimate motives unknown to Charles Perrault:

M. de Montragoux se rendit dans le Perche pour recueillir l'héritage de son cousin d'Outarde, tué glorieusement d'un boulet de canon à la bataille des Dunes, tandit qu'il jouait aux dés sur un tambour.

[41] *O.C.*, VI, pp. 34.
[42] *O.C.*, VIII, p. 160.
[43] *O.C.*, XIII, p. 16-17.
[44] *O.C.*, VIII, p. 11.

Avant de partir, M. de Montragoux pria sa femme de prendre toutes les distractions possibles pendant son absence.[45]

The grotesque nature of M. d'Outarde's death has nothing to do with the argument, yet it is an important part of the alibi France supplies for M. de Montragoux. But a digressive anecdote is generally longer than a clause. It is not a very sophisticated tool of aesthetic stimulation, but nonetheless provides unfailing amusement in two ways: a good anecdote surprises by its own subject matter or by its own stylistic merits, and it creates a contrast to its frame. The surprise is much sharper if the anecdote is organically integrated with the original topic, as in Giacomo Boni's causerie on his countrymen's religious life.

Les Italiens ne demandaient à leurs dieux que des biens terrestres et des avantages solides. ... Ce qu'ils exigeaient autrefois de leurs Dieux et de leurs Génies, ils l'attendent aujourd'hui de la Madone et des saints. Chaque paroisse a son bienheureux, qu'on charge de commissions, comme un député. Il y a des saints pour la vigne, pour les céréales, pour les bestiaux, pour la colique et pour le mal de dents. ... Les paysans exigent des miracles de leurs saints protecteurs et les couvrent d'invectives si le miracle tarde à venir. Le paysan, qui avait sollicité inutilement une faveur du Bambino, retourne à la chapelle et, s'adressant cette fois à l'Incoronata:

– Ce n'est pas à toi, fils de putain, que je parle, c'est à ta sainte mère.

Les femmes intéressent la Madre di Dio à leurs amours. Elles pensent avec raison qu'elle est femme, qu'elle sait ce que c'est et qu'on n'a pas à se gêner avec elle. Elles n'ont jamais peur d'être indiscrètes, ce qui prouve leur piété. C'est pourquoi il faut admirer la prière que faisait à la Madone une belle fille de la Riviéra de Gênes:

– Sainte mère de Dieu, vous qui avez conçu sans pécher, accordez-moi la grâce de pécher sans concevoir.[46]

Here both anecdotes are blended with the text so organically that they simply mark two steps which lead toward the same climax carefully planned by the narrator. They are so short and their content is such a fitting illustration of the speaker's conclusions that they do not appear to digress in any way. The contrast between two heterogeneous subjects is less distinct.

Although seemingly digressive, anecdote is seldom used only as literary padding. It has a purpose. It may, indeed, express the main idea more aptly by indirection. Meditating about the tragic passage of

[45] *O.C.*, XIX, p. 154.
[46] *O.C.*, XIII, p. 367-68.

time, France tells a deceptively casual anecdote which introduces the theme of death. Pierre Aubier, in the *Mémoires d'un volontaire*, returns home from *collège* to spend the summer vacation at his paternal home. He has grown more mature and his parents seem to be growing old. The boy's realization of the merciless flow of time has an intensive tragic undertone. The profoundly sad mood is emphasized by a contrasting anecdotal touch. Sobbing, Pierre embraces his mother. Her skimming ladle still in her hand, abruptly, she gives him the most recent news: his father, overcome by old age and pains, no longer can work in the orchard.

> . . . que l'aînée de mes sœurs était promise en mariage au fils du tonnelier et que le sacristain de la paroisse avait été trouvé mort dans sa chambre, une bouteille à la main; les doigts crispés serraient si fort le goulot qu'on crut qu'on ne les détacherait pas. Pourtant il n'était pas décent qu'on portât le sacristain à l'église avec sa bouteille de vin gris. En écoutant ma mère, j'eus pour la première fois l'idée sensible de la fuite du temps . . .[47]

Lamia's premonition of the divine wrath against Pilate is dissolved in an anecdote. To exploit this subject and, at the same time, make it sound more casual, France inserts a risqué anecdote between Lamia's two ironical warnings. Pilate's friend teases the retired administrator in a friendly manner, discussing in a light vein the influence of bizarre African deities on the religious whims of the Romans. His anecdote parodies the power of this influence, but its main goal is to dissipate the visionary irony in a lower, casual humor.

> L'Asie et l'Afrique nous ont déjà donné un grand nombre de dieux. On a vu s'élever à Rome des temples en l'honneur d'Isis et de l'aboyant Anubis. Nous rencontrons dans les carrefours et jusque dans les carrières la Bonne Déesse des Syriens, portée sur un âne. Et ne sais-tu pas que, sous le principat de Tibère, un jeune chevalier se fit passer pour le Jupiter cornu des Égyptiens et obtint sous ce déguisement les faveurs d'une dame illustre, trop vertueuse pour rien refuser aux dieux? Crains, Pontius, que le Jupiter invisible des Juifs ne débarque un jour à Ostie![48]

Again, the anecdote is almost invisibly woven into the theme of the conversation. The joke amuses the reader on its own merits, but also it

[47] *O.C.*, V, p. 358.
[48] *O.C.*, V, p. 231.

provides a desirable counterpoint to the grave irony of the anecdote. The fluid style, full of assonances and latent rhymes, helps to conceal the link between the two heterogeneous elements.

Frequently the seam between the subject on hand and the anecdote is more obvious. The anecdote may be pertinent, but the continuity is rougher:

> Un cercle de fer, de flammes et de haine entourait la grande cité révolutionnaire. Et cependant elle recevait avec magnificence, ... les députés des assemblées primaires qui avaient accepté la constitution. Le fédéralisme était vaincu; la République une, indivisible, vaincrait tous ses ennemis.
>
> Étendant le bras sur la plaine populeuse:
>
> – C'est là, dit Évariste, que, le 17 juillet 91, l'infâme Bailly fit fusiller le peuple au pied de l'autel de la patrie. Le grénadier Passavant, témoin du massacre, rentra dans sa maison, déchira son habit, s'écria: J'ai juré de mourir avec la liberté; elle n'est plus: je meurs.' Et il se brûla la cervelle.
>
> Cependant ... les bourgeois paisibles examinaient les préparatifs de la fête, ...[49]

Certainly both the historical anecdote and the sonorous description of the setting imply with grave irony that if the "end of freedom" had been the right time to commit suicide, the moment Passavant decided to settle his score with life was after all not so absurdly chosen; for what followed after his death, and especially after Bailly's execution,[50] was not exactly the restoration of freedom. Yet, technically, such a vague thematic association is an artificial bridge between the main subject and the digression. The digressions are not limited to clauses or short anecdotes; several of France's major works are as digressive as *Gil Blas, Candide, Tom Jones* or *Tristram Shandy.* The subject and the digressive nature of *La Rôtisserie de la Reine Pédauque* especially evoke these eighteenth century masterpieces. The comical circumstances which lead to the hiring of Abbé Coignard as preceptor of Jacques Tournebroche exemplify France's digressive technique. M. Coignard is earnestly explaining the excellent advantages of a literary education to M. Ménétrier: "Aussi ... le [Jacques] faut-il former aux bonnes

[49] *O.C.*, XX, p. 100.

[50] See "Bailly", Jean Sylvain (1736-1793), *Nouveau petit Larousse illustré* (Ed. Claude Angé et Paul Angé, Paris: Larousse, 1940) p. 1211.

lettres, qui sont l'honneur de l'homme, la consolation de la vie et le remède à tous les maux, même à ceux de l'amour, ainsi que l'affirme Théocrite."[51] Suddenly, the discussion is interrupted by the arrival of Catherine, compliant lacemaker popular among the male guests of the nearby *Petit Bacchus*, also patronized by M. Ménétrier.

– Monsieur Ménétrier, dit Catherine à mon père, venez dire un mot aux sergents du guet. Si vous ne le faites, ils conduiront sans faute frère Ange en prison. Le bon frère est entré tantôt au *Petit Bacchus*, où il a bu deux ou trois pots qu'il n'a point payés, de peur, disait-il, de manquer à la règle de saint François. Mais le pis de l'affaire est que, me voyant sous la tonnelle en compagne, il s'approcha de moi pour m'apprendre certaine oraison nouvelle. Je lui dis que ce n'était pas le moment, et, comme il devenait pressant, le coutelier boiteux, qui se trouvait tout à côté de moi, le tira très fort par la barbe. Alors, frère Ange se jeta sur le coutelier, qui roula à terre, emportant la table et les brocs. Le cabaretier accourut au bruit et, voyant la table culbutée, le vin répandu et frère Ange, un pied sur la tête du coutelier, brandissant un escabeau dont il frappait tous ceux qui l'approchaient, ce méchant hôte jura comme un diable et s'en fut appeler la garde. Monsieur Ménétrier, venez sans tarder, venez tirer le petit frère de la main des sergents. C'est un saint homme et il est excusable dans cette affaire.[52]

The leisurely discussion on the merits of humanistic education is first interrupted by Catherine's entrance, which forms a bridge between the main theme and the digression. The sudden deviation from the placid *causerie* on the merits of the arts and wisdom to the dramatic event at the *Petit Bacchus* creates a sharp, stimulating contrast. Although the farcical digression is contrived by the author for his own literary purpose, the reader may welcome the sudden switch from the abbé's slow-moving deliberations to the action at the *Petit Bacchus.* The reader immediately wants to know the outcome of Catherine's romantic entanglements. Within her digressive narrative are even internal digressions. Having read her account, the reader imagines that the peak of stimulation has been reached, that nothing can exceed the comical tribulations of the monk. But the long second bridge, which takes the reader back to the *rôtisserie*, adds yet further stimulus: the brief, ambiguous repartee between the innkeeper and Catherine is an

[51] *O.C.*, VIII, 13.
[52] *Ibid.*, pp. 13-14.

amusing mixture of irony and *gauloiserie*. Instead of exciting the pity of the jovial *rôtisseur*, Catherine delights him with the news that the lecherous monk will be out of the picture for a while, leaving Catherine to more honest men.

Il répondit net qu'il ne trouvait pas d'exuse à ce capucin et qu'il lui souhaitait une bonne pénitence au pain et à l'eau, au plus noir cul de basse-fosse du couvent dont il était l'opprobre et la honte.

Il s'échauffait en parlant:

– Un ivrogne et un débauché à qui je donne tous les jours du bon vin et de bons morceaux et qui s'en va au cabaret lutiner des guilledines assez abandonnées pour préférer la société d'un coutelier ambulant et d'un capucin à celle des honnêtes marchands jurés du quartier! Fi! Fi! [53]

Catherine, furious that she will get no support from M. Ménétrier, departs after antagonizing her practical admirer with irreverent and ambiguous insults to his male ego. The skillful diplomat Coignard immediately exploits the innkeeper's annoyance at Brother Ange. Encouraging M. Ménétrier's wrath against the uncouth monk, Coignard manages to replace him as Jacques's tutor, just as the humanist Ponocrates succeeds Tubal Holoferne to prepare Gargantua for the storms of life.

– Ce sera bien fait, dit l'abbé. Ce capucin est un âne, et il enseignait à votre fils bien moins à parler qu'à braire. Vous ferez sagement de jeter au feu cette *Vie de sainte Marguerite*, cette prière pour les engelures et cette histoire de loup-garou, dont le frocard empoisonnait l'esprit de votre fils. Aux prix où frère Ange donnait ses leçons, je donnerai les miennes; j'enseignerai à cet enfant le latin et le grec, et même le français, que Voiture et Balzac ont porté à sa perfection.[54]

The author returns to his original theme, to Jacques's education, and the action moves one step ahead. But even the return to the main stream of action does not mark the end of the digressions. Although characteristic of Coignard's brand of humanism, the final statement, "que Voiture et Balzac ont porté à sa perfection", is somewhat irrelevant. But the tapering off of the excitement produced by the digression and the return to the original topic are handled more suavely than the opening of the digression. Such a multitude of

[53] *Ibid.*, p. 14. See also pp. 170-172.
[54] *Ibid.*, p. 15.

heterogeneous topics seems to violate all the rules of unified composition. Yet the structure of the whole causerie is relatively homogeneous; the vague and amusing connection between Coignard's tutorship and the details of Catherine's and her Capucin's romantic tribulations is subtly established. Such passages may, with some justification, have inspired Blanck's term *Plauderstil.* But, of course, such passages represent only one aspect of France's style.

In some of France's works the anecdotal divagations play such an important role that their elimination would undermine whole chapters. The first chapter of *Histoire comique* could serve as another example: Without the anecdotes and amusing extemporaneous comments of Doctor Socrate Trublet, that great lover of theater and actresses, the whole chapter would shrink to less than half. A brief résumé will make it obvious. The main characters of the novel come together in the dressing room of Félicie Nanteuil, ingenue comedienne at the Odéon. Dr. Trublet, observing the wardrobe attendant tightening the corset of the actress, delivers a satirical, licentious comment of some three hundred words on corsets and their effect on feminine beauty.[55] His

[55] *O.C.*, XIII, 120-24. "Madame Michon rectifiait le corset. Et le docteur, subitement assombri, la regardait qui tirait sur les lacets.

– Ne froncez pas le sourcil, docteur, dit Félice, je ne me serre jamais. Avec la taille que j'ai, ce serait vraiment bête de ma part.

Elle ajouta, pensant à sa meilleure camarade du théâtre:

– C'est bon pour Fagette, qui n'a ni épaules ni hanches ... Elle est toute droite ... Michon, tu peux gagner encore un peu ... Je sais que vous êtes l'ennemi des corsets, docteur. Je ne peux pourtant pas m'habiller comme les femmes esthètes, avec des langes ... Venez passer votre main, vous verrez que je ne me serre pas trop.

Il se défendit d'être l'ennemi des corsets, ne condamnant que les corsets trop serrés. Il déplora que les femmes n'eussent aucun sense de l'harmonie des lignes et qu'elles attachassent à la finesse de la taille une idée de grâce et de beauté, sans comprendre que cette beauté consistait tout entière dans les molles inflexions par lesquelles le corps, après avoir fourni le superbe épanouissement de la poitrine, s'amincit lentement au-dessous du thorax pour se magnifier ensuite dans l'ample et tranquille évasement des flancs.

– La taille, dit-il, la taille, puisqu'il faut employer ce mot affreux, doit être un passage lent, insensible et doux entre les deux gloires de la femme, sa poitrine et son ventre. Et vous l'étranglez stupidement, vous vous défoncez le thorax, qui entraîne les seins dans sa ruine, vous vous aplatissez les fausses côtes, vous vous creusez un horrible sillon au-dessus de nombril. Les négresses, qui se taillent les dents en pointe et qui se fendent les lèvres pour y introduire un disque de bois, se défigurent avec moins de barbarie. Car, enfin, on conçoit

discourse is followed by a long, digressive session of theater gossip between Félicie and Madame Doulce, an elderly ex-comedienne. The two actresses discuss the Lesbian tendencies of the star Perrin. This enables Dr. Trublet to bring up the mythological sources of Lesbian love. He tells the Platonian "myth" of Jupiter splitting the too-powerful androgynes into men and women and the mythological women with four hands and four legs into two women. The separated halves have been trying to find each other ever since. Madame Doulce, suffering from a stomach irritation, asks for medical advice from the doctor. Félicie wants to know if the doctor's intimate knowledge of the feminine viscera is not a handicap in his erotic adventures. The question permits France to tell an expressive anecdote about Père Rousseau, the caretaker of the hospital autopsy room, who was in the habit of having his lunch on the table that held the corpse. Nothing disturbed his appetite. All he said was: "Je ne sais pas si c'est l'air de la salle qui le veut, mais je ne peux rien manger que de frais et d'appétissant."[56] Equally discursive is the conversation between the two actresses prior to Madame Doulce's exit. The composition of the novel would be improved if the contemplations on corsets or on androgyne were either entirely suppressed or at least substantially shortened. Yet, were this done, much pleasure would be sacrificed to an abstract aesthetic principle of creative economy.

A partial analysis of the first volume of *L'Histoire Contemporaine* reveals anarchy rather than unity in construction. For instance, the shocking *consilium abeundi* given to Firmin Piedagnel by Abbé Lantaigne is a smoothly integrated major digression. Although we find a minor reference to Piedagnel later in the text, the dramatic episode has no bearing upon the plot of "L'Orme du mail". It only further suggests the character of the abbé, which could have been described by more pertinent reference to his pastoral ambition to "put on purple stockings".[57] Yet the average reader, constantly entertained, hardly realizes to what extent the author has digressed. In fact, he might not

---

qu'il reste encore de la splendeur féminine à une créature qui s'est passé un anneau dans les cartilages du nez et dont la lèvre est distendue par une rondelle d'acajou grande comme ce pot de pommade. Mais la dévastation est entière quand la femme exerce ses ravages dans le centre sacré de son empire."

[56] Ibid., p. 131.

[57] *O.C.*, XI,p. 60; see also p. 60, n. 98 of this study.

be disturbed by the discovery that the whole work is a monumental *contaminatio*, a patchwork made of major digressive episodes. The first chapter of *L'Orme du mail* includes a longer discussion of the odious bishop Cautinus.[58] The second chapter describes the cited climax to Piedagnel's studies.[59] Chapter III is the memorable letter in which Abbé Lantaigne reports his junior colleague's fallacies and misdemeanors to His Eminence. His calculated exposé is full of digressive theological comments.[60] In Chapter IV, M. Guitrel's short, dogmatic controversy with the prefect Worms-Clavelin is followed by a digressive citation of the legend of Saint Agathe and the loss of her breast, which was "consecrated" to Jesus.[61] Chapter V parodies the enormous theological scholarship of Abbé Lantaigne, who tells the archbishop how to re-consecrate the church in which an alleged suicide was committed. Chapter VI is a longer caricature of General Cartier de Chalmont and of the army.[62] Only in Chapter VII does the protagonist, M. Bergeret, appear, discussing an obscure theological work and the conflict of man's reason with his Christian faith, which obliges him to believe in miracles.[63] Some of the chapters are pure interpolations and have absolutely nothing to do with the major theme. Such is the case in Chapter XII, which tells the story of the house of Queen Marguerite and Philippe Tricouillard,[64] and Chapter XV, in which M. Bergeret reads a five-thousand-word anecdote entitled "Substitut", developing a grotesque paradox and proving that the strongest political power in a bureaucratic state is impotent.[65] The following three volumes of the tetralogy are equally digressive and the twenty-five volumes of his collected works, do not contain a single example of what could be described as a literary cathedral. His longer works rather resemble horizontal mansions, not designed for the worship of an austere ascetic ideal, but for living in intimate association with sensual beauty and joy. Buried in neglected elegant parks they have

[58] *Ibid.*, p. 10.
[59] *Ibid.*, pp. 23-32.
[60] *Ibid.*, pp. 39-40.
[61] *Ibid.*, pp. 46-48.
[62] *Ibid.*, pp. 61-68.
[63] *Ibid.*, pp. 71-76.
[64] *Ibid.*, pp. 121-41.
[65] *Ibid.*, pp. 164-82.

many poetic mansards, and hidden terraces. Their walls are covered with ivy. Inside are irregular rooms with strikingly decorated nooks, and staircases supported by carved pillars which break the monotony of conventional design. Among France's major novels, perhaps only *Jocaste, Les Désirs de Jean Servien, Thaïs, Le Lys rouge*, and *Les Dieux ont soif* have what could be called, though not without considerable critical tolerance, an acceptable construction. But the first two novels mentioned have other shortcomings and do not belong among the author's major novels.

The lack of unified composition evident in his novels harmed France's literary renown as much as his scepticism. Cerf blames a great deal of France's "degeneration" on a lack of structure.[66] He attributes this shortcoming to the author's nihilism. "Having no convictions, France cannot simulate the serious interest in life which he does not possess. His works have no structure, for structure presupposes life and action. Structure is the framework of drama. Where there is no life, there is no drama, and no need of structure."[67] The critic's apodictically expressed findings are neither logically nor historically justified: an organic link between the author's strong convictions and composition does not seem to be an artistic *conditio sine qua non*. Superbly constructed commercial novels are often empty. And, in any case, France manifests strong convictions which spring from his integral wisdom and he symbolizes them in many dramatic conflicts. His own life was inspiring, active and even crusading enough to gain him recognition for several generations. True, some of his novels are very digressive, but it seems too orthodox to expect from a writer what one is entitled to require from a builder, for literary constructions never overwhelm the reader's aesthetic feelings in the same way as cathedrals, calculated to make an instantaneous impression on the observer's eyes and mind. Besides, whatever nonchalance of composition exists in France's novels disappears completely in the short story. Many among those included in the eight collections[68] are not inferior to the greatest

[66] Cerf uses the term structure in the same sense as rhetoric, i.e. composition.
[67] Cerf, *op. cit.*, p. 295; see also this study, p. 2.
[68] *Balthasar, L'Etui de Nacre, Les Puits de Sainte Claire, Clio, Sur la Pierre blanche, Crainquebille, Putois, Riquet et plusieurs autres récits profitables, Les Contes de Jacques Tournebroche,* and *Les Sept Femmes de la Barbe-Bleue.*

short stories written by Petronius, Boccaccio, or Voltaire. If his better short stories were arranged in the form of a "Tetrameron" the work would match in quality Boccaccio's masterpiece. France, who preached the return to the most characteristic genre of the French literary genius – *la nouvelle* –[69] elevated this genre along with other *conteurs* of his era to its ancient glory. A detailed analysis of the composition of stories such as "Balthasar", "Le Procurateur de Judée", "Le Jongleur de Notre Dame", "Le Saint Satyre", "Le Chanteur de Kymé", would reveal that they are written economically and that their forms are in most cases simple and dramatic molds for their subject matter. The perfect construction of France's short stories may make one wonder whether France was unable to use similar discipline in his novels or whether he had some aesthetic reason for not doing so. It may seem incredible that someone who stressed the necessity of an ingenious arrangement so strongly would not apply the same criterion to the architecture of a major work. But France may have justly felt that, in accepting as much rigid discipline in composition as he did in style, he would have sacrificed a great deal of his genuine originality. Had he accepted the laws of more rigid composition, works such as *Le Chat maigre*, his biographical *causeries* and satirical tetralogy, the *Histoire contemporaine* and *Les Opinions de M. Jerôme Coignard*, would never have appeared. French autobiographical literature would have suffered only a minor loss if France had not written his autobiographical *causeries*, and his literary reputation may even have gained had he not published *Le Chat maigre*. But, had his *Histoire contemporaine* never appeared because of its digressive nature, modern French satire would have been greatly impoverished. The suppression of all the anecdotes and references would drastically decrease the amount of aesthetic stimuli in works such as *Le Crime de Sylvestre Bonnard*, *Thaïs*, *Histoire comique*, *La Rôtisserie de la Reine Pédauque*, or even *La Révolte des anges*. This comment is not intended as an unreserved eulogy of digression. It merely points out that a venerated dogma, such as the classical unity of action, can be violated to advantage by an author who knows how and when to use a digression without losing sight of the main goal of art. For France, the goal of art is the same

[69] See p. 39, and n. 72.

as that of life – joy. If digression in the novel can create more joy than observance of the classical theatrical rules, why not digress? Stapfer, France's contemporary, was less dogmatic about the principles and goals of art than Cerf. Although he had no illusions about the discipline of France's composition, he still found certain merit in his digressive technique.

A vrai dire, la manière dont M. Anatole France compose ses livres ou plutôt ne les compose pas, ne saurait, en général, passer pour un modèle, et comme c'est par ses défauts, non par ses qualités, qu'on imite un auteur, des singes peu malins pourraient se figurer qu'il suffit de *ne pas* mettre dans ses récits une suite logique et serrée pour "faire du France". Mais ce n'est pas si facile que cela. S'il n'y a pas de vraie composition dans ses œuvres, il est probable qu'il y a autre chose, et de cette *autre chose* en effet il y a autant et plus qu'il n'en faut pour composer largement ce qu'on ne sera plus tenté de reprendre comme un vice, quand on y reconnaîtra la condition même des beautés que nous admirons.[70]

Despite the fluctuation in critical assessments of France's literary merits, the "autre chose" which Stapfer found and which Cerf was unable to appreciate, will endure in France's "poorly" constructed works. This "autre chose" will always await the reader for whom art is neither "life" nor "drama" nor "structure" but a path of joy and beauty.

Paying homage to his predecessor in his inaugural *discours* in the *Académie française*, a reserved Paul Valéry commends France precisely for this ingenuity of contrasts: "Admirons . . . cette grande capacité de contrastes."[71] The latter-day symbolist also makes a diplomatic allowance for the potential merits of an art, which, unlike his own, tended to conceal the style rather than the thought.

Son œuvre ne surprit que doucement et agréablement par le contraste rafraîchissant d'une manière si mesurée avec les styles éclatants ou fort complexes qui s'élaboraient de toutes parts. Il sembla que l'aisance, la clarté, la simplicité revenaient sur la terre. Ce sont des déesses qui plaisent à la plupart. On aime tout de suite en langage qu'on pouvait goûter sans trop y penser, qui séduisait par une apparence si naturelle, et de qui la limpidité, sans doute, laissait transparaître parfois une arrière-pensée,

[70] Stapfer, *op. cit.*, pp. 160-61.

[71] Paul Valéry, *Discours de réception à l'Académie française* (Paris, Gaillimard, 1927), p. 40.

mais non mystérieuse; mais au contraire toujours bien lisible, sinon toujours toute rassurante.[72]

France's elegant rhetorical arrangements and suave digressions contribute considerably to this "gentle and pleasant surprise" which radiates from every page of France's prose. Valéry also suggests that much of this surprise comes from France's light treatment of serious problems. He reticently "compliments" his illustrious predecessor's "art consommé de l'effleurement des idées et des problèmes les plus graves".[73] Yet France's ironic "effleurement" is often deeper than it seems. . . .

[72] *Ibid.*, p. 27.
[73] *Ibid.*, p. 28.

IV

HUMOR

A refined *esprit* prevails over the Gallic *rigolade* in France's humor. France is not a humorist who merely wants to satisfy the average reader's need for laughter. Humor plays a nobler role in his wisdom of joy and in his art. It is man's shield against the tragic *ananké.* It enables him to meet destiny, not with vacillating hope in Christian eternity, not with grave, stoic acceptance of nothingness, but with a wise smile, free of illusions.

Both France's subjects and his style are so pervaded with tragicomic accents, above all with irony, that Haakon Chevalier maintains that France's "ironic temper" is the key to his art.

> Irony . . . is in him a permanent attitude. It conditions . . . all that he says. It is the pattern of his response to experience. It is the pattern of his artistic expression. It is his originality, it is his virtue, his vice, his power, his insufficiency: it is the man.[1]

Everything in Chevalier's climactic statement tends towards a scholarly hyperbole. This hyperbole, like Cerf's speculative overstatements, helped to undermine France's literary significance.

The author's irony is certainly not so total and monolithic as the critic suggests. He must have other permanent attitudes besides irony. Perhaps Chevalier's notion of the ironic disposition itself is misleading. He defines it as "the product of certain radical insufficiencies of character and a mode of escape from the fundamental problems and responsibilities of life".[2] The "radical insufficiencies" are not only in France's character – Chevalier blames the sterility of the whole period,

[1] Chevalier, *op. cit.*, p. 214.
[2] *Ibid.*, p. 12.

during which France defined his wisdom, for having additionally compromised France's literary achievements. "Anatole France lived in a time in which there was no general vitalizing current of ideas that the artist could work in."[3] This claim does not seem to be completely substantiated either: France's major satires, conflicts or utopian topics reflect the influence of Darwin, Spencer, Comte, Renan, Marx, Engels. Their thoughts were as vitalizing as any current of urgent thoughts in human history. Diverse political events in the late 19th century aroused France's moral and social pathos. He also was influenced by the artistic trends of his day and they were not less vital than any of the literary tendencies of our century. Chevalier concludes that the alleged lack of vital ideas has impoverished France's human experience and affected his artistic vigor.

> Art is a way of expressing human experience, and it consequently reflects in some measure the quality and the validity of the individual artist's experience and the experience of the age which produced him as well. Upon reading Anatole France's work from beginning to end, as the record of a life's experience ... we are conscious of a certain poverty in range and variety of feeling, of a curious lack of vitality for all the freshness of the stream of prose that continued to flow for fifty years: most of all, of a too uniform application to life of a philosophy that is incomplete, tentative and increasingly monotonous.[4]

Art undeniably cannot grow from anything else than from man's experience – from life. But implying that art, like journalism, history, or any science, must express human experience, Chevalier seems to forget that art may profitably transgress the limits of historical experience to express dreams, or visions of past and future. He seems to underestimate the writer's humanism and overestimate the importance of moral and political engagement inspired by the bitter lessons of life. If the thematically and formally varied works of France suffer from "poverty in range" and "monotony", which of the life works of modern Western authors could escape the same condemnation? If France's practical philosophy of joy is "increasingly monotonous", which among the grave sermons of the authors committed to some ideology is not boring? By seeing in France's prose merely a result of

[3] *Ibid.*
[4] *Ibid.*, pp. 12-13

the author's ironic temper and a sterile age, Chevalier reduces France's life work to a bouquet of "wilted roses miraculously revived".[5] This view belongs among the narrower interpretations of the author's art. If we are to believe Chevalier, all of France's prodigious creations would be as futile as "the treatment of sick tooth roots", as Thomas Mann's Devil describes the sterility of our era.[6] In spite of all its skepticism, the religion France preaches is in many ways much more attractive than the grim world outlook of *littérature engagée.* Any critic may understand Chevalier's temptation to simplify things in the effort to find the common denominator in France's varied techniques and to declare one of them the only spring of his unusual creative force. After all, the author's general goal of life, joy, cannot be realized without irony.[7] But, besides irony, several other attitudes and experiences contribute to that bipolar joy. So although it would be an unpardonable oversight not to recognize the emiminent role of irony in France's art, we have to be aware that irony is not the master key to it, as Chevalier suggests, but one of several keys. This discussion leaves little doubt that, in France's prose, irony is not a mere figure of speech but an important aesthetic element inherent both in style and subject matter. Although it may channel a great deal of his verbal humor, irony often creates grave counterpoints to major themes, or stresses the insolubility of tragic conflicts. As sublime irony, it strikes serene or joyous accords.

Irony is not always the direct contrary of what is meant. Ironical statements may approach their opposite: some of the already described figures of speech are frequently ironic. But whether absolute or partial, the contradiction in irony is most often humorous: there is an abstract conflict between two different meanings, one expressed but not intended and the other intended but dissimulated, and the result

[5] *Ibid.*, p. 211.

[6] Thomas Mann, *Doctor Faustus, in: Gesammelte Werke* (Oldenburg, S. Fischer, 1960), p. 323.

[7] See this study, p. 26. See also Levaillant, (*op. cit.*, p. 143): "Reconnaître la médiocrité du réel ne signifie pas en effet qu'on s'en contente. Au cours des années de pause qui viennent, France va se consacrer à l'embellissement conscient de la vie banale, grâce à un optimisme tendre, conservateur et confortable, à un masque qui permet de voir clair et de paraître heureux, grâce à un alibi: l'humour."

– an unexpected verbal incongruity – causes laughter.[8] Irony may be motivated by various feelings: by love, hatred, contempt, indifference, by the desire to show the relativity of things, by the wish to change the mood. France smiles with approving, tender sympathy at the object of his wit or crushes it with a merciless sarcasm or bitter satire which may provoke a disgusted grin rather than laughter.[9] These limits define the vast empire of irony and satire France built while sharpening his wits as a writer for more than half a century. His judiciously divided sympathies gave his irony a wide range. He satirizes the French social classes – proletariat, bourgeoisie, aristocracy, nobility. He finds welcome targets for friendly and unfriendly irony in whores, saints, in God and the Devil, and in himself, whom he parodies with loving irony as Pierre Nozière. In one of his autobiographical causeries, he describes Pierre's childish desire to have a drum and the comical circumstances which hampered the fulfillment of this aspiration.

Pour qu'on ne s'y trompe pas, je voulais avoir un tambour, sans me sentir

[8] Scholars seem to imply that humor is a kind of surprise: The Aristotelian "deceived expectation", to which Maggi added "surprise" and „suddenness"; Hobbes' "sudden glory"; A. Zeisig's "theory of double shock"; Bergson's "contrast", in this case a sudden transition from one subject to another entirely opposite; Kant's sudden transformation of a strained expectation into nothing; Schopenhauer's "paradox" and "disappointment"; Martin's element of "unexpectedness" as well as "contrast'; Jean Paul's "sharply bursting out"; Pirandello's "awareness of contraries" and a "contrast between the ideal and the real" ; Spencer's "overflow" ; Lipp's "descending incongruity" ; Bains' "delivrance"; Levaillant's "contraire par le contraire" and "art de l'impropriété volontaire, du trop ou du trop peu", or Freud's "release" all imply a sudden shift from one contrasting element to another and the suprise linked with it. Although their theories do not agree on how such a stimulation is achieved and what kind of an enjoyment it is, they agree that a comical effect is a laugh-provoking, surprising contrast. Some writers also point out that we laugh instinctively and that laughter is a frequent symptom of human happiness. The quotations above are based on references in the following works: Max Eastman, *The Sense of Humor* (New York, Scribner, 1922), pp. 128, 138, 161, 170, 185, 191; Henri Bergson, *Laughter an Essay on the Meaning of Comic* (London, Macmillan, 1913); Luigi Pirandello, *L'Umorismo* (Florence, Battistelli, 1920) pp. 178-79; J. A. R. Thompson, *The Dry Mock, A Study of Irony in Drama* (Berkeley and Los Angeles, University of California Press, 1948), p. 75, nn. 24, 25 and Levaillant, *op. cit.*, p. 151.

[9] See also Levaillant, *op. cit.*, p. 151: "Aussi faut-il distinguer chez France ... deux intentions de l'humour valorisant, et ... dépréciatif."

aucune envie d'être tambour (1). Du métier je ne considérais ni la gloire ni les risques (2). Bien qu'assez versé, pour mon âge, dans les fastes militaires de la France (3), je n'avais encore entendu parler ni du jeune Bara mort en pressant ses baguettes sur son cœur, ni de ce tambour de quinze ans qui, à la bataille de Zurich, le bras percé d'une balle, continua de battre la charge, reçut du premier consul, à l'une des revues du décadi, une baguette d'honneur, et, pour la mériter, se fit tuer à la première occasion (4). ... Non, je ne voulais pas être tambour; je voulais plutôt être général, et, si je désirais ardemment une caisse et des baguettes noires, c'est que j'associais à ces objets mille images guerrières (5).

On ne pouvait me reprocher (6) alors de préférer le lit de Cassandre à la lance d'Achille (7). Je ne respirais qu'armes et combats; je me réjouissais dans le carnage (8); je devenais un héros, si les destins "qui gênent nos pensées" l'eussent permis. Ils ne le permirent point (9). ...

Comme je n'étais pas stoïque (10) je confiais souvent mon désir aux personnes capables de le satisfaire (11). Elles faisaient mine de ne rien entendre, ou me répondaient d'une manière vraiment désespérante.

– Tu sais bien, me disait ma chère maman, que ton père n'aime pas les jouets qui font du bruit (12).

Ce qu'elle me refusait par piété conjugale (13), je le demandai à ma tante Chausson, qui ne craignait nullement d'être désagréable à mon père (14). Je m'en étais fort bien aperçu, et c'est sur quoi je comptais pour obtenir ce que je désirais si ardemment. Par malheur, la tante Chausson, parcimonieuse, donnait rarement et peu (15).[10]

On the whole, the humor of this passage consists in the contrasts between the heroic dreams of the little boy and prosaic reality. This general effect is produced by a number of humorous details. There is a shade of sublime irony in the comically paradoxical desire to own a drum without wanting to be a drummer (1). France's seemingly serious tone in saying that the little boy did not try to assess the possible glory and risks of a drummer's career is ironical because little boys naturally would be unable to assess such factors with due responsibility (2). The remark that little Pierre was familiar with the military *fasti* is a touch of sublime irony. No doubt he was "interested" and "knew" a few melodramatic accounts of French heroism, probably from his children's books, but of course he was not a Michelet (3). This loving irony is juxtaposed with the satirized irony of fate: what France means by the term *fastes* is illustrated by the digressive account of the two drummers' heroic deaths (4). As if little Pierre had an

[10] *O.C.*, XIII, pp. 61-63.

instinctive premonition of the hazards dramatized in the two anecdotes, he surprises by revealing his comical dream: to be a general, someone who sends others to their deaths. The drum is just a symbol of everything related to the boy's heroic dreams (5). France enhances the humor of this passage with a series of ironical figures of speech, such as litotes (6, 10), a metonymy, which points out somewhat ambiguously the contrast between the ambitions of the young and of the old (7), hyperbole (8), metaphor (9), a new maternal litotes and understatement, "n'aime pas" (12), and an ironical *mot juste* (13). France's ironical euphemism, "confier son désir", seems to be an extremely delicate act hardly comparable to the bold statement of a lad determined to have a drum which would make everyone within earshot pray cynically for the annihilation of drum and drummer (11). With mock seriousness France reveals the boy's precocious diplomatic skill (14). But due to the irony of fate the young diplomat's Machiavellian scheme misfires: the purchase of expensive toys is not compatible with the spending policy of his aunt, who otherwise would have no scruples whatsoever about annoying the boy's father (15). But in spite of all these obstacles the boy's dream is fulfilled. Victoriously he marches down the street beating his drum, escorted by the faithful Mélanie. When they return home, the apartment is empty. Pierre's parents have left on a trip, leaving the boy alone with the servant girl. Now he learns the price of the fulfilled wish. His aunt and Mélanie try to console him, but he is so unhappy he will not eat his soup. However, the little boy is not going to starve to death: the *vol-au-vent* and the cream his mother ordered to console her son tempers his tragedy. All this is a subdued, gentle caricature which dramatizes with benign irony the joys and "griefs" of the little bourgeois.[11]

As an antithesis to this warm and playful irony, one might consider a remark passed by the gossipy funeral guest who, between the *Dies irae* and the following part of the mass, comments on the cause of the actor Chevalier's suicide:

[11] *Ibid.*, p. 68. In his last major work, *La Vie en fleur,* in which France describes his deliberations over his future career on the day of university registration, we find a very similar kind of self-caricature (*O.C.,* XXIII, pp. 431-32). Many examples of such jovial, tender irony can be found in all four autobiographical volumes, *Le Crime de Sylvestre Bonnard,* in the fairy tales, *Nos Enfants,* in *L'Etui de Nacre* and in all the collections of short stories.

– Alors, c'est pour Nanteuil qu'il s'est fait sauter le caisson. Une petite grue qui ne vaut pas son derrière plein d'eau chaude!

Le célébrant mit le vin et l'eau dans le calice et dit:

– *Deus qui humanae substantiae dignitatem mirabiliter condidisti* . . .[12]

Suddenly the funeral guest, summing up Mlle. Nanteuil's human worth soberly but with pithy vulgarity, puts Chevalier's love and suicide in a cruelly ironic light. He appears perhaps as a victim of his own imbecility, perhaps a victim of the power which inspired the actor's foolish love. The funeral rite provides a new target for the author's biting irony. His wit soars up from the common level to metaphysical satire, using the dead man, who shot himself for a tart, as a sample of "dignity" granted to man by God. The disharmony between the vulgar gossip and the august tone of the liturgical text creates a sharp tragi-comic contrast which echoes the central blasphemy of *Histoire comique*.

Between such sarcasm and Pierre Nozière's bitter fate, sweetened by cream pudding, are many kinds and many shades of irony. Their freshness and abundance mark all genres of France's prose including his historical monograph on Jeanne d'Arc and his journalism. Without the gently teasing tone and sarcastic flashes, the five volumes of *La Vie littéraire*, would today be a hodge-podge of dated literary critiques. But in the form of impressionist causeries they remain a colorful, mosaic of French literature.

The critic of *Le Temps* has little feeling for the exalted pathos of the Romantic generation. He comments in a light vein on the era when man took himself and his life very seriously and acquired a passionately solemn pose:

C'était le temps où les femmes portaient des boucles à l'anglaise et des manches à gigot. Les hommes étaient coiffés en coup de vent. Il leur suffisait pour cela de se brosser les cheveux chaque matin d'une certaine manière. Mais par cette artifice, ils avaient l'air de voyageurs errants sur la pointe d'un cap ou sur la cime d'une montagne, et ils semblaient perpétuellement exposés, comme M. de Chateaubriand, aux orages des passions, et aux tempêtes qui emportent les empires. La dignité humaine en était beaucoup relevée.[13]

[12] *O.C.*, XIII, p. 249.

[13] *O.C.*, VII, p. 402-03.

Such satire is not bitter. True enough, it mocks and ridicules and the grave statesman would probably be annoyed to read such an irreverent literary caricature of himself and of the life pose in which he and his era indulged. Yet it is not a satire nourished by bitterness or even hatred. The Romantics and their ideology are merely made ridiculous because of their sartorial styles, hair-dos, and pathos. In discussing the gloomy apostle of Romanticism, France did not feel the same impulse to devastate as he did when he reviewed the seventy-third edition of Ohnet's naturalistic novel, *Volonté*. In an essay polemically titled, "Hors de la littérature", France says mercilessly:

En vérité, plus je relis ce titre, plus j'y trouve d'intérêt. C'est sans contredit la plus belle page qui soit sortie de la plume de M. Georges Ohnet. Le style en est sobre et ferme, la pensée heureuse, claire, profonde. *Volonté, par George Ohnet*, soixante-treizième édition, que cela est excellement pensé, que cela est bien écrit!

J'avoue que le reste du livre m'a paru inférieur.[14]

Later in the same essay France continues in his caustic invectives against the would-be naturalist:

Je n'avais jamais lu encore un livre si mauvais: cela même me le rendit considérable, et je finis par en concevoir une espèce d'admiration. M. Ohnet est détestable avec égalité et plénitude; il est harmonieux et donne l'idée d'un genre de perfection. C'est du génie cela.[15]

France rarely comments on any political power, on any institution, or describes any type of politician, bureaucrat, general, scholar, priest, or judge without satirizing them. His irony and satire vary considerably in their tone and their intention. They can be urbane and almost apologetic, bitterly sarcastic, or even demagogical. The minister of finance, M. Martin-Bellème, meditates about the intricacies of his own budget and is somewhat annoyed that he has to defend in the senate budgetary measures which he would condemn if he were in the opposition. The passage is a subtle parody of the politician who is surprised and forced by circumstances to betray his own "principles" once he gets into power. The final paradox, "Ah! si l'on savait le peu que nous pouvons quand nous sommes au pouvoir!" [16] which sums up

[14] *O.C.*, VI, p. 385.
[15] *Ibid.*, p. 387.
[16] *O.C.*, IX, p. 372.

the reality of political life and which modifies the minister's spineless attitude, doubles the surprise produced by the irony of fate. Thus the satire becomes an almost tolerant caricature. What begins as a satirical revelation of a chameleon-like political leader ends with a "wise" recognition that political compromise is inevitable.

France's irony and political satire become demolishing in his *Histoire contemporaine* or in his political utopia, *L'Ile des Pingouins*, in which he describes one of the last fervent apostles of capitalism in Europe:

Le culte de la richesse eut ses martyrs. L'un de ces milliardaires, le fameux Samuel Box, aima mieux mourir que de céder la moindre parcelle de son bien. Un de ses ouvriers, victime d'un accident de travail, se voyant refuser toute indemnité, fit valoir ses droits devant les tribunaux, mais rebuté par d'insurmontables difficultés de procédure, tombé dans une cruelle indigence, réduit au désespoir, il parvint, à force de ruse et d'audace, à tenir son patron sous son revolver, menaçant de lui brûler la cervelle s'il ne le secourait point: Samuel Box ne donna rien et se laissa tuer pour le principe.[17]

The satirist elevates capitalism to a religious cult and makes martyrs of stubborn capitalists, identifying "la moindre parcelle" of the capitalist's fortune with a superhuman principle worth more than human life.

By reflecting a work's universal symbolism, sublime and grave irony may reach a higher aesthetic level. Neither the writer in his commentary nor his characters intentionally say the contrary of what they intend to say. The discrepancy originates in the course of fate. The irony of fate is a case of pure surprise in the narrow sense of the term. Just the reverse of what is expected happens. The almost incredible result, which takes the reader by surprise, is frequently an ironic paradox or ambiguity. In "Le Procurateur de Judée", Lamia's teasing of Pontius Pilatus, who describes the administrative problems created by the peculiarities of the Jewish cult, presents an intuitive vision of Pilate's role in Christian history.

Je ris, dit Lamia, d'une idée plaisante qui, je ne sais comment, m'a traversé la tête. Je songeais qu'un jour le Jupiter des Juifs pourrait bien venir à Rome et t'y poursuivre de sa haine. Pourquoi non? L'Asie et l'Afrique nous ont déjà donné un grand nombre de dieux.[18]

[17] *O.C.*, XVIII, p. 401.
[18] *O.C.*, V, p. 231.

The reader, from his historical perspective, is amused at the accuracy of Lamia's mocking prediction. But the irony of fate casts much darker and longer shadows on Pilate's and Lamia's symposion. The two protagonists, the omnipresent but forgotten Galilean and his reluctant Roman judge, personify this irony. France's Pilate compromises his Roman political career by his continuous opposition to what he considers Jewish religious fanaticism and political bigotry yet, ironically, Christian tradition marks him as the villain of the tragedy at Golgotha. Had he saved the life of the unknown son of God, as he wished, the whole Christian dogma would have collapsed. It is a further irony that if Pilate's superiors, including the emperor, had listened to a Roman rather than to Jewish plotters, the empire and the civilization Pilate believed in might not have had to face the fateful challenge of Christianity. It is equally ironic that Pilate has enough historical insight or ingenious naïveté to see the threat to Rome coming from Palestine:

> On ne viendra pas à bout de ce peuple. Il faut détruire Jérusalem de fond en comble. Peut-être, ... me sera-t-il donné de voir le jour où tomberont ses murailles, ... où l'on semera le sel sur la place où fut le Temple. Et ce jour-là je serai enfin justifié.[19]

"Justified" from the pagan and Roman point of view, he means and "justified" from this point of view he is indeed – by the author. Ironically, it is too late. There are no more Pagans and no empire. The final chord is a grave ironic paradox. Apropos of his love for the Jewish dancer Maria Magdalena, Lamia asks the former procurator if he recalls the young "thaumaturge" whose sect the seductive Jewess joined. He called himself Jesus of Nazareth. Pontius puts his hand to his temple with the air of a man who concentrates very deeply. After a few moments of silence, he mutters: "Jésus? ... Jésus, de Nazareth? Je ne me rappelle pas."[20] Thus all the previous ironic implications are topped by Pilate's unawareness of his key role in the most significant historical event of his era.

M. Bergeret's plea for indulgence to the hot-tempered M. Mazure, who wants to publish the scandalous histories of prominent families,[21]

[19] *Ibid.*, p. 235-236.
[20] *Ibid.*, p. 238.
[21] *O.C.*, XI, pp. 283-287. See also this study, p. 203, especially n. 21.

acquires a paradoxically ironical meaning. As soon as the tolerant scholar comes home, he catches his wife *in flagranti* with his favorite disciple. Although he recommends indulgence to others, he has none for his own wife. He leaves her despite her plea for forgiveness. Indulgence could not provide him with the freedom he seeks. In "Le Roi boit", Pierrolet, the small, illiterate secretary of the Burgundian *messire* Guillaume Chappedelaine, does not cry "Le roi boit!" on the day in Epiphany in 1428 when his master, appointed that year the King of Epiphany, lifts his goblet. Pierrolet thus violates a tradition and, according to the same tradition, he must be punished by having his face blackened. The young Armagnac boy draws his dagger, kills his pro-English master and disappears before the amazed participants in the ceremony have time to catch him. He joins the company of Captain La Hire, is seen by Jeanne d'Arc capturing an English captain in the battle of Patay and the murderer is knighted. Thus, ironically and paradoxically, his crime leads to his fortune and his success in life.[22] Leila's prayer for death in order to taste life and for guilt in order to find joy reveals the tragic irony of immortality.[23] The torment of love suffered by the young Abyssinian monarch provides an ironic catharsis. By overcoming his sensual love for Balkis, Balthasar finds wisdom and divine love.[24] Thus his serene revelation approaches sublime irony.

Grave irony excites regrets, anger, or fear; sublime irony arouses loving sympathy, understanding, or melancholy joy, like that inspired by "Le Jongleur de Notre Dame". The cheerless life of the humble juggler Barnabé is full of misery. France, pretending that human suffering was justly imposed upon man for Adam's fall, interprets with simulated naiveté the divine verdict, implying that each man should not suffer more than his "share". With regretful irony, he compares his hero with other products of God's creative bungling, the tree and the grasshopper, which are forced to suffer through every winter half-dead.[25] In spite of all this, Barnabé bears no grudge against human destiny and with his own irony naively eulogizes his condition to an

[22] *O.C.*, XIII, pp. 87-94.
[23] *O.C.*, IV, p. 193. See also this study, pp. 164-202.
[24] *O.C.*, IV, p. 148.
[25] *O.C.*, V, p. 288.

itinerant monk: "Tel que vous me voyez, je me nomme Barnabé, et je suis jongleur de mon état. Ce serait le plus bel état du monde si on y mangeait tous les jours."[26] The monk, missing the subtle irony, protests against Barnabé's statement and claims that there is nothing to equal monastic life. Barnabé answers humbly, recognizing the charms of monastic life with words full of deference.

– Mon Père, je confesse que j'ai parlé comme un ignorant. Votre état ne se peut comparer du mien et, quoiqu'il y ait du mérite à danser en tenant au bout du nez un denier en équilibre sur un bâton, ce mérite n'approche pas du vôtre. Je voudrais bien comme vous, mon Père, chanter tous les jours l'office, et spécialement l'office de la très sainte Vierge, à qui j'ai voué une dévotion particulière. Je renoncerais bien volontiers à l'art ... pour embrasser la vie monastique.[27]

Barnabé is ready to give up the drudgery of his special métier at any time. It is difficult to decide whether the hero himself is or is not aware of the latent irony in all he says. Maybe only France, the reader, and, in the final instance, the Virgin and God, see the two farcically contrasting "professional merits" in quite a different light. This seems to be confirmed by the miraculous ending. Barnabé's naive statements are, perhaps without his intention or realization, extremely subtle and ambiguous. They have two levels of irony: the first is a sublime irony which contradicts with warm sympathy the juggler's belittlement of his art and the second is a latent blasphemous irony which parodies the monk: the cleric's repeated and righteous flattery would, after all, bore even a saint. The ironic element in the miracle described at the end of "Le Jongleur de Notre Dame" rests in the fact that the monks who seek God through asceticism and a lifetime of devotion do not find Him, while the perspiring juggler, whose act of worship is a demonstration of his art, finds grace.

Grave and sublime irony are masterfully amalgamated in the finale of "Le Chanteur de Kymé". Grave is the irony of the artist's fate in Homer's time as in any era: the public fortunate enough to listen to the greatest of the Bards fills him with despair and inspires his suicide.[28] Sublime irony in this passage springs from the parody of Homeric

[26] *Ibid.*, p. 290.
[27] *Ibid.*, p. 291.
[28] See Ch. VI, pp. 154-55.

diction harmoniously integrated with France's vision of the ancient setting. The account of the Bard's last day of life describes his arrival at the home of the wealthy patron. The old Homer ascends the staircase chiseled in the rock leading up to the town of Hissia, where he is to sing at Mégès' feast. His host greets him:

Sois le bienvenu. Quels chants sais-tu dire? (1)
Le Vieillard répondit:
– Je sais (2) la Querelle des rois qui causa de grands maux aux Achéens (3), je sais (4) l'Assaut du mur. Et ce (5) chant est beau (6). Je sais (7) aussi Zeus trompé, l'Ambassade et l'Enlèvement des morts. Et ces (8) chants sont beaux (9). Je sais encore six fois soixante (11) chansons très belles (12).
De cette manière, il faisait entendre qu'il en savait beaucoup. Mais il n'en connaissait pas le nombre (13).[29]

The previously cited opening epical accusative (1) evokes the ancient charm of the *Iliad*. It is, in fact, an *imitatio*[30] of its opening: the quarrel of the kings which caused many evils to the Achaeans is the Homeric wrath which *myri' Achaiois algen etheken*.[31] One is surprised by the charming parody of the Bard's *sit venia verbo* commercial: "Et ce chant est beau" (6). This praise of his own product has the undeniable flavor of the stereotyped lines of the epic poems offered to Mégès (9, 12). The primitivistic anaphorae, "Je sais . . . Je sais" (2, 4, 7, 10), their counterparts, "Et ce . . . et ces" (5, 8), the final hyperbolic numeral (11) used by the old Bard, and France's ironic interjection (13), contribute to the sublime gaiety of the poetic text.[32] It is written in rhythmical prose and some of its parts vaguely parody the dactylic or anapestic rhythm of ancient poetry: ". . . la Querelle des rois qui causa de grands maux aux Achéens" or ". . . mur, Et ce chant est beau". Or: "Mais il n'en connaissait pas le nombre."[33]

Irony dominates in France's humor but it is not its exclusive feature. In many comical scenes irony is blended with farce. The Aristotelian

[29] *O.C.*, XIII, p. 18.
[30] For the meaning of *imitatio* see Ch. X.
[31] *Homeri Opera* (Oxford, Clarendon Press, 1951) Ch. I., v. 2.
[32] See p. 55n. 66.
[33] For a detailed analysis of France's poetic technique see Chapter VI, particularly pp. 149-58.

definition of humor, "ugliness which is not painful",[34] explains why we laugh when seeing or reading a farce. A similiar idea is spelled out in two Indian medieval works on humor. *Dasarupa*, a Sanskrit treatise on the forms of the drama dating from the tenth century, says: "Mirth (hasa) is caused by one's own or another's strange actions, words or attire"; *Sahitya Darpana* or *Mirror of Composition* states that the comic may "arise from the fun of distorted shapes or other dramatization, words, dresses, gestures etc."[35] The author may create a farcical effect by a certain type of topical overstatement, understatement, or other exaggerated dramatization. Such distortions must not provoke pity but only the sense or "instinct of humor".[36]

Without theorizing about elementary sources of various types of humor France knows how to treat farce and yield farcical effects. Almost all of the typical Francean heroes are somewhat "distorted" from the normal, even in his miniature literary caricature where the farcical element is limited to a few features. In *Le Petit Pierre*, France portrays one of his former teachers, M. Grepinet, as follows:

> Je le vois comme s'il était assis devant moi. Doué d'un gros nez et d'une lippe disgracieuse, il ressemblait à Laurent de Médicis, non par la libéralité de ses mœurs, mais par la laideur de son visage.[37]

Even the reader who has never seen the portrait of the ugly Lorenzo, and cannot therefore visualize his nineteenth century replica at Collège Stanislas, may be inclined to smile, because France settled his score with a former teacher and because the educator's ugliness was so illustrious. In *La Vie en Fleur*, Pierre Nozière's friend, Fontanet, characterizes *le père* Bugnet, one of the professors at the Faculty of Law, in a few satirical words: "C'est un vieillard sordide. Il lui coule perpétuellement du nez une roupie qu'il recueille dans un mouchoir rouge, grand comme un drap."[38] The comic effect depends on the adjective "sordide" and on the outsized handkerchief. Red handkerchiefs are used by peasants and country innkeepers and the vision of a sloppy jurisprudent with a red sheet spread to absorb the flood

[34] Eastman, *op. cit.*, p. 124.
[35] *Ibid.*, p. 163.
[36] *Ibid.*, p.236.
[37] *O.C.*, XXIII, p. 248.
[38] *O.C.*, XXIII, p. 433.

from his ever-welling nose is dominantly farcical. The source of surprise is the professor's unappetizing appearance, in one word, "ugliness which is not painful", or "humiliation" of a superior by a subordinate.

Among France's major farcical characters is the alcoholic "poet-scholar", Marquis Tudesco of Venice. Tudesco tells anyone and everyone about his translation of Torquato Tasso's *Gerusalemme liberata*, an unacknowledged contribution to human culture. This tiding, usually offered at the least suitable moment, is his perennial preamble to a request for a loan. He implies that such a respectable achievement is worthy of unlimited generosity and will perhaps provide a source of income to satisfy all his creditors. When Jean Servien becomes *maître d'études*, the marquis visits him during the noon hour in the college guest hall, which is full of pupils and their wealthy parents. Everybody turns to look at the bizarre old fellow as he loudly details his insolvency to Servien. Before he has time to appeal to the young teacher's generosity, his victim is recalled by the prefect. The marquis, whose needs are evidently immediate, seizes the chance to canvass the assembly of well-to-do parents. He opens his campaign for funds with the following prologue:

– Mesdames et messieurs, dit-il, j'ai traduit dans la langue française, que Brunetto Latini disait être la plus délectable de toutes, la Jérusalem délivrée, le chef-d'œuvre glorieux du divin Torquato Tasso. J'ai écrit ce grand ouvrage dans un grenier sans feu, sur du papier à chandelle, sur des cornets de tabac ...

Alors, d'un des coins du parloir, un rire d'enfant partit comme une fusée.

M. Tudesco s'arrêtta et sourit, les cheveux épars, l'œil noyé, les bras ouverts comme pour embrasser et bénir; puis il reprit:

– Je dis: le rire de l'innocence, c'est la joie du vieillard infortuné. Je vois d'ici des groupes dignes du pinceau du Corrège et je dis: heureuses les familles réunies en paix dans le sein de la patrie! Mesdames et messieurs, excusez-moi si je vous tends le casque de Bélisaire. Je suis un vieil arbre foudroyé.

Et il tendait de groupe en groupe son feutre pointu où, dans un silence glacial, tombaient une à une de menues pièces d'argent.

Mais tout à coup le préfet des études saisit le chapeau et poussa le vieil homme dehors.

– Rendez-moi mon chapeau, criait M. Tudesco au préfet qui s'efforçait de restituer les pièces blanches aux donateurs; rendez le chapeau du vieil homme, le chapeau de l'homme blanchi dans les études.

Le préfet, rouge de colère, jeta le feutre dans la cour et cria.
– Filez, ou je vous fais arrêter.[39]

Tudesco's melodramatic description of the technical obstacles he surmounted to translate the masterpiece could be tragicomical if it were not just a farcical lie. The erudite and somewhat ambiguous *captatio benevolentiae*, addressed to his donors-to-be, is farcical not only because the tone of such a humanistic address is incompatible with begging, but because of the setting the marquis chose for his humble plea. The surprise reaches a climax when the beggar's bizarre pointed hat suddenly becomes Belisarius's helmet.[40] The parallel between the Byzantine soldier who almost become the Emperor of the Roman Empire and the parasitic humanist begging slyly in a plush college creates a grotesque contrast.

In France's collection of farcical characters, one of the most successfully drawn is M. de Montragoux, the innocent Bluebeard.

M. de Montragoux ne portait pas sa barbe en pointe comme son grand-père à la Cour du roi Henry II; il ne la portait pas en éventail comme son bisaieul, qui fut tué à la bataille de Marignan. Ainsi que M. de Turenne, il n'avait qu'un peu de moustache et la mouche; ses joues paraissaient bleues; mais, quoi qu'on ait dit, ce bon seigneur n'en était point défiguré, et ne faisait point peur pour cela. Il n'en semblait que plus mâle, ... Bernard de Montragoux était un très bel homme, grand, large d'épaules, de forte corpulence et de bonne mine; quoique rustique et sentant plus les forêts que les ruelles et les salons. Pourtant, il est vrai qu'il ne plaisait pas aux dames autant qu'il aurait dû leur plaire, ... Sa timidité en était la cause, sa timidité et non pas sa barbe. Les dames exerçaient sur lui un invincible attrait et lui faisaient une peur insurmontable. ... Voilà l'origine et la cause initiale de toutes ses disgrâces. En voyant une dame pour la première fois, ... il restait devant elle dans un sombre silence; ses sentiments ne se faisaient jour que par ses yeux, qu'il roulait d'une manière effroyable. Cette timidité l'exposait à toutes sortes de disgrâces, et surtout elle l'empêchait de se lier d'un commerce honnête avec des femmes modestes et réservées, et le livrait sans défense aux entreprises des plus hardies et des plus audacieuses ...[41]

[39] *O.C.*, III, p. 133-134.
[40] Belisarius, a Byzantine general during Justinian's rule, defeated the Persians, the Vandals, and the Ostrogoths. According to the false historical account adopted by Marmontel in his *Bélisaire,* the general was blinded and reduced to begging.
[41] *O.C.*, XIX, pp. 133-134.

The keynote of the farce is the digressive double litotes, not on the hero's moustache but on the elaborate facial ornaments of his two ancestors. Further farcical effects are produced by an ironical eulogy of the lord's rotundity and by the attribution of his ogling of women to shyness rather than to untamable lust. The farce is heightened by the marriage of this shy murderer to an overblown bear-dancer with a doubly ambiguous name, Colette Passage. After having exchanged her furry partner for the obese nobleman, Mademoiselle Passage automatically becomes a *dame de qualité*.[42] Bluebeard's portrait also stimulates by ironical overstatements and understatements such as "ce bon seigneur", "très bel homme . . . de forte corpulence", "peur insurmontable", "toutes sortes de disgrâces", or "enterprises des plus hardies".

The pious sinner, Verlaine, was the model for farcical portraits of Gestas and Choulette. Here we see the Parnassian convert – Gestas in a grotesque, mystical fit of penitence:

> La voix de son repentir et de sa honte lui criait: "Cochon! cochon! Tu es un cochon!" Et il admirait cette voix irritée et pure, cette belle voix d'ange qui était en lui mystérieusement et qui répètait: "Cochon! cochon! Tu es un cochon!" Il lui naissait un désir infini d'innocence et de pureté. Il pleurait; de grosses larmes coulaient sur sa barbe de bouc. . . . Docile à la parole du maître qui a dit: "Pleurez sur vous et sur vos enfants, filles de Jérusalem", il versait la rosée amère de ses yeux sur sa chair prostituée aux sept péchés et sur ses rêves obscènes, enfantés par l'ivresse.[43]

An angelic voice, which keeps calling "Cochon!" provides a farcical contrast: such an accusation is not what one would expect from the herald of divine grace. France's picture of a Parisian loafer whose satyr-like beard is soaked with tears of mystical penitence is a mixture of farcical and tragic elements. The parallel between the laments of the daughters of Jerusalem and those of Gestas, who mourns the corruption of his innocence by the seven mortal sins and by his obscene dreams, is another tragicomic touch. The subsequent prayer for the miraculous return of his innocence "Mon Dieu, donnez-moi de redevenir semblable au petit enfant que j'étais",[44] heightens the effect. A

[42] *Ibid.*, p. 134.
[43] *O.C.*, V, pp. 330-331.
[44] *Ibid.*, p. 331.

few minutes later, Gestas makes several vain attempts to find a confessor in an empty church. The farce reaches its climax in a controversy with the sexton, after which Gestas is thrown out of the church. When the robust sexton tells him the *curé* is not available, Gestas demands in turn: "Le premier vicaire, . . . Le second vicaire, . . . le dernier vicaire." At the response, "Allez-vous-en!" Gestas moans:

– Ah ça! est-ce qu'on va me laisser mourir sans confession? C'est pire qu'en 93, alors! Un tout petit vicaire. . . . Dites à un prêtre qu'il vienne m'entendre en confession. Je lui promets de lui confier des péchés plus rares, plus extraordinaires et plus intéressants, bien sûr, que tous ceux que peuvent lui défiler ses péronnelles de pénitentes. Vous pouvez l'avertir qu'on le demande pour une belle confession.[45]

The hero's faith contains much sublime naiveté and his expulsion from the church has a tragic accent, but the whole conflict, especially the hyperbole concerning the theological excellence of Gestas's sins, is a typical sample of Francean buffoonery. In France's work, there are many other clowns or characters with at least a few farcical features. The caricatures of many comic heroes are emphasized by some farcical distortion.[46] Some of them resemble, because of their naiveté, the characters from the old legends, from the *fabliaux*, or from *Decameron*. Others imitate the characters from eighteenth century philosophical novels and short stories: still others are inspired by the fabulous and naive aspects of popular fairy tales.

Farcical action are frequent features of Francean aesthetic surprise. They range from tame bourgeois humor suitable for reading in the nursery to titillating *gauloiseries* and even risqué obscenities.

Recalling the memorable achievements of his youth, France relates how the little Pierre-Anatole, inspired by Rabelais, tried to imitate Gargantua's stew. Filled with "une irrésistible envie d'accomplir une action étonnante", the restless Pierre wanders into the deserted kitchen.

[45] *Ibid.*, p. 334.

[46] One can find farcical elements in characters such as M. Fellaire de Sisac, M. Godet-Laterasse, the general Télémaque, Pierre Nozière, Mélanie, Sembobitis, M. Pigeonneau, Paphnuce, Célestin, Saint Bertaud, Coignard, M. d'Astarac, Brother Ange, Choulette, M. Schmoll, Mme Marmet, Buffalmacco, the tailor Rabiou, Crainquebille, Bluebeard, and many other characters in *Les Sept Femmes de la Barbe-Bleue,* in *L'Ile des Pingouins,* and in *La Révolte des anges.*

Suddenly he is inspired by the *civet de lièvre* bubbling on the stove: he will cook a giant stew to rival that of Gargantua, using all the animals in his toy Noah's Ark. Hiding the *civet* in the broom closet, spilling the sauce but burning only four fingers and two knees, the young chef tosses the contents of his ark, including Noah, into a casserole and puts it on the fire.

Je jouissais par avance de l'émerveillement de Mélanie, quand cette simple créature, croyant trouver le lièvre, qu'elle avait apprêté, découvrirait en son lieu, le lion et la lionne, ... l'éléphant et sa compagne, enfin toutes les bêtes échappés du déluge, sans compter Noë et sa famille que j'avais fricassés avec elles par mégarde. Mais l'événement trompa mes prévisions. Une puanteur insupportable ... ne tarda pas à se répandre dans tout l'appartement, ... Ma mère, suffoquée, courut à la cuisine pour en chercher la cause et trouva la vieille Mélanie qui, tout essouflée ... tirait du feu la casserole où fumaient horriblement les restes noircis des animaux de l'arche.

– Ma "castrole!" ma belle "castrole!" s'écria Mélanie ... avec l'accent du désespoir.[47]

The farcical menu is of course seasoned with generous doses of verbal irony, but basically the whole passage is pure farce.

France can channel pure farce into his work even through his style. Michel-Angelo Polizzi's letter to M. Bonnard illustrates how superlative adjectives and adverbs, subjunctives of unusual verbs, and exaggerated epistolary clichés can become vehicles of farcical verbosity:

Illustrissime seigneur,

Je possède en effet l'incomparable manuscrit de la Légende dorée, qui n'a point échappé à votre lucide attention. Des raisons capitales s'opposent impérieusement et tyranniquement à ce que je n'en désaississe pour un seul jour, pour une seule minute.[48]

Frequently, France's buffoonery approaches the level of indecency. He does not hesitate to introduce humor which Stephen Leacock would designate as archeo-comical or paleocomical.[49] In *Les Sept Femmes de la Barbe-Bleu* there are parodies of risqué "archeofarce". Describing the prenuptial merrymaking to honor Bluebeard's future wife, Jeanne

[47] *O.C.*, XXIII, p. 28.
[48] *O.C.*, II, p. 298.
[49] Stephen B. Leacock, *Humour: – its theory and technique with examples and samples,* (London, Lane, 1935) p. 9.

de Lespoisse, and her family and lover, France parodies crude medieval jests. This form of low farce heightens the literary surprise produced by other features such as irony and *gauloiserie*:

Le chevalier de la Merlus se déguisait une fois en diable, une autre fois en fantôme ou en loup-garou, pour effrayer les dormeurs, mais il finissait toujours par se couler dans la chambre de la demoiselle Jeanne de Lespoisse. Le bon seigneur de Montragoux n'était pas oublié dans ces jeux. Les deux fils de Mme des Lespoisse mettaient dans son lit de la poudre à gratter et brûlaient dans sa chambre des substances qui répandaient une odeur fétide. Ou bien encore ils plaçaient sur sa porte une cruche pleine d'eau, de telle manière que le bon seigneur ne pouvait tirer l'huis sans renverser toute l'eau sur ta tête.[50]

In this passage, France ironically censures the licentiousness of the archaic pranks and unsophisticated libertinage and thus blends a more refined humorous tone with vulgar humor. The reader's primary surprise and amusement are provoked by the childish moral crudities and the author's ironical pretense of indignation only enhances their effect. The beginning of "Crainquebille" reads like a nineteenth century version of the *Farce de Maître Patelin.* We laugh at the vegetable peddler's professional tribulations and at his legal infractions largely because of their farcical aspects. The irony and the sarcasm enter only later. Crainquebille's final personal tragedy springs from a farcical situation. The memorable purchase of a bunch of leeks by the stingy Madame Bayard and her delayed payment are pure farce. Crainquebille's conflict between the exercise of his private right to collect fourteen sous and his duty to obey a bossy *flic* enforcing a minor traffic regulation does not foreshadow a tragedy of any consequence. Madame Bayard's sly art of bargaining and the peddler's conflict with his petty, vulgar customer, his folksy sales talk, the policeman's comical refrain, "Circulez!", Madame Bayard's secondary conflict with the policeman, the cause of her delayed payment, evoke the slapstick humor of *commedia dell'arte.*[51] At first, the whole conflict seems to be absurd: would it

[50] *O.C.*, XIX, p. 150.
[51] *O.C.*, XIV, pp. 13-14. "–Ils ne sont guère beaux, vos poireaux. Combien la botte?
– Quinze sous, la bourgeoise. Y a pas meilleur.
– Quinze sous, trois mauvais poireaux?

matter whether Crainquebille lost his fourteen sous and kept moving or stayed where he was, violated the silly regulation and were finally paid? Of course it would be unjust to penalize him for either decision and that is precisely what ultimately gives his decision to wait for his money tragic dimensions. The reader is amused and moved at the same time by this amalgamation of farce and growing tragedy.

Farce, usually a lower aspect of humor, can only rarely reach the more elevated heights of irony. Yet in literature, it is an unfailing source of entertainment, especially for the average reader who, as France emphasizes, likes to read without the slightest intellectual effort. France's balanced blend of irony and farce is probably one of the factors which account for his popularity in the wider circle of readers, for the large number of editions and translations of his works. Yet France is not a humorist who compromises his art in trying to appeal to the masses who merely want to laugh. Stapfer comments on the rare alliance of France's formal perfection with humor: "La perfection classique de la forme est si grande chez M. Anatole France, qu'on pourrait hésiter à voir en lui un humoriste; car l'humoriste est, en bonne définition, le contraire d'un artiste . . ."[52] And Chevalier, who condemned France's ironic temper, felt he went too far in some of his statements. The ironic man, apparently incapable of a satisfying aesthetic synthesis, is in the final paragraph of *The Ironic Temper* de-

Et elle rejeta la botte dans la charrette, avec une geste de dégoût.

C'est alors que l'agent 64 survint et dit à Crainquebille:

– Circulez! . . . .

– Faut encore que je choisisse la marchandise, répondit aigrement la cordonnière.

Et elle tâta de nouveau toutes les bottes de poireaux, puis elle garda celle qui lui parut la plus belle et elle la tint contre son sein comme les saintes . . . pressent sur leur poitrine la palme triomphale.

– Je vais vous donner quatorze sous. C'est bien assez. Et encore il faut que j'aille les chercher dans la boutique, . . . elle rentra dans la cordonnerie où une cliente, portant un enfant, l'avait précédée.

A ce moment l'agent 64 dit pour la deuxième fois à Crainquebille:

– Circulez!

– J'attends mon argent, répondit Crainquebille.

– Je ne vous dis pas d'attendre votre argent; je vous dis de circuler, . . .

Cependant la cordonnière, . . . essayait des souliers bleus à un enfant de dixhuit mois dont la mère était pressée.

[52] Stapfer, the cited article, p. 240.

clared to be "the best writer of his time".[53] The critic asks himself, "Must we not admit him to the gallant company of Boccaccio, and Erasmus and Chaucer and Rabelais and Montaigne?"[54] Chevalier also says in his conclusion: "Anatole France's works will for a long time, probably, give superior pleasure to choicest spirits, a delight intimate, subtle, profound."[55] If such an allowance does not contradict some of his previous conclusions, at least it radically modifies their harsh verdict. The harmony of beauty and wit is typical of the French literary tradition. Like Molière, Montesquieu, Voltaire, France embodies the French genius for combining artistry with "esprit".

[53] Chevalier, *op. cit.*, p. 221.
[54] *Ibid.*
[55] *Ibid.*

V

AMBIGUITY, SYMBOLIC AMBIGUITIES, PARADOX, CONTROVERSY AND CONFLICTS

France, the polemist, seems incessantly preoccupied with conflicts and France, the *homme de métier*, incessantly sharpens them stylistically with an abundance of inventive contrasts. It is interesting to speculate whether the polemist or the stylist has the upper hand.[1] It is quite evident that France's taste for ambiguity and paradox reflects both his fascination with conflict and his aesthetic delight in acute contrast. The stylist and the polemist are inseparable: his ambiguities and paradoxes and conflicts will be analyzed in this chapter as integral counterpoints.

Like irony, both paradox and ambiguity are based on a latent contrast or contradiction, but in each this contradiction plays a different role. In irony, only the implication which contradicts the expressed meaning is valid; in ambiguity, both, or possibly several, meanings are defensible, whereas in the paradox, what is plainly said is intended and true, or passes for truth, though it seems logically impossible or improbable. There is no dissimulation involved: conventional experience is refuted, but wisdom agrees unless it is the case of pure contradiction.

An ambiguity may sometimes result from the lack of precision in

[1] Analyzing France's intellectual constitution, Levaillant states (*op. cit.*, pp. 825-826): "... les contradictions ne lui manquent pas plus qu'à Voltaire ou Diderot. Elles se détruisent l'une l'autre au courant de sa vie, c'est parce que la pensée sceptique figure une dialectique incomplète: comment choisir entre les antinomies? Les circonstances, les impondérables de l'esprit peuvent faire adopter celle qui avait été rejetée naguère. La réalité toujours double recèle une contradiction fondamentale, qu'au niveau même du style toutes les formes de la dissonance tentent chez France d'exprimer: les mots et les tours en contradiction avec la pensée, les adjectifs s'opposant l'un l'autre, l'humour et les jeux, les feintes de l'ironie ont pour but de manifester la dualité des choses, ... Pourtant l'œuvre de France paraît bien centrée, ..."

formulating an idea, from an omission, from ignorance of exact connotation, or it may be intended to disguise other meanings. What is implied may be more important than what is directly expressed, or it may only carry a suggestion of the comical, satirical, frivolous, or even obscene. This twist or direct incompatibility of the two meanings contained in one statement appeals to the human delight in play, in conflicts and tricks.[2] But ambiguity does not have to be only a comical duplicity. By implying contradiction it may become a kind of verbal sleight-of-hand: it kills two birds with one stone, but sometimes the very stone which kills the first bird feeds the second, either by accident or design.

Like France's irony, his ambiguities cover a very wide range, from fleeting and comic trivia to symbolic echoes of the main themes. Such an echo was in the ambiguity of Thaïs's last words, "un vampire! un vampire!" Compare their aesthetic significance to the ambiguous pun in the name of the learned royal physician, Professor Quillebœuf from "La Chemise". While the first has a symbolic meaning, the latter is pure buffoonery, a low joke.[3] Such a name suggests that the professor's medical art can knock down an ox; the other two implications are obviously obscene. The phallic skittle either alludes to the monumental tool of the professor's virility or to its impotence – *bœuf* being emasculated. The ambiguity of Thaïs's last words, in spite of their derision, has a grave philosophical pathos: Thaïs in a mortal coma may or may not recognize the fanatic monk who finally "sees the light" and is sorry for all the joy and beauty he missed and destroyed. He confesses his love and tries to seduce the dying Thaïs. Her fearful exclamation refers to the repulsive appearance of the lecherous ascetic, but also to the result of his religious zeal; Paphnuce is a vampire in persuading her to give up her youthful beauty and joy for an absurd religious mortification and premature death. Such an ambiguity expresses the universal meaning of the novel. It epitomizes the whole bizarre tragedy. It accuses every fanatic who preaches asceticism and masochism,

[2] Eastman, (*op. cit.*, p. 227) quotes James Drever who lists "play" among man's instinct tendencies.

[3] *O.C.*, V, p. 212 and *O.C.*, XIX, p. 319; Quilleboeuf could also refer to the place name (Normandy, itself renowned for the indulgence of its inhabitants in ambiguities).

and who ignores the joy and beauty of life. The two examples illustrate the aesthetic sweep of ambiguity, from vulgar to sublime. In naming his heroes ambiguously or symbolically France imitates the classical tradition. *Nomen omen* says a Latin proverb. Parodied aristocratic names such as Comte de Maubec de la Dendelynx, or grotesque names such as Doctor Obnubile, Queen Glamorgana, Councilor Chaussepied, general Télémaque, the obscene Tricouillard, are sheer buffoonery. Ambiguous names chosen to characterize the hero are often rather common – Bergeret, Bonnard, or Boni; the skeptical scholars, who are delighted to embarrass the honest bourgeois by finding immense merits in evil and repulsive hypocrisy in conventional good, are ironically called "little shepherd", Goodman or Goodfellow. Sometimes the satirical accent is stronger, as in the case of Mazure, the archivist from *L'Histoire contemporaine*, whose name caricatures his interest in archeology. France chose the names Worms-Clavelin for the smooth master of dubious diplomacy, alluding probably to the concordat of Worms, the memorable medieval agreement between the spiritual and secular powers. Clavelin may be an allusion to *la clavelée*, meaning sheep pox, and implies that the adroit Judeo-Masonic prefect is an infected sheep in the eyes of the satirized Church. Fulgence Adolphe Bussart d'Esparrier from *La Révolte des Anges* suggests rapacity. The name of the lucky candidate for the bishopric, Guitrel, may have been chosen because *gui* is the symbol of good luck. Tournebroche, Jacques Ménétrier's nickname, invites a twofold interpretation, one professional, the other erotic, and both comical. France is well aware of the aesthetic value of such deliberately chosen names. Discussing the nickname of the Countess de Gueldre, France says: "Elle se nommait de son nom de baptême, Auréliane, mais ses amis l'appelaient Liane, lui donnant de la sorte le nom qui convenait à sa grâce flexible."[4]

The ambiguous name vaguely resembles the ancient *epitheton constans* or more rarely, the modern *leitmotif*. Repeated, it loses its force but, in an unexpected context, it may regain it because of an unprecedented contradiction or parallel between the name and the content. Many minor Francean ambiguities express the same mischief as the ambiguous names. In *Sur la Pierre blanche*, the disciples of

[4] *O.C.*, VII, p. 633.

Boni, the archeologist, discuss the unexpected course of Boni's exploration. Boni, who organized excavations to find archeological monuments of royal, republican, and imperial Rome, discovered instead unexpected traces of paleontological life. Joséphin Leclerc comments on the new discoveries in a learned harangue in which he suddenly interpolates a question posed by one of the scholar's devotees:

Ainsi, mon cher Giacomo Boni, non content de chercher dans le Forum les monuments des Empereurs, ceux de la République et ceux des Rois, vous vous enfoncez maintenant dans les terrains qui portèrent une flore et une faune disparues, vous creusez dans le quaternaire, dans le tertiaire, vous pénétrez dans le pliocène, ... On s'inquiète, dans les salons, *des profondeurs où vous descendez. La comtesse* Pasolini *ne sait plus où vous vous arrêterez;* et l'on vous représente, dans un petit journal satirique, sortant par les antipodes et soupirant: *Adesso va bene*! [5]

In such a context the "innocent" question becomes a verbal *salto* which turns a scholarly conversation into a gallant adventure; the final hyperbolic account on the explorer's "soundings" which may lead him to the Antipodes verges on *gauloiserie.*

A gently comic incident in "Balthasar" also involves a double meaning. The royal advisor finds his young king thoughtful. When he asks him if he contracted a trade treaty with their seductive hostess, Queen Balkis, he does not know about the recent conversation between the two monarchs.

Balthasar étendit les bras vers elle et s'écria:

– Laissez-moi prendre la petite plume qui s'est posée sur votre cou et je vous donnerai la moitié de mon royaume avec le sage Sembobitis et l'eunuque Menkéra. ...

Quand le mage et l'eunuque revinrent, ils trouvèrent leur maître dans une attitude pensive, ...

– Seigneur, n'auriez-vous conclu un bon traité de commerce? demanda Sembobitis.[6]

Ironically, the royal suitor's proposition could be called so, and thus the term "business treaty", acquires a roguish meaning, of which Sembobitis is not aware. In both cases, the ambiguity lies in the different shades of interpretation. Such ambiguities are subtler than the

[5] *O.C.*, XIII, p. 370, italics are mine except for the Italian salutation.

[6] *O.C.*, IV, p. 126.

puns illustrated earlier. France does not limit the use of ambiguity to erotic subjects. Frequently his ambiguities surprise through satirical innuendoes. In "Gallion", France indirectly mocks the Christian doctrine of transubstantiation. Annaeus Mela, a pagan pantheist, defends some of the pagan religious myths saying that one should not interpret them as literally as simple people, who see tangible gods everywhere – Ceres in wheat or Bacchus in wine. "Il ne faut pas prendre à la lettre, dit-il, tout ce qu'on rapporte des dieux. Le vulgaire appelle le blé Cérès, le vin Bacchus. Mais où trouverait-on un homme assez fou pour croire qu'il boit et mange un dieu?"[7] In "Crainquebille", the lawyer Lemerle, a nationalist candidate in his district, pleads for Crainquebille. His simple client had disobeyed an order from the officious policeman Matra to keep moving. The attorney, who does not want to irritate the police force, thinks that his case provides a good opportunity to play lip service to the army. While pleading for the poor peddler, he tries to gain his adversary's political support:

> Il commença sa plaidoirie par l'éloge des agents de le Préfecture, "ces modestes serviteurs de la société, qui, moyennant un salaire dérisoire, endurent des fatigues et affrontent des périls incessants, et qui pratiquent l'héroïsme quotidien. Ce sont d'anciens soldats, et qui restent soldats. Soldats, ce mot dit tout . . ."[8]

The word "soldier" indeed says everything. It implies not only the military virtues of gallantry and obedience, but also, as France hints, the red tape, bossism and stupidity, traditionally attributed to all armies and to professional soldiers. In *L'Orme du mail*, Abbé Lantaigne realizes that the archbishop was making fun of him when he asked him how to reconsecrate a church in which a suicide had been committed. "L'archévêque me trompait! Cet homme ne dira donc jamais la vérité, hors sur les degrés de l'autel où, prenant la sainte hostie dans ses mains, il prononce ces paroles: *Domine, non sum dignus*!"[9] Thus the liturgical formula gets a new twist: not only is the archbishop not "*dignus*" in the theological sense, but in fact he is a true rascal, at least in the eyes of Abbé Lantaigne.

Sometimes, ambiguities in the style of ancient oracles ironically

[7] *O.C.*, XIII, p. 402.
[8] *O.C.*, XIV, p. 27.
[9] *O.C.*, XI, p. 19.

foreshadow the unexpected. The veracity of M. Roux's words on militarism and human barbarity will soon be confirmed, though not on the battlefield. M. Bergeret's unworthy disciple, who is completing his military service, tells his master about the man's atavistic urge to use the bayonet:

Enfin j'ai l'amour de l'humanité. Mais, dès qu'on me fiche un fusil dans la main, j'ai envie de tirer sur tout le monde ... Il suffit de donner à un homme une baionnette au bout d'un fusil pour qu'il l'enfonce dans le ventre du premier venu et devienne, comme vous dites, un héros.

La voix méridionale de M. Roux vibrait encore quand madame Bergeret entra dans le cabinet de travail, où ne l'attirait point d'ordinaire la présence de son mari ... elle avait sa belle robe de chambre. ...[10]

And, figuratively, the young soldier, equipped with a vital "bayonet", will do precisely what he says a man with a bayonet enjoys doing: he will become the *héros-Eros* of Madame Bergeret and "liberator" of M. Bergeret.

The comical touch so prevalent in ambiguities may be hardly noticeable or even absent. France gently parodies Jean Servian's romantic suffering by doleful symbols. The hero, who had fallen in love with a glamorous actress, stands at night overlooking the river and pathetically contemplates his hopeless love.

Quand il fut sur le quai désert, il arracha une feuille à une branche qui pendait d'un platane. Puis, ... il jeta cette feuille dans le fleuve et il la regarda couler au fil de cette eau argentée par la lune. ... C'était son propre emblème. Il s'abandonnait, lui aussi, au courant d'une passion brillante et qu'il croyait profonde.[11]

Overwhelmed by sentimentality, the young martyr of love is carried like a floating leaf by an unknown force to an unknown destination, or rather destiny, buried in the impenetrable darkness of the future.

Gamelin's prayer, "Sainte guillotine, sauve la patrie!"[12] is grimly prophetic. It will be at least partly answered and Gamelin himself will be beheaded to save the fatherland. The contrast between the two salvations, one invoked in the prayer and the other achieved by the liquidation of the fanatic extremists, is, of course, only of minor tragic

[10] *Ibid.*, p. 230.
[11] *O.C.*, III, p. 54.
[12] *O.C.*, XX, 204.

significance. Its purpose is to remind the reader once more of the universal theme of *Les Dieux ont soif*. Profound ambiguities, symbolizing fundamental problems in man's life, are a *conditio sine qua non* of any great literature. The parallel between the mad Orestes and the fanatic Gamelin is a major symbolic theme in France's *chef d'œuvre*. France suggests this parallel when the poor painter Gamelin explains to the *citoyenne* Rochemaure his figural composition of Orestes and Electra.

He cites the passage of Euripides' *Orestes* which inspired his work and explains the core of the tragic situation which he tried to express visually.[13] The symbolism is emphasized later when Gamelin is appointed people's juror through the influence of Mlle Rochemaure and sends hundreds of his fellow men to the guillotine, including the woman who helped him obtain his responsible position and his own brother-in-law. Gamelin's political fanaticism is a replica of the crazed Orestes' persecution by the Erinyes. Suffering under the unpardonable illusion that his merciless "justice" is the best service to humanity and a mortal blow to corruption, the painter becomes an anti-social monster. Throughout the novel Gamelin grows more and more like the Orestes on his canvas. The repeated returns to this tragic *leitmotif* leave no doubt about the universal meaning of France's theme.

The title of "L'Humaine tragédie" clearly symbolizes the nature of man's fate: like *Fra* Giovanni, man seeks truth and cannot find it. And when, in a moment of divine intuition, he can catch a glimpse of it, it not only blinds him but he discovers that it is an optical illusion.[14] Like *Fra* Giovanni, man should revere the Creator who gave man all joy and wisdom, who made man imperfect and then penalized him for it, but he should also love the source of his damnation, the devil.[15] He alone gives man's fate the indispensable seal of tragedy, without which life would be dull. This is strikingly similar to Camus's Sisyphean heroism dramatized equally by extensive poetic ambiguities. *La Révolte des anges* is France's great pagan confession: like his beauty and freedom-loving Prometheus-Lucifer-Satan, man should shake off the yoke put on him by the bigoted Judeo-Christian demi-

[13] See pp. 220-21.
[14] *O.C.*, X, pp. 194-197.
[15] *Ibid.*, p. 211.

urge, Iehovah alias Iadalbaoth, and should rediscover Dionysian joy, Apollonian harmony and the charming Muses. However, man should not dissipate his genius like Lucifer in trying to overthrow the tyranny of Iehovah. He should not revolt against one master by replacing him with another. He should ignorc Ichovah and embrace the sublime ideals of the friendly gods.[16]

L'Histoire contemporaine and *L'Ile des Pingouins* are satirized symbols of a degenerate French society. Their heroes typify the classes of this society, the clergy, the army, the professional administrators, the corrupt political parties and the rulers. "Le Chanteur de Kymé" poetically dramatizes the eternal degradation of an artist by the vulgar society for which he creates.[17] In *Les Opinions de M. Jérôme Coignard*, in *La Rôtisserie de la Reine Pédauque*, in *Sur la Pierre blanche*, in *Crainquebille*, everywhere the reader finds these symbolical ambiguities which reveals the aesthetic and philosophical perspective of France's humanistic wisdom. Had he not symbolized a convincing teleology, France's polished craft would be sterile, and he would not stand as a master in his era and beyond his era. He is clearly aware that the Rabelaisian "cracking of the marrow bone" is one of the most rewarding aesthetic gratifications and that only through the wealth of its hidden meaning can a literary work survive. (This commentary merely illustrates France's symbolist technique. His wisdom and his tragic vision of the tragic beauty of life, expressed symbolically throughout his work are analyzed in other passages of this work, particularly in Chapter I).

But symbolism is not the only means of injecting great themes into literature. The aesthetic role of paradox in France's art is comparable to that of ambiguity; both features express a latent contrast, both have a wide range. Paradox may rest in a minor antonym, it may be elevated to aphorism, or it may rise to a major speculative controversy and reveal tragic incongruity of man's destiny. Like ambiguity, it may become the focal point of the work of art. The importance of this technique in France's art is perhaps the natural reflection of basic paradoxes in his own wisdom. France thinks that the best thing about

[16] See pp. 192-94.
[17] See pp. 154-55.

good is evil, that suffering is the source of joy, and that one must be unhappy to be able to be happy.[18]

Most frequently paradox and the contradiction are considered as synonyms. Yet in this analysis an effort will be made to maintain the distinction defined earlier. But it is nonetheless difficult to draw a clear dividing line between paradox and contradiction. They are often so close that it seems preferable to discuss them simultaneously. This can be illustrated by the following example. When little Pierre Nozière tells his mother that he is going to settle in the botanical gardens, become a famous hermit, and have calling cards printed announcing that he is a saint from the calendar, the mother modifies her son's religious zeal by saying: "Mon petit garçon a perdu la raison à l'âge où l'on n'en a pas encore."[19] This is only a paradoxical pun which sounds like a logical contradiction – one cannot lose something one does not have. Yet the contradiction is an illusion produced by the juxtaposition of two idiomatic hyperboles. Paraphrased, Madame Nozière's statement becomes a platitude: My little boy is foolish ("a perdu la raison") at a foolish age ("à l'âge où l'on n'en a pas encore").

The same kind of humorous effect is achieved by the statement: "M. Dubois à qui j'ai gardé le nom, me contentant de lui retrancher un titre nobiliaire, que d'ailleurs il ne portait pas."[20] Here the contradiction is real but it soon becomes obvious that lacking a title did not prevent the vain M. Dubois from using it. And thus the "contradiction" merely becomes satirical comment on his hero's snobbery. The inconsistency of Saint Valéry and his disciples, who fought against paganism and spread the gospel in France, is satirized by the following description of their zeal: "Ils ont lutté contre la barbarie avec une énergie féroce."[21] At first sight one is inclined to take it for a pure paradox: A determined, almost mad fight for or against any cause is not impossible. But France implies that crusaders for the cause of Christian love were not eradicating religious barbarism, they were spreading it. It would be paradoxical indeed if, by their violence, they had managed to spread love and spiritual refinement. Since they

[18] See pp. 35-6.
[19] *O.C.*, III, p. 243.
[20] *O.C.*, XXIII, p. 563.
[21] *O.C.*, X, p. 436.

did not, the discrepancy between their goals and their achievements remains a contradiction. Their actions can be described as the exorcising of the Devil by Beelzebub. Religious fanaticism is also parodied in the description of monastic life among the Egyptian Cénobites. "... les cénobites renfermés chacun dans une étroite cellule, ne se réunissaient qu'afin de mieux goûter la solitude."[22] The ancient monastic rallies held to help the ascetics enjoy the bliss of solitude sounds like a contradiction *par excellence*. On the other hand, if such meetings were designed to demonstrate the superiority of solitude over the company of other unkempt zealots, such a statement may be considered a paradox. If France writes: "Ta sœur n'avait pas mauvais cœur mais elle était égoiste et violente",[23] he may try to surprise by a paradox. There may be a grain of paradoxical truth in the judgment of Mother Gamelin. On the other hand, her words may be just a contradiction typical of this brainless heroine of the commonest stock. Whether a contradiction or a paradox, this statement contributes to her caricature. In his sketch of M. Crottu, a former teacher, France again uses the contradiction as a means of satirical characterization, but it too can be regarded as a paradox. "Son humeur acerbe s'exerça avec une ardeur nouvelle sur mes erreurs et fautes; mais c'était surtout ce que je faisais de bien qu'il ne me pardonnait pas."[24] It is absurd to punish the student for his excellence, but it is a commonplace that a mediocre man prefers mediocrity to excellence.

If the incompatibility of the two incongruous elements is less evident, the aesthetic surprise is less intense, or the paradox survives rather as an aphorism without any paradoxical content. It seems that there is hardly any contradiction in a statement such as "Il était trop prudent pour n'être un peu égoiste."[25] Yet any attempt to bridge virtue and vice brings the expression close to paradox. Carrying the idea a step further, one could conclude in the style of La Rochefoucauld that the celebrated prudence is no more than despicable selfishness in disguise. Again, there is potential paradox in the words: "... il faut taxer la farine et guillotiner quiconque spécule sur la nourriture."[26]

[22] *O.C.*, V, p. 5-6.
[23] *O.C.*, XX, p. 22.
[24] *O.C.*, XXIII, pp. 317-318.
[25] *O.C.*, VI, p. 182.
[26] *O.C.*, XX, p. 20.

The taxation of flour by the state would perhaps affect the price of flour to the consumer just as much as the capital offense of commercial speculation. The statement satirizes the perennial discrepancy between individual and collective moral codes and also confirms the ancient practical wisdom, *Quod licet Iovi non licet bovi.*

Usually, a well conceived paradox is a subtler aesthetic surprise than a mere contradiction. Its validity accentuates the shock of discrepancy. Authors such as Voltaire, Wilde, or Shaw, whose creative strength stems from intelligence and wit, have always seasoned their observations with this literary spice. Whether France is commenting on intangibles, on nature, on society, on man, his wisdom or his prejudices, he discovers paradoxical incongruities in every aspect of life. For instance, in practical philosophy: "Nous ne sommes heureux que parce que nous sommes malheureux";[27] ". . . la souffrance est la sœur de la joie";[28] "L'avenir est dans le présent, il est dans le passé."[29] Morality: "La vertu n'est pas une innocente";[30] "Cette coutume de faire l'aumône est contraire à la bienfaisance . . . et à la charité."[31] Love: "Nous voulons être aimées, et, quand on nous aime, on nous tourmente ou on nous ennuie";[32] "En femmes il eut toujours aimé la nouveauté; mais une femme nouvelle n'était plus une nouveauté pour lui et la monotonie du changement lui pesait."[33] Education: "Comme je n'étudiais rien j'apprenais beaucoup";[34] "Les sciences sont bienfaisantes, elles empêchent les hommes de penser."[35] Political life: "Il détestait la république et donnait tous les jours sa vie pour elle."[36] On ironic somersaults of human destiny: "La courtisane . . . mourut sans désirs et quitta saintement ce monde illusoire";[37] "L'apostat vécut comme un saint."[38] In most cases the author astonishes not only by the validity of

[27] *O.C.*, XII, p. 446.
[28] *Ibid.*
[29] *O.C.*, VI, p. 294.
[30] *O.C.*, VI, p. 514.
[31] *O.C.*, XII, p. 240.
[32] *O.C.*, IX, p. 109.
[33] *O.C.*, XIX, p. 248.
[34] *O.C.*, VI, p. 446.
[35] *O.C.*, IV, p. 141.
[36] *O.C.*, V, p. 397.
[37] *O.C.*, VII, p. 370.
[38] *O.C.*, VII, p. 625.

contradiction but by economy of form or by a striking word choice. If France stated that man cannot fully realize what happiness is unless he has experienced its opposite, most of the surprise would vanish. If he said that the future is the result of the past and the present, no one would be amazed. If Pontius Pilate had said merely: "Je suis un partisan dévoué de la douceur" instead of "je ne me suis opiniâtré que dans la douceur"[39] the spell would be gone. It is evident that many paradoxical aphorisms depend entirely on the brilliance of the artists's style: their inherent logical contradiction is only illusory and verbal.

France takes delight in satirical blasphemies, in crossing swords with convention and hypocrisy. He often attacks a corrupt practice which, however, is so common that no one would ever dare to question it. By thus spelling out the discrepancy between accepted reality and hallowed ideal, France's onslaught appears to threaten the very foundation of "solid" social and political order; it sounds like sacrilege. In such a case, the stylistic treatment, which pervades the very marrow of the topic, gives birth to a conflict – an extended paradox. These paradoxes are usually not expressed aphoristically and constitute major portions of text; a more accurate term for them would be paradoxical controversies. France's prose is full of passages in which one can often find a grain of wisdom but which, from the point of view of convention, are shocking. Because he views things from the comical side, he is rarely pathetic; the discrepancies become targets of his wit. In controversies he favours the indirect attack *à la* Voltaire. Instead of openly attacking war, militarism and military heroism, for instance, France speaks through his hero and ironically approves of murder. Chatting in M. Paillot's book store with other regular visitors, the archivist, M. Mazure, and M. de Terremondre, M. Bergeret suddenly learns that the eighty-year-old widow, Mme Houssieu, was strangled in bed. When M. de Terremondre, touched by the unexpected news, points out that at the moment when the crime was committed, the conversationalists were having a quiet talk in M. Paillot's bookshop, the learned man almost approvingly declares killing to be a natural act, and adds that it would not be sensible to expect that anything as banal as a murder would put a stop to all conversation in the radius

[39] *O.C.*, V, p. 226.

of a few miles of the victim. An act inspired by the most criminal thoughts cannot but have natural consequences. Killing is as natural for beasts as it is for humans. In fact, even today, just as in primitive societies, murder may contribute to the social prestige of many a felon. "Le meurtre a été longtemps estimé dans les sociétés humaines comme une forte action et il subsiste encore dans nos mœurs et dans nos institutions des traces de cette antique estime."[40] At this point M. Bergeret is interrupted and challenged to specify the mysterious traces. This, of course, is precisely what he is waiting for: he points out that society honours soldiers in the name of the fatherland for collective crimes which seem so shocking on the individual level. He views the behaviour of the human race dispassionately just as a zoologist may generalize on instincts and life patterns of an animal species. All human actions are inspired by hunger or love. Hunger taught the barbarian how to kill; it forced him to raid and fight wars. Modern man is no different.

Les peuples civilisés sont comme les chiens de chasse. Un instinct corrompu les excite à détruire sans profit ni raison. La déraison des guerres modernes se nomme intérêt dynastique, nationalités, équilibre européen, honneur. ... il n'est pas un peuple au monde qui ne soit souillé de tous les crimes. ... Si toutefois il subsiste encore un honneur dans les peuples, c'est un étrange moyen de le soutenir que de faire la guerre, c'est-à-dire de commettre tous les crimes par lesquels un particulier se déshonore: incendie, rapines, viol, meurtre. Et quant aux actions dont l'amour est le mobile elles sont pour la plupart aussi violentes, aussi furieuses, aussi cruelles que les actions inspirées par la faim, en sorte qu'il faut conclure que l'homme est une bête malfaisante.[41]

So much for the murder of Mme Houssieu. Most readers would find

[40] *O.C.*, XI, pp. 186-187.

[41] *Ibid.*, pp. 187-88. Levaillant (*op. cit.* pp. 704) comments extensively on France's pessimism concerning the vitality of social passions and the tragic inevitability of individual and collective murders. Discussing France's treatment of Mme. Bergeret's speculations on adultery, the same critic (*ibid.*, pp. 446-447) illustrates the typically Francean technique of extended paradox: "Madame Bergeret réfléchit-elle sur son adultère, c'est pour conclure qu'il représente 'une expansion de sa vie conjugale, un rayonnement de son foyer', le résultat d'un 'matronal orgueil,' supposant, 'impliquant, cet état de mariage que le monde honore, que l'Eglise sanctifie, et qui assure à la femme sa sécurité privée et sa dignité sociale.' C'est une idéalisation ironique de l'adultère, le paradoxe intégrant dans la valeur: mariage, la contre valeur: adultère." (Levaillant's footnote not retained).

it shocking that someone should counter conventional remarks on a neighbour's murder with the declaration that murder is really quite in harmony with principles current in the international community, principles which bring successful "murderers" top social honours. Yet at the same time they feel that M. Bergeret's scathing necrology is not entirely impertinent. Besides, from his other actions, they know that he is a tenderhearted man. The reader's conventional morality and social sense are challenged by the reasoning of the learned speaker. The scholar's satirical pacifism is quite a special case; although the controversial statements are made with tongue-in-cheek, one can see a certain logic beyond their apparent absurdity. To do so, one must be willing to correct one's own illusions about the publicly honored military virtues and the collective massacres executed by modern armies with indescribable barbarism. Accepting M. Bergeret's premise, one can formulate the whole controversy in the following terms: if society venerates murderers on the collective level, it is about time to manifest more esteem for them on the individual level. Finally, sharpening it to a paradox-aphorism, one could say that in honouring soldiers, we honour licensed killers; or that heroes who murder without compulsion deserve bigger statues than soldiers who murder by government decree. Thus the unexpected conflict between a common opinion and its logical consequence offers enlightening amusement. But, even if resented, M. Bergeret's logic provokes a certain aesthetic surprise or shock through satirical abrasion.

In the opening controversial dialogue of *Jocaste* France may engender similar excitement. M. Longuemare is conducting painful experiments on live frogs to prove that the stoic doctrine concerning pain is an absurdity and that pain is actually blessing. An ironic counterpoint of this argument is the paradoxical behaviour of the heroine: this modern Jocaste, who is going to murder her husband, feels a sincere indignation over the fate of frogs killed in the course of a scientific experiment:

– Quoi! monsieur Longuemare, vous mettez des grenouilles dans vos poches? Mais c'est dégoutant!

– Rentré dans ma chambre, mademoiselle, j'en fixe sur une planchette, et je lui découvre le mésentère, que l'excite. . . .

– Et que vous sert de torturer ainsi de pauvres animaux?

– A édifier ma théorie expérimentale de la douleur. Je prouverai que les stoïciens ne savent ce qu'ils disent et que Zénon était un imbécile. ... Il niait la sensation. Et tout n'est que sensation. ... D'ailleurs il est extrêmement avantageux pour les animaux d'être doués de la faculté de souffrir.

– Vous plaisantez! A quoi peut servir la douleur?

– Elle est nécessaire, mademoiselle. C'est la sauvegarde des êtres. Si, par exemple, la flamme ne nous causait pas, dès la première atteinte, une excitation intolérable, nous nous rôtirions tous jusqu'aux os sans nous en apercevoir. ... Et c'est une beauté que la souffrance, ...[42]

In spite of its obvious logic, at first most of us would instinctively agree with Hélène that man could be happier if pain did not exist. The statement that pain is not only practical but even beautiful intensifies this eulogy of suffering.

The most frequent disseminators of controversial ideas in France's work are his typical heroes: M. Bonnard, Nicias, Jérôme Coignard, Choulette, M. Bergeret or Doctor Trublet. The last, for instance, pleads for stupidity because it is a natural disposition of the happy man and a blessing of civilized society.[43] Among the other paradoxes observed by the doctor: human society puts such a high premium on life, whereas life in nature is worthless;[44] atheists are not the enemies of the Church; there have been many of them right within the pale of the Church and several have rendered inestimable services to the papacy.[45] In the discussion on the form of burial of the actor Chevalier and on the degree of his responsibility for self-inflicted violence this confirmed determinist passes many controversial remarks.[46] Such a light approach to the grave issues of life is effective. It may provoke a more intense reaction than, say, Zola's heavy handed social protests or the crusading writers' sermons.

An extended paradox is often an integral part of France's conflicts. A keen reader of Homer, he knows that one of man's deeply rooted instincts is his desire *aei aristeuein kai hypeirochon emmenai allon*,[47]

[42] *O.C.*, II, pp. 3-4.
[43] *O.C.*, XIII, p. 132.
[44] *Ibid.*, p. 170.
[45] *Ibid.*, p. 212.
[46] *Ibid.*, pp. 281-84.
[47] *Homeri Opera* (*op. cit.*), Chant VI, v. 208.

and that man's rivalry, pugnacity, anger, repulsion, disgust[48] drive him to seek and enjoy conflicts. Conflicts of all kinds will always find a grateful public. Individual murders, heroic massacres, or pugilistic contests, whether held in the sports arenas or parliaments of civilized nations, thrill both the active participants and curious observers. The newspaper editor does not need to be a psychologist to know that a heated argument between politicians, a lovers' quarrel in a café, a sidewalk polemic between drunkards or an intricate legal investigation of a corrupt branch of industry or labor, defending itself shrewdly against "unsubstantiated" accusations, will be welcomed eagerly by the public. Aesthetically, conflicts are merely acute contrasts, in which the two contraries clash. Violent or non-violent conflicts climax any series of literary adventures or intrigues: without them there is no vital literature.

Francean conflicts usually spring from the author's humanism and his speculative delight in challenging social or religious taboos. His theologians cherish a hope that Satan will finally be saved by infinite divine grace.[49] Paradoxes, major and minor, characterize the theological conflict between *Fra* Giovanni and Doctor Subtil in "L'Humaine Tragédie".

– Tu prétends que la pauvreté est un grand bien, et tu ôtes aux pauvres une part de ce grand bien en leur faisant l'aumône.

Et fra Giovanni songea et dit:

– L'aumône que je fais, je la fais à Notre-Seigneur Jésus-Christ dont la pauvreté ne peut être diminuée. Car elle est infinie, elle sort de lui comme une source inépuisable, ... En donnant aux pauvres, je ne donne point aux hommes, mais à Dieu, comme les citoyens payent l'impôt au podestat, et l'impôt est pour la ville. ... Et ce que je donne est afin de paver la cité de Dieu.[50]

The tormented monk's profound paradox is his ultimate love of Satan for the very suffering and damnation the prince of darkness has im-

[48] Eastman, *op. cit.*, pp. 225-27.

[49] *O.C.*, X, p. 7. "Il pensait que le diable était mauvais sans l'être absolument et que son imperfection naturelle l'empêcherait toujours d'atteindre à la perfection du mal. Il croyait apercevoir quelques signes de bonté dans les actions obscures de Satan, et, sans trop l'oser dire, il en augurait la rédemption finale de l'archange méditatif, après la consommation des siècles."

[50] *O.C.*, X, p. 150.

posed upon him.[51] France symbolized his spiritual legacy by the revolt of the enlightened Lucifer against the jealous demiurge Ialdabaoth. Even if more successful than their mythical war, glorified by Nectaire,[52] a new revolution against the divine tyrant paradoxically would not solve anything. He has to be destroyed by a more civilized and permanent process than a revolution: his reactionary rule can be overthrown only in man's liberated heart and by his return to pagan joy.[53] France contemplates the irremediable imperfections of human justice in "Les Juges intègres", a dogmatic conflict between judges personifying opposing legal systems, one dogmatic, the other dynamic. The premises of both orders are debatable. True equity perhaps cannot exist in an arrangement as relative as man's political and moral life.

Le premier juge dit:
– Je m'en tiens à ce qui est écrit. La première loi fut écrite sur la pierre, . . .
L'autre juge répondit:
– Toute loi écrite est déjà périmée. Car la main du scribe est lente. . . .
PREMIER JUGE. – La loi est stable.
SECOND JUGE. – En aucun moment la loi n'est fixée.
PREMIER JUGE. – Procédant de Dieu, elle est immuable.
SECOND JUGE. – Produit naturel de la vie sociale, elle dépend des conditions mouvantes de cette vie.
PREMIER JUGE. – Elle est la volonté de Dieu, qui ne change pas.
SECOND JUGE. – Elle est la volonté des hommes, qui change sans cesse. . . .
PREMIER JUGE. – La justice est parfaite quand elle est littérale.
SECOND JUGE. – Quand elle n'est spirituelle, la justice est absurde.[54]

This conflict of the two equally legitimate and equally vulnerable principles is eternal. France can only point out the relativity of any human justice. But in the conflict between man and principle he is

[51] See pp. 181-78.
[52] *La Révolte des anges,* Chs. XVIII - XXI.
[53] See pp. 193-94. Theological controversies also add to the scope of literary surprise in *Thaïs, L'Etui de nacre, La Rôtisserie de la Reine Pédauque,* the *Histoire contemporaine,* and *L'Ile des Pingouins.* The deliberation in heaven concerning the validity of the Penguins' baptism is one of the most memorable. Political and philosophical controversies are concentrated rather in *L'Histoire contemporaine,* in *Sur la Pierre blanche, Crainquebille, Les Dieux ont soif,* and *Les Opinions de M. Jérôme Coignard.*
[54] *O.C.*, XIV, pp. 162-165.

always on the side of life, man and his joys. His sarcasm in the face of hypocrisy, revealing the moral squalor of politicians or of religious dignitaries, for instance, may excite the reader's sense of honesty, or decency as intensely as the most revolting acts of physical violence. The reader is incensed by the expulsion of the indigent, frail, and brilliant Piedagnel from the seminary. Reviewing the scholastic record of Piedagnel, the head of the seminary, Abbé Lantaigne, concludes that the boy, who is interested in Parnassian poetry, lacks the theological spirit and therefore is not eligible for an ecclesiastic career. M. Lantaigne is torn inwardly by his sympathy for the boy's intelligence, and he prays for the moral strength to expel the boy from the institution. The superior gives the boy the honor of assisting at the morning mass and then, after the service, gives him the *consilium abeundi.*[55] Although the decision is solely the priest's own, he tries, even in his own eyes, to make God responsible for it. At its face value his attitude smacks of Jesuitic casuistry. The conflict between the boy's literary talents and the cold and tested policy of the Church is essentially tragic: it cannot be solved without crushing the boy on the threshold of his adult life. The vitality of the literary portraits intensifies the moral conflict for the reader. In spite of the human disgust he feels for the priest's decision and his method of announcing it, he still sees a certain wisdom in it: the student's talents and propensities leave no doubt that as a future priest he would be in constant theological conflict with the inflexible authority of the Church which M. Lantaigne serves with such impersonal loyalty. Since the seminary is not a charitable institution, why should it invest in a potential apostate who evidently lacks the desired "theological spirit"? Abbé Lantaigne's de-

[55] *O.C.*, XI, pp. 20-21. "Le supérieur du séminaire, qui revêtait sa douillette, lui fit signe de rester, et le regarda avec tant de noblesse et de douceur que l'adolescent reçut ce regard . . . comme une bénédiction. . . .

– Mon enfant, dit M. Lantaigne, en célébrant cette messe, que je vous ai demandé de servir, j'ai prié Dieu de me donner la force de vous renvoyer. Ma prière a été exaucée. Vous ne faites plus partie de cette maison.

En entendant ces paroles, Firman devint stupide. . . . Il voyait vaguement, dans ses yeux gros de larmes, la route déserte, la pluie, une vie noire de misère et de travail, une destinée d'enfant perdu. . . . Il regarda M. Lantaigne. La douceur résolue, la tranquillité ferme, la quiétude de cet homme le révoltèrent. Soudain, un sentiment naquit et grandit en lui, . . . la haine du prêtre, une haine impérissable et féconde, une haine à remplir toute la vie."

cision may have saved the boy a much worse crisis at a later stage of his life. Nonetheless, a superior who could put human values above the impersonal principles and interests of an institution might have encouraged the boy's literary talents and advised him to follow another career after the completion of his secondary education. But anger not reason, is provoked by M. Lantaigne's *calotin* method of hiding beneath the hypocritical halo of divine will. The reader's instinctive respect for spiritual freedom may also rebel against the rigid thought control and merciless screening of future Church servants by militant members of the Church. He rebels against the inhuman institution which strives to prejudice the young hearts and minds of its future servants. One may experience a chain of similar reactions in reading the conflict of the poor vegetable peddler, Crainquebille. One's pity for him grows as fast as one's hatred for the police, "justice" and society, if one may term "society" his few customers, all of whom crush him mercilessly by false incrimination and shallow prejudice. "Monsieur Thomas" and "Vol domestique" are also full of such conflicts and controversies. Typical Francean heroes are elderly scholars who do not engage in violent conflicts. Even in his literary fresco of the French national crises, France does not rely too heavily on violence. Comparing the picture of the French Revolution in *Les Dieux ont soif* and in the *Tale of Two Cities*, G. R. Havens says:

> In *Les Dieux ont soif*, Anatole France in no way sought to give a vivid, melodramatic, primarily pictorial impression of great events, like for example the Revolutionary trials, imprisonments, and executions which fill the pages of Dicken's famous *Tale of Two Cities*. Instead with classic Racinian restraint, the French author preferred to keep these striking scenes "off-stage", ... concentrating his attention on the more normal, day-by-day, humdrum details of life ... too often forgotten by historians.[56]

Perhaps France may indulge in the aesthetics of violent conflict less than writers like Shakespeare, Schiller, or Dumas père, but he does not underestimate in the least the surprise such actions may produce. In fact, in works such as *Jocaste, Les Désirs de Jean Servien, La Rôtisserie de la Reine Pédauque, L'Histoire Comique, L'Ile des Pingouins,*

[56] G. R. Havens, "Anatole France and the French Revolution" *American Society Legion of Honor Magazine,* Vol. XXVI, p. 233.

Les Dieux ont soif, and in some of his short stories, such as "Balthasar", "Histoire de Doña Maria d'Avalos et de Don Fabricio, duc d'Andria" or "Komm l'Atrébate", the bloodshed easily rivals that immortalized in the works of the above authors.

France makes forceful use of the shock of violence in his naturalistic description of the absurd "execution" of Jean Servien. During the last revolutionary convulsions of the defeated Paris *Commune*, Jean Servien is caught by a retreating group of revolutionaries commanded by an old woman. This bloodthirsty *cantinière* persuades her fellow rebels to execute Jean as a Versailles spy. He is put to the wall but the few riflemen lack the heart to kill him. Finally, the fanatical commander kills the young man with her own hand:

Elle avait traversé la bataille, cette fille! elle avait bu à même les tonnaux défoncés et dormi sur le dos, pêle-mêle avec les hommes, au milieu de la place publique rougie par l'incendie. On ne faisait que tuer autour d'elle, et on n'avait encore tué personne pour elle. Elle voulait qu'on lui fusillât quelqu'un, à la fin! Et elle criait en trépignant:

– "Feu! feu! feu!"

Les fusils s'armaient de nouveau et les canons s'abaissaient; mais les Vengeurs de Lutèce manquaient d'entrain; leur chef avait disparu, ils étaient dispersés, ils fuyaient, . . . la fête était finie. Ils voulaient bien, tout de même, fusiller ce bourgeois-là, avant d'aller se cacher chacun dans son trou.

Jean essaya de dire: "Ne me faites pas souffrir!" mais la voix s'arrêta dans sa gorge.

Un des Vengeurs regarda du côté du Pont-au-Change et vit les fédérés qui lâchaient pied.

Il dit, en se mettant l'arme à l'épaule:

– F. . . . . s le camp, nom de Dieu!

Ils hésitaient. Quelques-uns s'en allaient.

Alors la cantinière hurla:

– Sacrés c . . . . . s! c'est donc moi qui lui ferai son affaire.

Elle se jeta sur Jean Servien, lui cracha au visage; se livra du geste et de la voix à des farces d'une obscénité frénétique et lui mit le canon du revolver sur la tempe. Alors il sentit que tout était fini et il attendit.

Pendant une seconde il revit mille choses; il revit les allées plantées de vieux arbres où sa tante le menait promener jadis; il se revit lui-même petit enfant heureux et étonné; il se rappela les châteaux qu'il construisait avec des écorces de platane . . . Le revolver partit. Jean battit l'air de ses bras et tomba la face en avant. Les hommes l'achevèrent à coups de baïonette, puis la femme dansa sur le cadavre en poussant des cris de joie.

> La bataille se rapprochait. Une fusillade nourrie balaya le quai. La femme partit la dernière. Le corps de Jean Servien resta étendu sur la voie déserte. Son visage avait pris une expression de tranquillité étrange; il y avait à la tempe un petit trou à peine visible; du sang et de la boue souillaient ces beaux cheveux qu'une mère avait baisés avec tant d'amour.[57]

In imagination the reader experiences a whole range of emotion from anger to helpless repugnance. He is shocked by the vulgar bestiality of the possessed woman. He is revolted by any revolutionary mob and any human bestiality which may crush in a minute the most precious human values, yet at the same time he is urgently reminded that many of his fellow men are like wild beasts in the jungle. For a while he is filled with powerful hatred and sympathy. He also senses the fragility of his own destiny, which cannot resist the violent outbursts of his unknown fellow men. The contrast between the love of the woman who gave Servien life and the absurd hatred of the one who took it away intensifies the shock of violence.

In addition to Hélène's suicide after the poisoning of her wealthy husband, there is a thrillingly described murder in *Jocaste*: Mr. Haviland's scheming butler, Groult, tries in vain to obtain the death certificate of Samuel Ewert from Tancrède Reuline, a shrewd sharper. Ewert, descendent of a late benefactor of Mr. Haviland's family, is the legatee of the poisoned man. Groult, surprised that the Jewish usurer is clearly aware of his scheme to get illegal possession of a substantial part of his late master's estate, attacks the blackmailer with his switch blade knife. France extends the tension by his ambiguous comment on the knife. describing it as destined not only for the butler's personal use but also for the service of his fellow man. But then, without pause, France shows what kind of service this instrument of fellowship will perform: it will be used to murder Groult's "fellow man", Reuline.[58] Although he treats this climax with economy and

[57] *O.C.*, III, pp. 176-179.

[58] *O.C.*, II, pp. 93-94.

"– Donne l'acte, vieux juif, ou je t'étrangle!

Il était furieux de rencontrer un obstacle ... Reuline, jaune et maigre, sec et semblant rendre l'âme à chaque souffle, se raidit et résista avec le muscle et la souplesse d'un homme exercé par de fréquentes querelles avec les marins qui lui portaient leur montre en gage pour aller boire. Cette résistance augmenta la fureur de Groult, qui vit rouge et tira son eustache. C'était un méchant couteau

laudable dramatic pace, France profitably turns naturalist to emphasize all the gruesome details. The fight-to-the-death is made terrifyingly vivid by name-calling, a death threat and Groult's gradual loss of self-control. The suspenseful remarks on Reuline's muscular strength, on his fighting skill, and on Groult's knife, emphasize how little is needed to preserve or lose one's precious and worthless life. Reuline's incidental wound, the first sight of blood, the struggle of the two men, Reuline's cries and Groult's panic, prolong the suspense before the final stabbing. The gruesome physical reactions of the dying man, even his facial expression, extend to the limit the reader's horror at the murder.

Perhaps the most powerful literary shock produced by a theme of violence in France's work is the repulsive and unexpected finale to the "Histoire de Doña Maria d'Avalos et de Don Fabricio, duc d'Andria." The heroine is caught *in flagranti* with her lover, the duc d'Andria, by her husband, Prince Venos, and his armed body guards. Don Fabricio, fighting half naked, is killed. The prince, calling his wife "Puttana!" then "Puttaccia!" and finally "Sporca puttaccia!" sadistically revels in her fear. But his adulterous wife soon regains her Spanish *sang froid*, starts whistling to irritate her husband, and tells him that she had not been to confession for two years. When asked if she wants to confess her sins, she replies that it is useless and that she does not regret anything. She throws herself on the dead body of her lover, kisses him passionately on the lips, and her husband drives his sword through her body. Not satisfied with one more mortal stabbing, he runs his sword through his wife's stomach and chest several times. The prince has the naked bodies of the two lovers displayed publicly in the courtyard of the palace, where the dogs lick his wife's wounds.

---

pointu, ... Groult l'avait sans cesse dans la main pour son usage personnel et le service d'autrui. Le vieillard, glissant pour se dégager, alla tomber contre l'angle de la cheminée, qui lui fit une blessure au front. ... Ce sang et les cris de Reuline lui firent faire le coup de la peur. Avec une lucidité singulière, il choisit sa place et enfonça la lame du couteau dans le poitrine du vieillard. Puis, pendant une minute, qui lui parut indéfinement prolongée, il ne remarqua rien. L'homme était là, sous son poing, roulant des yeux verts, la bouche ouverte et résistant de tout ses muscles; puis après cette minute-là, enfin, il lâcha prise, s'affaissa, ferma et rouvrit convulsivement les mains. ... Alors ses traits n'exprimaient plus rien de violent. Il avait l'air de sourire malicieusement. ...

This seems like a sufficiently grim climax to a grim melodrama, but France has something even more repulsive in store to enhance the shock:

Les corps restèrent honteusement exposés. Vers la fin de la nuit, comme il ne venait plus de curieux, les valets se retirèrent.

Un moine dominicain, qui s'était tenu tout le jour devant la porte, se glissa dans l'escalier à la lueur fumeuse des torches de résine qui s'étaignaient, rampa jusqu'aux degrés où gisait Doña Maria d'Avalos, se jeta sur le cadavre et le viola.[59]

The reader, previously excited by the description of the passionate act of adultery, by the final act of violence of the jealous husband, by his vulgarities delivered in Italian, by the provocative dialogue between the Prince and his wife, and by her amazingly persuasive show of loyalty to her dead lover, is finally nauseated by this act of the necrophile who may have been spying on Maria.[60]

Chevalier's strange suicide in *L'Histoire comique* belongs in the same category of aesthetic excitement. This hero surprises his mistress, Félicie, as she is about to give herself to her new lover Ligny. Chevalier commits suicide in their presence, expressing a strange last will: "Écoutez, et n'approchez pas! cria Chevalier d'une voix forte. Je vous défends d'être l'un à l'autre. C'est ma dernière volonté. Adieu, Félicie."[61] With his self-destruction he succeeds in destroying the young love of those who made him choose death rather than life. The dead Chevalier remains forever the invisible witness of all their later attempts to consummate their love. The scene shocks the reader's taste and at the same time stirs his compassion for the frustrated Chevalier; it may also provoke some irrational contemplations on divine justice and awaken a fearful premonition of mysterious fate.[62]

Violence is not exclusively tragic. The "homicide" committed by M. Coignard, for instance, is a farcical skirmish.[63] In spite of the two dead bodies and the injured banker, the colourful violence and turmoil produce mirth rather than anger or aesthetic pity, especially since the

[59] *O.C.*, X, p. 247.
[60] See also p. 164, n. 13 and p. 201.
[61] *O.C.*, XIII, pp. 188-189.
[62] See pp. 97-8, 160.
[63] See p. 53, n. 55.

descriptions of the killings are interspersed with the abbé's flamboyant oratory.[64] When Komm L'Atrébate returns incognito to his former territory, on which the Romans have built a new town, he is strongly tempted to provoke a brawl.

Il s'approcha dans l'idée de faire quelque violence. Une vieille survint, qui glapit aigrement:
– Passe ton chemin. Ce n'est pas une maison pour les paysans qui puent le fromage. Va retrouver tes vaches, bouvier!
Komm lui répondit qu'il avait eu cinquante femmes, les plus belles parmi les femmes atrébates, et des coffres pleins d'or. Les courtisanes se mirent à rire et la vieille cria:
– Au large, ivrogne!
Et la vieille semblait un centurion armé du cep de vigne, tant la majesté du Peuple romain éclatait dans l'Empire!
Komm, d'un coup de poing, lui brisa la mâchoire et s'éloigna tranquille, tandis que l'étroit couloir de la maison s'emplissait de cris aigus et de hurlements lamentables.[65]

In this passage, Komm's violence is an integral part of his absurd conflict with the ancient *Madame*. A touch of *gauloiserie*, a digressive sneer at the Roman "civilization", and musical effects, "cris aigus et de hurlements lamentables", each help to dramatize the turmoil provoked by Komm. The mere prelude to a conflict is a traditional literary stimulus.[66] Readers have always enjoyed plans of heroic deeds, strategic ruses or criminal plots, and all that leads up to them. The parody of Komm's intrepid heroism behind the enemy lines is preceded by an exciting account of his vigilant preparation for the secret return to his native settlement. Before entering the heavily fortified

[64] *O.C.*, VIII, pp. 174-175. "Odieux traitant ... tu prétends que cette maison est tienne? Pour qu'on te croie, pour qu'on sache qu'elle est à toi, inscris donc sur la porte ce mot de l'Evangile: *Aceldama,* qui veut dire: *Prix du sang* .... Larron, bandit, homicide, écris avec le charbon que je te jetterai au nez, écris de ta sale main, sur ce seuil, ton titre de propriété, écris: Prix du sang de la veuve et de l'orphelin, prix du sang du juste, *Aceldama*. Sinon, reste dehors et laisse-nous céans, homme de quantité."

[65] *O.C.*, XIII, p. 52.

[66] Although integrated with the conflict, heroism, adventure and danger often have their independent aesthetic value. They may stimulate even if they do not lead to a conflict, as, for instance, in accounts of the Kon-Tiki expedition. Of course, one could debate whether such adventures do not symbolize man's conflict with nature rather than his harmony with it. But the relative rareness of such features in France's work does not invite a detailed analysis.

town, the Celtic chieftain cautiously hides in the forest all his jewels and anything that could betray his identity. Then, disguised as a simple peasant, he passes through the gate guarded by his enemies.

The opening of "La Muiron", which tersely sums up Napoléon's war ruse, exemplifies the thrill of any shrewd and daring intrigue.

> Depuis plus de trois mois Bonaparte était sans nouvelles de l'Europe quand, à son retour de Saint-Jean-d'Arc, il envoya un parlementaire à l'amiral ottoman, sous prétexte de traiter l'échange des prisonniers, mais en réalité dans l'espoir que sir Sidney Smith arrêterait cet officier au passage et lui ferait connaître les événements récents, si, comme on pouvait le prévoir, ils étaient malheureux pour la République. Le général calculait juste.[67]

Throughout his writing France exploits the raw material of violent and non-violent conflicts, converting them into fresh aesthetic values with a wide range of effect. They may simply strike a spark of indignation or grotesque surprise; they may reach tragic dimensions and symbolize an eternal incongruity of man's fate. Havens is certainly right in pointing out France's tendency to keep melodrama and the culminating points of violent conflicts "off-stage". This is in harmony with his classicism and with his resentment of the naturalist lack of taste. On the other hand, France's pagan sensuality has an undeniable naturalist trait. We must not forget that, without scenes of violence, many of the short stories would not exist; had France avoided violence in *La Rôtisserie de la Reine Pédauque*, it would have become merely another series of *causeries* like the *Opinions de M. Jérôme Coignard*; *L'Ile des Pingouins* and *La Révolte des Anges* would be insipid without the dramatic power of their underlying violent themes.

The nature and solution of Francean controversies and conflicts put in proper perspective the critical accusations that France is a superficial dilettante and lacks strong convictions. For all their irony, France's controversies – moral, political, teleological or metaphysical – are speculatively responsible. They contradict the critics who consider his ironic skepticism sterile and nihilist. It is not destructive to draw man's attention to the sandy ground on which he builds his speculative castles. France's pagan dualism, his contemplative verve, combined

[67] *O.C.*, XIII, p. 95.

with his taste for satirical paradox, challenge many illusions cherished for centuries by Christian puritanism and its offshoots. These controversies and paradoxes show man the path which may lead to the rediscovery of lost values. The treatment of the same conflicts invalidates the charge that France failed to express the "drama" of life.[68] The conflicts in *L'Histoire contemporaine*, in "Crainquebille", in "Le Chanteur de Kymé", in *La Révolte des anges*, in *Les Dieux ont soif*, in *Thaïs*, all prove that he sees both the absurd tragedy and the charm of life. In a materialistic age, France's controversial meditations reopen many forgotten humanist horizons, and help the reader find a gratifying purpose in this paradoxical life and its intriguing dilemmas.

[68] See p. 88.

VI

POETIC TECHNIQUE

Quite often the reader of France's prose has an illusion that he reads poetry. Yet it may or may not be an illusion. Sometimes the narrator's tone soars from the valley of prose to the poetic heights. It is no longer prose, it is a luminous verse.[1] This metamorphosis is achieved by rhythm, rhymes, assonances, sonorous alliterations, euphonies, harmonies, and accords – all designed to create a characteristic melody or mood. France's poetization of prose has not been critically appraised to the same extent as other traits of his art. The only major critical work exclusively devoted to France's style is Robert Blanck's study *Anatole France als Stilkünstler in seinen Romanen.*[2] Blanck approached France's art grammatically and also explored its imagery and antithesis. Several pertinent remarks are in Lanson's *L'Art de la Prose.*

[1] The term "free verse" has in this study the same meaning as in Maurice Grammont's *Petit traité de versification française* (Paris, Colin, 1958), p. 68. Different concept of free verse as defined by Mathurin M. Dondo in his *Vers libre, a logical development of French verse* (Paris, Champion, 1922, p. 81), was considered but rejected.

Dondo defines such *vers libre* as "*prose rhythmique* wrongly *vers libre.* It represents fragments of prose rhythmically devided into lines. The rhythmic units are strongly accented so as to leave no doubt about their divisions, but an equality of time is not sought for in the recurrence of the ictus." Dondo's terminology was not used especially because he calls rhythmical prose which cannot be arranged into lines (this may include, for example, *cursus*) simply prose. This could lead to terminological confusion because the distinction between rhythmical prose (*cursus*) and entirely non-rhythmical prosaic narrative is eliminated. Besides, Dondo's comment on prose seems to be somewhat contradictory: "Prose which to deserve the qualification of artistic, must possess its rhythmic pattern, although this pattern is but dimly felt and faintly suggested." In other words, the concrete rhythm is a mere illusion, it cannot be specified and the rhythmic "pattern" does not exist.

[2] See pp. 13 and 225.

Lanson refers to France's prose as "cette musique", and finds that its musical harmony is produced especially by an unspecified "rhythme léger" and "la phrase onduleuse et souple".[3] But it is Lanson's contemporary, A. H. Becker, who first points out the specific rhythmical groups in France's musical prose in his article on *La Révolte des anges*. Analyzing Nectaire's account of the world's destiny in Chapters XVIII - XXI, Becker arranges large portions of the text metrically. He characterizes these chapters as four frescoes drawn by a powerful but precise hand and flooded with charming light. This effect is largely achieved

[3] Gustave Lanson, *L'Art de la prose* (Paris, Librairie des Annales politiques et littéraires, 1908), pp. 273-74. He analyzes the following text from *Le Mannequin d'osier:*

"Les ormes du Mail revêtaient à peine leurs membres sombres d'une verdure fine comme une poussière, et pâle (1). Mais, sur le penchant du coteau, couronné de vieux murs, les arbres fleuris des vergers offraient leur tête ronde et blanche ou leur rose quenouille au jour clair et palpitant qui riait entre deux bourrasques. Et la rivière, au loin, riche des pluies printanières, coulait blanche et nue (2), frôlant de ses hanches pleines les lignes des grêles peupliers qui bordaient son lit, voluptueuse, invincible, féconde, éternelle (3), vraie déesse, comme au temps où les bateliers de la Gaule romaine lui offraient des pièces de cuivre et dressaient en son honneur, devant le temple de Vénus et d'Auguste, une stèle votive où l'on voyait, rudement sculptée, une barque avec ses avirons (4). Partout, dans la vallée bien ouverte, la jeunesse timide et charmante de l'année frissonnait sur la terre antique. Et. M. Bergeret cheminait seul, d'un pas inégal et lent, sous les ormes du Mail. Il allait l'âme vague (5), diverse, éparse, vieille comme la terre, jeune comme les fleurs des pommiers, vide de pensée et pleine d'images confuses, désolée et désirante, douce, innocente, lascive, triste, traînant sa fatigue, et poursuivant des Illusions et des Espérances dont il ignorait le nom, la forme, le visage (1).

(1) Mis en valeur par l'asymétrie.

(2) Nudité mythologique à demi évoquée, imprécise.

(3) Rhythme d'invocation rituelle, de litanie: ce chapelet d'épithètes donne à la phrase un peu de la gravité d'un hymne antique.

(4) La mélodie s'est attenuée pendant cette évocation archéologique. Elle reprend aussitôt: la phrase qui suit est d'une étonnante délicatesse musicale.

(5) Toute la fin de la phrase est d'une structure desserrée, vague, abandonnée, comme la pensée dont elle est l'expression: sans éclat de sonorités, doucement décolorée comme cette pensée."

Lanson's stylistic *explication de texte* is very sensitive, yet he does not specify the meter of the ritual invocation or of the grave ancient hymn miraculously invoked by the text, nor does he indicate the concrete constituents of the musicality. The term "la phrase onduleuse et souple" is too general. If the passage creates a musical effect, it has to contain at least some elements of rhythm and harmony without the specific indication of which the formal analysis of the passage would seem to be incomplete.

by an omnipresent rhythm. "D'un bout à l'autre, . . . on y rencontre des vers et même des séries de vers, vers de six, sept, huit, dix, douze syllabes, vers blancs, cela va sans dire, mais parfaitement constitués, . . ."[4] Becker abundantly illustrates all types of metres and cites lines of seven syllables:

Je l'admirai, je l'aimai
Je vécus dans la lumière . . . ,
Et des éclairs s'allumaient
A la pointe de leurs lances . . .

ten-syllable lines, such as "De mon front sortaient deux cornes naissantes . . . / Sur ses pas naissaient les fleurs et les fruits."[5] But hexameters flow most freely from Nectaire's lips. Of course, by hexameters Becker means alexandrines. This may seem somewhat confusing, because the cited lines usually have only four, not six, measures. They echo many of France's poetic models. Some, as Becker points out, are hardly noticeable, but most are thoroughly "hammered out":

. . . il y en a de classiques qu'on dirait empruntés à une épître de Boileau ou de Voltaire: *Il est entre La Saône et les monts Charolais* . . . Cet autre ne vient-il pas d'une idylle de Chénier: *L'Olbios l'Erymanthe et l'orgueilleux Cratis?* Musset signerait celui-ci: *Sur ses lèvres brillait le rubis des grenades.* Et ce dernier enfin est du pur Baudelaire: *La face violette et la langue pendante.*[6]

Becker believes that France used rhythmical prose because it simply pleased his ear and stimulated his imagination. The artist also hoped that such poetic *élan* would inevitably surprise the reader. Another reason may have been that the prose writer France, whose first literary efforts were the *Poèmes dorés* and *Les Noces Corinthiennes*, was carried away by the melody and cadences of traditional rhythms. And finally, France perhaps framed an existing poem in a novel to increase its aesthetic value.[7] Becker does not indicate that he is aware of

[4] A. Becker, "La Prose rythmée dans 'La Révolte des anges' ", *Mercure de France,* May 16th, 1914, p. 320.
[5] *Ibid.*, pp. 322-24. Becker's parenthetical notes not based on the Calmann-Lévy edition have not been retained.
[6] *Ibid.*, p. 324.
[7] *Ibid.*, p. 325.

rhythmical passages in other parts of *La Révolte des anges* or in the other works. Only the reader who knows that he reads a poem rather than prose can fully appreciate the formal ambiguity of the text. Becker recognized it, identified the poem's meters, and assessed the poetic charm of the rhythmical prose. But such rare humanist discoveries are reserved only for the slow and patient reader with genuine aesthetic interest.

Gabriel Des Hons added much to Becker's conclusions. His thorough comparative study, *Anatole France et Jean Racine ou la clef de l'art francien*,[8] evaluates France's debt to the tragedian and reveals the extent to which many of France's works are pervaded with rhythmical fragments of prose which are identical Racinian lines.

So far only little has been added to Becker's and Des Hons' findings on France's poetic technique. Later critics examining the lyricism of France's prose usually refer to the passage cited above which Lanson analyzed in *L'Art de la prose.* A frequently cited example of poetization is the lyrical account of Paphnuce's pilgrimage along the vital stream of the Nile.[9] Several critics have commented on its qualities, without specifying the technical sources of its musicality. Although this narration is not the most striking example of a unified rhythmical pattern, even this sample can be arranged into free verse. The latent rhythm accounts for only a part of its musical harmony for the passage also contains many assonances, alliterations, harmonies, accords, and even rhymes. The arrangement of any rhythmical prose into a relatively regular rhythmical pattern presents some difficulties: often several arrangements are possible and they are not always the most

[8] Paris, Colin, 1927. See this study, p. 211, n. 10.

[9] *O.C.*, V, p. 28. "Au matin, il vit des ibis immobiles sur une patte, au bord de l'eau qui reflétait leur cou pâle et rose. Les saules étendaient au loin sur la berge leur doux feuillage gris; des grues volaient en triangle dans le ciel clair et l'on entendait parmi les roseaux le cri des hérons invisibles. Le fleuve roulait à perte de vue ses larges eaux vertes où des voiles glissaient comme des ailes d'oiseaux, où, çà et là, au bord, se mirait une maison blanche, et sur lesquelles flottaient ou loin des vapeurs légères, tandis que des îles, lourdes de palmes, de fleurs et de fruits, laissaient s'échapper de leurs ombres des nuées bruyantes de canards, d'oies, de flamants et de sarcelles. A gauche, la grasse vallée étendait jusqu'au désert ses champs et ses vergers qui frissonnaient dans la joie, le soleil dorait les épis, et la fécondité de la terre s'exhalait en poussières odorantes."

suitable or the only formal mold for the recitation of such prose. The rhythmical arrangements reveal latent stylistic ambiguities in the prose and one of the possible aesthetic stimulations produced by style. This rhythmical ambiguity can be illustrated with the text. Its beginning could be arranged in perhaps two or more rhythmical variations. One possible arrangement of the beginning is as follows:

... il vit des ibis immobiles (8)
sur une patte, au bord de l'eau qui reflétait (12)
leur cou pâle et rose. Les saules étendaient (12)
au loin sur la berge leur doux feuillage gris; (12)
des grues volaient en triangle dans le ciel clair (12)
et l'on entendait parmi les roseaux ... (10)
le cri des hérons invisibles.[10]

Another possibility would be:

... il vit des ibis immobiles (8)
sur une patte, au bord de l'eau (8)
Qui reflétait leur cou pâle et rose. (9)

The following sentence could be arranged into one ten-syllable and one five-syllable line. This arrangement creates an elegiac effect and thus expresses the melancholy of the whole passage. "Le fleuve roulait à perte de vue (10) / ses larges eaux vertes" (5). Another alternative would be a more dynamic arrangement into three five-syllable lines which would emphasize the force of the running waters: "Le fleuve roulait / à perte de vue / ses larges eaux vertes ..." The whole passage could be arranged into similar rhythmical groups.

The application of Grammont's theories on the effects of sounds may perhaps explain other formal features of the above text.[11] The

[10] The figures in parentheses indicate the number of syllables in each line.

[11] The reservations of conservative critics concerning similar analyses of sound effects are quite legitimate. In *Theory of Literature* (New York, Harcourt Brace, 1949, p. 164) René Wellek and Austin Warren comment on Grammont's study as follows: "While the study of Grammont is open to the charge of mere subjectivity, there is still, within a given linguistic system, something like a 'physiognomy' of words, a sound-symbolism far more pervasive than mere onomatopoeia." A concrete interpretation of specific euphonies is usually a point of contention. The critic who rejects the analysis of such aesthetic features may be limited to saying the obvious, while the critic who does not avoid the issue can always be accused of reaching debatable conclusions.

musicality is a result, not only of rhythm, but also of a harmonious phonetic composition. For example, the series of clear dominantly short *i*'s, il vi de zibis im:ɔbi:l, followed by a series of variated grave *o*'s, o bɔ:r də l'o, (i.e., both open and closed *o*'s), creates a pleasing contrast. The first series onomatopoetically suggests the symphony of the shrieking calls of water birds ("le cris des hérons invisibles"). At the same time it may express their grace.[12] The latter series may suggest the more powerful sound of flowing water, especially in connection with the liquid *l*'s, which suggest the "fluidity, flowing, sliding".[13] One may hesitate to interpret the *r*'s in the analysed passage as Grammont interprets the consonant in his study, namely, as "un grincement" or "un grondement".[14] If the *r*'s in this passage contribute to the dramatization of the subject matter, it may seem that they express the glorious vitality of creation which overwhelms the ascetic pilgrim, Paphnuce.[15] The *m*'s and *n*'s produce an impression of "douceur, molesse, ... langueur".[16] The euphony is increased by numerous assonances, alliterations, echoes, and internal rhymes such as: *il vit - ibis - gris - des grues - parmi - cri - de vue; leur cou - leur doux; et l'on - hérons; de fleurs - de leurs; terre - poussières*, etc. These features contribute to the harmony and to the "velvety" smoothness of France's prose just as much as to its cadence. In the cited passage, the rhythm, vocal harmony, consonantal euphonies, rhymes, assonances, and alliterations underscore the lyrical mood and dramatize the poetry of a vast setting in condensed form.

In other cases, such factors may rather emphasize the dramatic climax of an unexpected action, as in the grotesque description of M.

[12] Grammont, *op. cit.*, p. 132. "... les voyelles claires sont particulièrement désignées pour exprimer des idées légères, gaies, riantes, douces, gracieuses, idylliques ..."

[13] *Ibid.*, p. 139

[14] *Ibid.*

[15] Yves Le Hir, in his *Esthétique et Structure du vers français d'après les théoriciens, du XVIe siècle à nos jours* (Paris, Presses Universitaires de France, 1956), p. 167, cites René Ghil's *Traité du verbe,* in which Ghil quotes P. Mersenne (1588-1648). Mersenne feels that the *r*'s express "Les choses rudes, dures, les actions véhémentes et impétueuses ..." However, Le Hir himself is most skeptical about the value of such phonetic interpretations, calling Ghil's key to the interpretations of sounds and Ghil's disciples' theories "mythes paralinguistiques".

[16] Grammont, *op. cit.*, p. 139.

d'Astarac's sudden invasion of the Christmas idyl at the *Rôtisserie de la Reine Pédauque.* The passage is arranged to reveal the rhymes and assonances, which in this passage have a significant aesthetic function. The doggerel-like rhymes parody a sorcerer's incantations.

C'est le moment, dit mon père, de déboucher une de ces bouteillles, que je tiens en reserve pour les grandes fêtes (1)

> qui sont la Noël, les Rois
> et la Saint-Laurent.
> Rien n'est plus agréable
> que de boire du bon vin
> quand on est tranquille chez soi,
> et à l'abri des importuns. (2)

A peine avait-il prononcé ces paroles, que la porte s'ouvrit et qu'un grand homme noir aborda la rôtisserie, dans une rafale de neige et de vent (3).

> – Une Salamandre! une Salamandre!
> s'écriait-il. Et, sans prendre
> garde à personne,
> il se pencha sur le foyer
> dont-il fouilla les tisons
> du bout de sa canne,
> au grand dommage
> de frère Ange,
> qui, avalant des cendres
> et des charbons
> avec son potage,
> toussait à rendre l'âme (4).
> Et l'homme noir
> remuait encore le feu, en criant:
> "Une Salamandre! . . . Je vois une Salamandre,"
> tandis que la flamme agitée
> faisait trembler au plafond son ombre
> en forme de grand oiseau de proie (5).
> Mon père était surpris (6) et . . .[17]

The frame (1, 6) is in prose but even its opening passage is partly integrated in the rhyme-scheme, "Le moment" rhyming with "Saint-Laurent" and with the more distant "vent". A partly rhymed transition: the serene atmosphere (2) suddenly vanishes with the appearance

[17] *O.C.*, VIII, p. 38. The numbers indicate the integration of the rhymed passages and prose.

of the black man changing into mystery and excitement. The dark intruder's entrance is described in prose but many consonantal and vocalic accords elevate the prose to a poetic level (3). The account of the stranger's Mephistophelean performance lightly parodies, in a fairy-tale manner, a wizard's magic spell, yet its grotesqueness does not destroy the tension and the premonition of mystery (4). The last lightly rhythmical and gravely sonorous passage, and the image of the dark bird of prey on the ceiling, leave no doubt that the forces of evil have been unleashed (5). The surprise, created initially by M. d'Astarac's arrival, his search for an unknown, invisible supernatural being, and the ghastly shadow-play on the ceiling, is intensified by the careful orchestration of the *éclatant a*'s and nasals, by the smooth *l*'s and, above all, by the thundering *r*'s in "sans prendre", "à rendre l'âme", or in "noir remuait encore", and to some extent in the refrain-like "Une Salamandre! Une Salamandre!" Such sounds may evoke crackling flames and thunder, the traditional theatrical sound effects which accompany the entrance of the devil. The symmetrical harmonies[18] such as

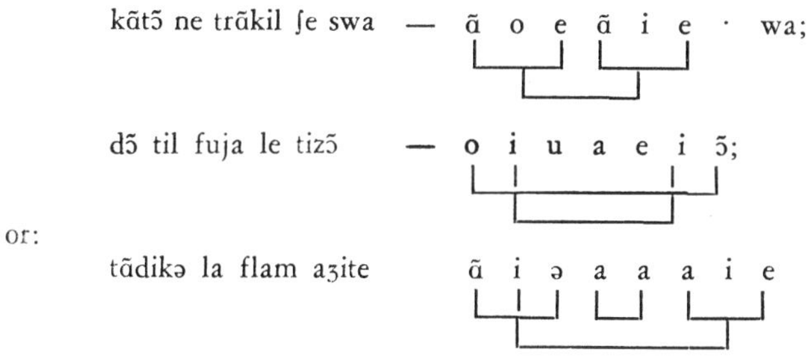

many internal rhymes (moment - Laurent - grand - vent, tiens - rien, dont - tisons, cendres - rendre, etc.), and many consonantal and vocal accords[19] in words (p*ro*noncé - *rô*tisserie, p*ar*ole - *ra*fale, p*or*te - ab*or*da, tre*mbl*er - o*mbr*e, *fla*mme - p*la*fond, plaf*on*d - *son* - *om*bre, *oi*seau - pr*oi*e, etc.), are a significant part of this blend of the grotesque with poetry. If for no other reason than M. Ménétrier's reaction, we can see

[18] The term, "harmony", is used here in the same sense as defined and illustrated in Grammont's *op. cit.*, pp. 142-45.

[19] The term, "accord", is defined in Jean Hytier's *Les techniques modernes du vers français* (Paris, Presses Universitaires de France, 1926), pp. 50-53.

that the black man's act near the fireplace was calculated to surprise, as were all the stylistic ornaments in the author's narration (6).

In his short stories, France often skillfully parodies hagiographical poetry. He imitates its topics as well as its short meters and the primitively charming assonances and rhymes written by medieval monks or "poets". The following passage from "Balthasar" illustrates this stylistic technique. The text is arranged to make the rhymes obvious

Et les trois mages
continuèrent ensemble leur voyage.
L'étoile qu'ils avaient vue en Orient
les précédait jusqu'à ce que, venant
au-dessus du lieu où était l'enfant,
elle s'y arrêta. Or, en voyant
l'étoile s'arrêter, ils se réjouirent
d'une grande joie. Et, entrant
dans la maison, ils trouvèrent
l'enfant avec Marie, sa mère,
et, se prosternant, ils l'adorèrent.
et, ouvrant leurs trésors,
ils lui offrirent de l'or,
de l'encens et de la myrrhe,
ainsi qu'il est dit dans l'Evangile [20]

The internal "rhyme", "ainsi qu'il - l'Evangile", puts a climax to this subtle satire of poetry. Naturally, all "lines" do not always have a rhymed or assonanced counterpart; in this sequence "réjouirent", for example, is isolated. One may object that some of the cited rhymes may be coincidental; that prose in any language contains many rhymes because the number of vowels and diphthongs is relatively limited; that similar endings of all parts of speech must therefore necessarily repeat, and that vocal and consonantal accords, harmonies, assonances, and rhymes are inevitable. Yet in prose, in which rhymes and assonances are not intended, the distribution of identical vowels and related consonants is quite irregular and the narrative is rather dissonant.

Citing *Le Mannequin d'osier*, Lanson suggests that the rhythm of one of the sentences gives the text the gravity of an ancient hymn. It seems that France tried to imitate not only the subject matter and

[20] *O.C.*, IV, p. 148.

diction but also the meters of ancient poetry. There is good reason to believe that France may have played with the idea of a possible return to the charms of ancient cadences. In *L'Ile des Pingouins* he satirizes medieval poetry and its techniques by imagining Virgil's meeting with Dante. The Mantovan, who calls Dante "mon Etrusque", comments that even Roman children too young to pay admission to the public baths would laugh at Dante's masterpiece. One of the reasons for Virgil's resentment of this poetry, written in a vulgar dialect unknown to him, was that it introduced rhymes: "Mes oreilles furent plus surprises que charmées d'entendre que, pour marquer le rythme, il ramenait à intervalles réguliers trois ou quatre fois le même son. Cet artifice ne me semble point ingénieux; . . ."[21] There is no doubt that France agrees. As a critic, he ridicules Théodore de Banville, whose *Petit traité de Poésie française* overemphasizes the significance of rhyme in poetry. He calls Banville's conclusions the "metaphysics of a nightingale".[22]

It would be logical that, in parodying the naive rhyming of medieval legends, France would try to confront their crudity with the harmony, free beauty, and euphonious lyricism of ancient bucolic poetry. He attempted to contrast the two poetic styles in "Le Saint Satyre", a mythological legend on one of France's favorite themes, the clash of the Christian and the pagan cultures. In an ingenious stylistic reflection of this clash, France describes the Christian protagonist, *Fra* Mino, in short, rhymed and assonanced lines, and stylizes the pagan satyrs and nymphs in rhythmical, euphonious prose which echoes the ancient poetic meters. The rhythmical passages try to revive the atmosphere of ancient pastoral poetry as France knew it from Virgil, Ovid, and Theocritus. France, like anyone who had studied Latin and Greek at school every day for many years, had the ancient meters, dactylic hexameters in particular, in his blood, and it was not difficult for him to imitate such cadences in modern French, half in parody, half in admiration. The learned abbot of Santa Fiora, who, paradoxically, rose above his brothers through his humility, is gently caricatured in the following sketch:

[21] *O.C.*, XVIII, p. 168.
[22] Le Hir, *op. cit.*, p. 134.

Fra Mino s'était élevé
par son humilité
au-dessus de ses frères;
et, jeune encore, il gouvernait
sagement le monastère
de Santa-Fiora. Il était pieux.
Il se plaisait à prolonger
ses méditations et ses prières;
parfois
il avait des extases.
A l'exemple de saint François,
son père spirituel, il composait
des chansons en langue vulgaire
sur l'amour parfait
qui est l'amour de Dieu.
Et ces ouvrages ne péchaient
ni par la mesure ni par le sens,
car il avait étudié
les sept arts libéraux
à l'Université de Bologne.[23]

At this moment, a melancholy theme of his lost love and his youth begins and with it a new, elegiac rhythm and tone. Instead of the medieval "low" meter of a primitive lithurgical chant, a "pagan" echo, so dear to France, resounds in his "prose":

Or un soir, comme il se promenait sous les arcades du cloître, il sentit son cœur s'emplir de trouble et de tristesse au souvenir d'une dame de Florence qu'il avait aimée lorsqu'il était dans la première fleur de la jeunesse, et que l'habit de saint François ne protégeait pas encore sa chair. Il pria Dieu de chasser cette image. Mais son cœur resta triste. Les cloches, pensa-t'il, disent comme les anges: AVE MARIA; mais leur voix s'éteint dans la brume du ciel.[24]

One can see in "comme il se promenait" a six-syllable line; in "sentit-son cœur s'emplir de trouble et de tristesse" an alexandrine; in "et que l'habit de saint François" an eight-syllable line; in "les cloches, pensa-t-il, disent comme les anges" an alexandrine, and in "leur voix s'éteint dans la brume du ciel" a ten-syllable line. Yet even if one reads the text to underscore these rhythms, the illusion of the dactylic meter remains. It may be partly because of the elegiac alternation of

[23] *O.C.*, X, p. 15.
[24] *Ibid.*, pp. 15-16.

longer and shorter lines and also because certain fragments of the text vaguely resemble the dactylic cadence: "sous les arcades du cloître", "au souvenir d'une dam(e) de Florence", "Il pria Dieu de chasser cette image", or "Les cloches, pensa-t-il, disent comme les anges . . ."

Naturally, France did not observe any rigid metrical rules in using the dactylic and anapestic meters in his prose. He was too much of an artist to make it a slave of an inflexible prosodic canon. But he often appears to have imitated the ancient cadence.[25] In another example from the "Saint Satyre", the medieval Christian hero is again parodied in rhymed and assonanced free lines:

Fra Mino resta longtemps prosterné
devant l'autel; mais il lui fut
impossible de prier
et, dans le milieu
de la nuit,
il sentit peser sur lui
cette torpeur qui avait accablé
les disciples de Jésus-Christ
au jardin des Oliviers.
Et, tandis
qu'il demeurait étendu
sans courage ni prudence, . . .[26]

Here the rhyming ceases and the rhythmical, harmonious prose, with the repeated, ambiguous motif, "nuée" and its phonetic variation, "une", begins. "Une nuée" gradually dissolves in the darkness into "multitude de nuées" and finally becomes "nudité": "Il vit comme une nuée blanche s'élever au-dessus du tombeau de saint Satyre et bientôt il reconnut que cette nuée était faite d'une multitude de nuées dont chacune était une femme."[27] Again, the anapests (or dactyls or spondees) resound vaguely from "multitude de nuées dont chacune était une femme". The playful dance of the yearning nymphs and lusty satyrs is echoed in the rhythm and euphony of the following sentence:

[25] Considering the metrical licenses permissible, not in epical but in lyrical ancient prosody, such as diastole, anacrusis, catalexis, anaclasis, corruption, protraction, synapheia, or systole, one could arrange longer passages of France's rhythmical prose in hexameters and occasionally in elegiac distychs. But no doubt such arrangements would be as debatable as specific interpretations of concrete euphonies.

[26] *O.C.*, X, pp. 17-18.

[27] *Ibid.*, p. 18.

Elles flottaient dans l'air obscur (8);
à travers leurs légères tuniques (9)
brilliaient leurs corps légers (6) [28]

The gay movement is emphasized by the accumulation of light *e*'s and *i*'s and the growing desire is dramatized by the accelerated rhythm of the nine-syllable line and by the graver vowels in "flottaient", "obscur", "corps". The *l*'s in expressions such as "flottaient", "l'air", and "leurs légères" onomatopoetically suggest the meaning of the words. The rhythm occurs throughout the whole story, including the subsequent erotic interlude which belongs among the most alluring seduction scenes in nineteenth century literature. Not all of its lyrical intensity can be attributed to the stylistic art; the erotic subject alone is poetic, but at least half of its charm is a result of sensitive stylization. The tormented *Fra* Mino observes that the dancing nymphs are not alone. Young naked men trail them, beating the clearing with their buck hoofs. The account of their playful but determined chase can be arranged metrically as follows:

Leur nudité laissait (6)
paraître l'effroyable ardeur de leurs désirs. (12)
Cependant
les nymphes fuyaient: sous leurs pas rapides (10)
naissaient des prés fleuris et des ruisseaux. (10)
Et chaque fois qu'un capripède (8)
étendait
la main sur une d'elles et la croyait saisir (12)
un saule
s'élevait soudain pour cacher la nymphe (10)
dans son tronc creux comme un(e) caverne (8)
et le blond feuillage s'emplissait (9)
de murmures légers et de rires moqueurs. (12) [29]

In the following long sentence rhythm is less evident, and the poet relies on different technical effects. "Quand toutes les femmes se furent cachées sous les saules, les capripèdes, assis sur l'herbe soudaine, soufflèrent dans leurs flûtes de roseaux et en tirèrent des sons dont toute créature eût été troublée." [30] Then, rhythm reoccurs but only intermittently:

[28] *Ibid.*
[29] *Ibid.*
[30] *Ibid.*

Les nymphes charmées
passaient la tête entre les branches (8)
et peu à peu, quittant leurs ombreuses retraites (12)
s'approchaient, attirées, par la flûte irrésistible.
Alors les hommes-boucs se jetèrent sur elles (12)
avec une fureur sacré. (8)
Dans les bras de l'insolent agresseur, les nymphes
s'efforcèrent un moment encore de railler et de se moquer.
Puis elles ne rirent plus. La tête renversée,
les yeux noyés de joie et d'horreur, (9)
elles appelaient leur mère, ou criaient: (10)
"Je me meurs", ou gardaient un silence farouche. (12) [31]

The musical effects in this passage are so obvious that they could serve as classical examples of onomatopoeia: "sous leurs pas rapides", or "de murmures légers et de rires moqueurs". The nasals in "la nymphe dans son tronc" express lethargy[32] or the diphthongs in "les yeux noyés de joie" may suggest the fusion and harmonious undulation of charming curves. The *e*'s and *i*'s and the darker *eu*'s, the liquids and the nasals in "elles appelaient leur mère, ou criaient: 'Je me meurs' ", dramatize the feverish pace, voluptuousness, and climax of erotic ecstasy. The lascivious ambiguities, "effroyable ardeur", "un saule s'élevait", "tronc", "caverne", "ombreuses retraites", "flûte irresistible", celebrate the sacred lust and the advent of Eros. This poem in prose is one of the stylistic precedents of Nectaire's "hexameters" in *La Révolte des anges*. France uses the same technique extensively, usually to intensify lyrical topics.

Certain subjects are naturally lyrical, others can be made lyrical through style, and still other prosaic topics cannot be poetized. It is often difficult to determine whether a lyrical effect springs from the style or from the content itself. A lyrical echo in an epic narrative, a reflective pause in the turmoil of dramatic action, may lead to a delicate aesthetic surprise. Perhaps the evocation of a cherished memory, or an arrow of desire piercing prosaic reality, is enough to create a lyrical mood. Like symbolism or rhythm and rhymes in prose, topical lyricism may not be fully felt by all readers. In "Le Chanteur de Kymé", France

[31] *Ibid.*

[32] Grammont, *op. cit.*, p. 136. "Lorsque les nasales sont plus nombreuses que les orales, le voilement du son par la nasalité devient la qualité dominante et le timbre passe au second plan; si bien que l'ensemble devient propre à exprimer la lenteur, la langueur, l'indolence, la mollesse, la nonchalance . . . ."

dramatizes his vision of Homer's last days spent touring the Greek coast. Homer's last recital, in the town of Hissia, is interrupted by a row between two boastful cowherds. The fatigued poet feels an intense *taedium vitae* and wishes to merge with the eternal elements. He leaves, cursing the house with the contempt of an immortal singer who had thrown pearls to swine. The eternal night, perhaps as soothing and poetic as the one which envelops him, beckons, inviting him to surrender the noisy prose of life and to merge with the divine powers which inspired his immortal poetry. Of course, the lyrical effect is produced by the subject itself, but one cannot separate it from the stylistic arrangement. Rhythm enhances the poetry of the bard's meeting with his gods. The first two seven-syllable lines could be the opening of an ode. The illusion of the Homeric meter continues.

Alors d'une voix plus grande (7)
que tous les bruits du combat (7)
il maudit cett(e) maison injurieuse (10)
et ces hommes impies. (6)
Puis, pressant sa lyr(e) contre sa poitrine, (10)
il sortit de la demeure (7)
et marcha vers la mer (6).
le long du haut promontoire. (7)
A sa colère succédaient (8)
une profonde lassitude (8)
et un âcre dégoût des hommes et d(e) la vie (12)
Le désir de se mêler aux Dieux (9)
enflait sa poitrine. Une ombre douce, (9)
un silence amical et la paix de la nuit (12)
enveloppaient toutes choses. (7)
A l'occident, vers ces contrées (8)
où l'on dit que flott(ent) les ombres des morts, (10)
la lune divine, (5)
suspendu(e) dans l(e) ciel limpide, (7)
semait de fleurs argentées (7)
la mer souriante. (5)
Et le vieil Homèr(e) s'avança (8)
sur te haut promontoire (6)
jusqu'à ce que la terre, (6)
qui l'avait porté si longtemps (8)
manquât sous ses pas.[33]

[33] *O.C.*, XIII, p. 23. Other metrical arrangements in the same passage are possible. See also pp. 103-104 of this study.

Many a modern man would envy Homer for such a rendezvous with the mythical gods. For France, who often satirized funeral pomp, the poet's farewell may have been an unattainable dream. Contributing to the lyrical effect are frequent elegiac short lines, which contrast with the long to create the effect of a funeral march. The theme of death is accented by the accumulation of the dark *os*'s, gravely ominous *ous*'s, liquid consonants and the moaning nasals, ("à l'occident vers ces contrées où l'on dit que flottent les ombres des morts"), periphrases, and finally, the poetic contrast between "les ombres des morts" and the "fleurs argentées la mer souriante". We can agree unreservedly with Becker that France, the prose writer, never completely gave up versified diction. We find many rhythmical and rhymed passages in his earliest works, such as *Jocaste* and *Le Chat Maigre*. The Verlainian influence mentioned by Shanks[34] is evident in the following passage from *Le Chat Maigre*:

Le jour des Rois, vers quatre heures, Rémi,
passant avec le poète Dion sur la place
Saint-Sulpice, regarda les coulées de glace
qui recouvraient à demi
les quatre évêques de pierre
et l'eau gelée sous leurs pieds, . . .
le moraliste suivait
le bord sans fin de la vasque de pierre.
Sur la place déserte, une jeune ouvrière,
attardée sans doute par quelque aventure,
coupait le vent avec la vive allure . . .
et le moraliste tournait encore.
Les talons sonores de deux gardiens
de la paix troublaient seuls un bruit
monotone le silence de la nuit.
A une heure et demie
le philosophe s'éloigna pour relire
sous un réverbère le billet parfumé.
"Vous êtes brun et je suis blonde;
vous êtes fort et je suis faible.
Je vous comprends et je vous aime." [35]

[34] Shanks, Lewis Piaget, *Anatole France* (Chicago, The Open Court Publishing Company, 1919), p. 225.
[35] *O.C.*, II, p. 204-5.

The result of the latent rhythm, harmony, euphonies, assonances, and rhymes in France's prose is a radiant impressionism. With some justification, Fernand Gregh, citing the same passage Lanson analysed in *L'Art de la prose*, says: "Cela est frémissant comme du Claude Monet, et cela pourrait avoir, quant aux mots, été écrit par Jean de la Fontaine."[36] Reading the opening of Chapter IX of *Le Lys rouge*, one could easily draw a parallel between France's text and Claude Monet's painting, *La Gare St. Lazare*,[37] the rhymed title of which would probably appeal to France. The prose could be arranged as follows:

Le rapide de Marseille était formé
sur le quai, où couraient
les facteurs et roulaient
les camions dans la fumée et le bruit
sous la clarté livide qui tombait
des vitrages. Devant les portières
ouvertes, les voyageurs en long manteau
allaient et venaient.
A l'extrémité de la galerie
aveuglée de suie et de poussière,
apparaissait, comme au bout d'une lunette,
un petit arc de ciel. Grand comme la main,
l'infini du voyage. La comtesse Martin . . .[38]

The atmosphere in the painting depends on the illusion of evanescent clouds of smoke in the subdued light under the glass roof. The contrasting dark but luminous shades, the vague perspective of the two trains, contribute to this melancholy of departure and of distance. Such an effect in the text is created by the rhythm and the drab assonanced series which pervade the whole fragment: "formé - le quai - fumée - clarté and était - couraient - roulaient - tombait - allaient - venaient". Their monotony suggests the rattling of the wheels, the squeaking of the rails, coming and going, and, above all, the illusion of the engine puffing steam into the twilight of the station. Both the literary fragment and the painting attempt to create both a convincing

[36] Gregh, Fernand, "Le Style" (*Les Annales politiques et littéraires*, July-December, 1924), p. 421.
[37] *L'Histoire de la Peinture Moderne, de Baudelaire à Bonnard* (text by Maurice Reynal, Genève, Albert Skira, 1949), p. 28.
[38] *O.C.*, IX, p. 99.

atmosphere and clearly demonstrate the same effort to create a harmonious effect. The harmony in the picture is produced by a certain symmetry of lines and by the repetition of forms (two engines, two lamps, two parts of the huge glass roof, the angle of the glass roof and the angles of the two lamp tops and two columns of smoke), and by contrast (in this case a balanced arrangement of dark and light colors). The literary harmony is created by a certain textual symmetry, contrasting subject matter (clarté - galerie aveuglée de suie) and by the colorful sounds of words, rhymes, assonances and accords (rapide - livide; vitrage - voyage; portières - voyageur - poussière; bruit - galerie - suie; dans - devant - man(teau) - grand, and the two series cited above). The painting, like the text, captures *l'infini du voyage*, shrouded in smoke and steam. Although the painter and the writer use entirely different tools, their works obviously have much in common: a taste for the same subject matter, an effort to project the transcendental value inherent in the subject, extensive use of contrast, linear rhythm and repetition, adoration of light, poetical exploitation of the twilight, disciplined understatement, and an identical lyrical vagueness.

In most instances, the musical euphonies, rhymes, and cadences must have been intended by the author, who was so closely associated with the Parnassians and whose first love was poetry. Yet it seems that his technique of rhythmical and rhymed prose often was spontaneous. In the case of rhythmical prose this has been well proved, particularly by Beker. Musical effects, rhythm, and rhymes are so natural to France that they occur even in his critical essays. This may be the case in France's meditations about French prosody in his essay on Jean Moréas.

L'incessante métamorphose de tout
ne surprend ni n'effraye. Elle est naturelle.
Les formes d'art changent
comme les formes de la vie.
La prosodie de Boileau et des classiques
est morte. Pourquoi la prosodie
de Victor Hugo et des romantiques
serait-elle éternelle?
Je ne vois guère
que les vieux lions
de 1830

s'il en est encore
pour gémir de ce qui se passe
aujourd'hui en poésie.
Les révolutionnaires
s'étonnent seuls qu'on fasse
des révolutions . . .[39]

Although France could not say like Ovid "Et quod temptabam scribere, versus erat",[40] one could say that whatever he begins to write often ends in the poetic: ". . . toute la réalité se poétise, se dépouille de sa brutalité, s'allège de sa matérialité",[41] says Lanson, who ascribes this effect primarily to France's brilliant style. His poetic technique justifies Walton's comparison between the Greek plastic arts and France's style. This critic points out that France's Atticism is more than the mere observance of rules designated by Cicero and the neoclassicists. Estimating to what extent France's love of Greek art marked his style, Walton says:

If anything, the prose of France imitates the purity of line of Greek statuary rather than the complex quality of Greek prose with its highly flexible word order, its host of synonyms and restrictive particles. His presentation of ideas tends to follow the spoken principle of the dialogue, to retain that balance of natural speech which is characteristic both of French classical, and of Attic, prose. Hellenism in his style is a luminous ideal rather than a technique.[42]

It is not too much to say that, even if all other literary merits were disregarded, France would rank with the classics of French literature for his style alone. In one respect, however, the results of this analytical illustration of France's style contradicts Walton's conclusion: France's "Atticism" is not only an esoteric ideal which he worships from the distance, it is also a practical goal which could not be attained without a brilliant "Attic" technique. If France succeeded in charming his readers more than most of his contemporaries, his extraordinary stylistic skill had a major share in this success.

[39] *O.C.*, VII, p. 528.
[40] *The Oxford Book of Latin Verse,* (ed. by H. W. Garrod), Oxford, Clarendon Press, 1912, No. 206, p. 233.
[41] Lanson, *op. cit.*, p. 274.
[42] Walton, Loring Baker, *Anatole France and the Greek World* (Durham, N.C., Duke University Press, 1950), p. 243.

VII

EROTICISM AND *GAULOISERIE*

Right from the beginning of his literary career France was aware of the irresistible fascination of love. Eros is "le dieu qui crée incessamment le monde, le père de la vie et des destins ..." and it is by "... l'amour fatal, par ses luttes cruelles que l'univers s'anime ..."[1] Readers have always been stimulated by old and new versions of erotic adventures, ranging from the sublime to the pornographic. The idyllic matrimonial love of Philemon and Baucis or the adulterous elopement of Helen and Paris, the Ovidian strategy and art of love, the tragedy of Tristan and Isolde or Romeo and Juliet, the spiritual adoration of Dante for Beatrice, the libertinage of Boccaccio, the erotic pathos of Werther, the frustration of Julie and Saint-Preux, the perversity of the Marquis de Sade and the bourgeois lust of Madame Bovary, – the appeal of these will endure as long as man's sexual instinct.[2]

France's wisdom of love is much more cultivated than Zola's naturalistic interpretation of sex but more dynamic than, for example, Huysmans' decadent eroticism. His treatment of love has the light-hearted touch of Boccaccio. France seldom excites by eroticism alone; he prefers to blend it with other elements. By projecting the So-

[1] *O.C.*, I, p. 132.

[2] J. Y. T. Greig (*The Psychology of Laughter and Comedy*, London: Allen and Unwinn, 1923, pp. 80, 81), says: "If the race is not to die out, we must take pleasure in the sexual, ... and it is not enough that we should take pleasure in sex only when we participate ... performing the sexual act ... we enjoy the sexual when it is removed to a greater or less 'distance' from ourselves, when we only dream about it, tell or hear stories about, investigate it scientifically, or contemplate it in the mood of the artist. A hint of the sexual, addressed to any of our senses, starts off in us behaviour which must be called sexual. ... and from ... this behaviour comes our pleasure."

phoclean myth of Jocaste and Laios into the nineteenth century, he makes a travesty of the theme. He introduces eroticism into his version of Euripides' *Orestes*, changing Electra into Elodie, the bloodthirsty mistress of his eighteenth-century Orestes - Gamelin. The more he is stained with his victims' blood, the more she craves his doomed flesh. He dramatizes the tragic marriage of Daphné and Hippias, destroyed by the promise made to God by Daphné's fanatical mother, Kallista, a Christian convert.[3] He parodies mystical "sexless" love in *Thaïs*, in his "Scolastica", a faithful *imitatio* of the Latin text by Grégoire de Tours,[4] and in his version of "Sainte Euphrosine". The tragic theme in *Histoire comique*, Chevalier's suicide in the presence of his mistress, its effect on Félicie's romance and the actor's burial[5] make a sarcastic comment on the instinct stronger than man's will to live. The young France records the intensity of erotic torment in Jean Servien's love dreams; this anaemic but sensitive and stubborn lover is racked by love in his imagination as vividly as Werther, Des Grieux, or even Othello.

Il fut content à la pensée qu'elle mourrait un jour et que rien alors ne resterait plus d'elle, rien de ses formes, rien de sa chaleur, et qu'on ne verrait plus les jeux magnifiques de la lumière dans sa chevelure, sur ses yeux et sur sa chair tantôt mate et tantôt nacrée. Mais ce corps, qui lui donnait tant de colère, était jeune, tiède et souple pour longtemps encore, et plus d'un, à qui il serait offert, le sentirait frémir et s'animer. Elle existerait pour d'autres sans exister pour lui. Cela était-il tolérable? Oh! quelles délices de plonger un poignard dans ce sein tout chaud! oh! la volupté de bien tenir cette femme renversée sous un genou et de lui dire entre deux coups de couteau:
– Suis-je ridicule, maintenant? [6]

For the shallow actress Jean Servien's remote adoration is merely a flattering but insignificant tribute to her popularity; the boy's love dreams are amusing, even desirable, but not worthy of fulfilment. The older France and his older hero know far better how to bewitch a young and beautiful star from the *Comédie française*. The growth of love between the elderly cavalier Brotteaux and Rose Thévenin, though tragic, radiates a tender erotic wisdom and a restrained *galant* charm.

[3] *O.C.*, I, pp. 325.
[4] See p. 212.
[5] See pp. 97-8, 136 and n. 62.
[6] *O.C.*, III, p. 96.

La Thévenin s'était rapproché du vieux Brotteaux. Elle savait que est homme avait mené grand train autrefois, et son imagination paraît de ce brillant souvenir la pauvreté présente du ci-devant financier, qu'elle jugeait moins humiliante, étant générale et causée par la ruine publique. Elle contemplait en lui, ... les débris d'un de ces généreux Crésus que célébraient en soupirant les comédiennes ses aînées. Et puis les manières de ce bonhomme ... lui plaisaient.

– Monsieur Brotteaux, lui dit-elle, on sait que jadis, dans un beau parc, par des nuits illuminées, vous vous glissiez dans des bosquets de myrthes avec des comédiennes et des danseuses, au son lointain des flûtes et des violons. ... Hélas! elles étaient plus belles, n'est-ce pas, vos déesses de l'Opéra et de la Comédie-Française, que nous autres, pauvres petites actrices nationales?

– Ne le croyez pas, mademoiselle, répondit Brotteaux, et sachez que, s'il s'en fût rencontré en ce temps une sembable à vous, elle se serait promené, seule, en souveraine et sans rivale, pour peu qu'elle l'eût souhaité, dans le parc dont vous voulez bien vous faire une idée si flatteuse ...[7]

Their second and last rendezvous takes place in the Luxembourg Palace, the revolutionary jail: "Vous ici mon enfant. La joie de vous y voir m'est cruelle ..."[8] The shadow of death and the bars separating Rose and Brotteaux make a tragedy of the actress's muted confession.

Eroticism and the themes of death and of futility are lyrically blended in the description of the first passion shared by the sculptor Dechartre and Thérèse Martin-Bellème one afternoon in a lonely villa in Florence.[9] An almost transcendental peace veils their romance. All

[7] *O.C.*, XX, p. 131.

[8] *Ibid.*, p. 245. For Rose's confession see this study, p. 52 and n. 51. See also Levaillant (*op. cit.*, p. 782): "N'embrassant dans la Thevenin, mais à travers la grille de la prison, que l'image de toutes les femmes qu'il a aimées, appréciant encore, mais enchaîné déjà pour l'échafaud, la gorge de sa voisine, il veut seulement, sans pathétique et sans pessimisme explicite, que les images qu'il sait fuyantes de la chair le divertissent de l'insipidité de la vie et de la menace de la mort." (Levaillant's notes not retained.)

[9] *O.C.*, IX, p. 210. "Ils montèrent un escalier si tranquille sous un bandeau grec, qu'il semblait avoir oublié le bruit des pas. Il poussa une porte et fit entrer Thérèse dans la chambre. Sans rien voir, elle alla droit à la fenêtre ouverte qui donnait sur le cimetière.

Au-dessus du mur s'élevaient les cimes des pins, qui ne sont pas funèbres sur cette terre où le deuil se mêle à la joie sans la troubler, où la douceur de vivre s'étend jusqu'à l'herbe des morts. Il la prit par la main et la mena à un fauteuil. Elle resta debout et regarda la chambre qu'il avait préparée pour

eternity is caught in a fleeting moment of approaching sensual excitement. The staircase which leads to the room of their reunion has forgotten the sound of footsteps. The eternal counterpoint of life and death resounds assonantly from "fenêtre ouverte qui donnait sur le cimetière" and from the suggestively phallic symbols, "Au-dessus du mur s'élevaient les cimes des pins." Thus *mort* and *amor* fatefully fuse, joy and mourning meet at this lovers' tryst near the cemetry. The grave alliance is further suggested by the oxymoron, "tristesse aimable", by the lost joy of "gaietés passées", and "grâce évanouie" and finally by the euphonious "l'ombre de Rosalba", an allusion to a seventeenth century Italian painter of delicate pastels.

A subtle touch of eroticism accents the premonition of death in "Le Chanteur de Kymé". One of the last rays of sun in the life of the old Homer is his meeting with a young girl. During his final grand tour along the Greek coast, after an exhausting night pilgrimage, the poet rests near a fountain, eating onions in the morning sun. After he finishes his breakfast, a young girl comes to the fountain for water. At first she is frightened of the stranger but, realizing that he is a bard, tired and old, she feels pity and respect. She draws some water to her cupped hands and carries the refreshing drink to the lips of the old man. Confronted with youth and living beauty, he imagines the erotic bliss her future husband may experience in union with her.

Alors il la nomma fille de roi; il lui promit une longue vie et lui dit:
– Jeune fille, l'essaim des désirs flotte autour de ta ceinture:. Et j'estime heureux l'homme qui te conduira dans sa couche. Et moi, vieillard, je loue ta beauté comme l'oiseau nocturne qui pousse son cri méprisé sur le toit des époux. Je suis un chanteur errant. Jeune fille, dis-moi de bonnes paroles.[10]

Both content and form express a haunting melancholy. The gallant bard's poetic improvisation is inspired by the contrast between the girl's fresh beauty and happiness and his own exhaustion and the

---

qu'elle ne s'y trouvât pas trop perdue ni à l'aventure. Quelques lés de vieille indienne, à figures de comédie, mettaient sur les murs la tristesse aimable des gaietés passées. Il avait accroché dans un coin un pastel effacé qu'ils avaient vu ensemble chez l'antiquaire, et que, pour sa grâce évanouie, elle appelait l'ombre de Rosalba."

[10] *O.C.*, XIII, p. 16. See also above p. 59 and n. 81.

vision of the nearing end. The drink from her hands is the last ray of joy he experiences.

The Ovidian pastoral vision of *Fra* Mino in the "Saint Satyre"[11] belongs among the most memorable seduction scenes in nineteenth century literature. France successfully evokes the atmosphere of erotic life in an era which did not see in the act of love a replica of the original sin but a most natural step toward the simplest and strongest joy. Bizarre erotic themes are in "La Dame de Vérone", whose heroine falls in love with the charming, melancholy devil, and in *La Rôtisserie de la Reine Pédauque*, in which the young humanist, Jacques Tournebroche, becomes intimate with the "Salamander", Jahel. Although the latter adventure seems merely an innocent, youthful dalliance with this allegedly immortal beauty, Jacques's romance is perhaps more profound than just the eager exploration of feminine flesh:

Elle était en chemise et cette clarté de la lune s'égouttait comme du lait sur ses épaules nues. Elle se coula à mon coté; m'appela des noms les plus tendres et des noms les plus effroyablement grossiers qui glissaient sur ses lèvres en suaves murmures. Puis elle se tut et commença à me donner ces baisers qu'elle savait et auprès desquels tous les embrassements des autres femmes semblent insipides.

La contrainte et le silence augmentaient la tension furieuse de mes nerfs. La surprise, la joie d'une revanche et, peut-être jalousie perverse, attisaient mes désirs. L'élastique fermeté de sa chair et la souple violence des mouvements dont elle m'enveloppait, demandaient, promettaient et méritaient les plus ardents caresses. Nous connûmes, cette nuit-là, des voluptées qui, par leur excès, confinaient à la douleur.[12]

Jahel's amourous inventiveness is such that it transforms the minor sin of Jacques's youth into an unforgettable lesson in the art of loving. The whirl of erotic bliss which seizes the young Cabalist makes him aware of distinct and precious nuances in erotic *savoir faire*, nuances he had never savored in his earlier adventures with a prostitute. He also realizes the paradoxical relationship which exists between voluptuousness and pain. He learns that the purely physical experience may transgress the limits of animal lust and unleash joy, jealousy, and melancholy. The erotic excitement of France's lyrical voluptuousness

[11] See pp. 151-53.
[12] *O.C.*, VIII, 244-247.

is enriched, spiritually, by Jacques's thoughts and emotions, and stylistically by poetic diction.

France treated both seriously and mockingly all kinds of adultery. Madame de Caillavet, stylized as Thérèse Martin-Bellème, belongs with Anna Karenina and Madame Bovary among the significant literary heroines of the late nineteenth century. The "Histoire de Doña Maria d'Avalos et de Don Fabricio, duc d'Andria" is melodrama, adultery blended with violence, climaxed by the rape of a dead body.[13] In "La Fille de Lilith", France, introducing the supernatural, creates the unusual character of an eternal adulteress, whose erotic adventures are paradoxically beyond sin and theological punishment. According to an obscure Judaic myth, Leila was begotten in the union of Adam and his first wife, Lilith, who preceded Eve. Therefore Leila is not only unaffected by the theological consequences of original sin; she is immortal. Disseminating despair through the ages among her many husbands and lovers, she prays for sin and death, which alone could lead her to salvation and peace.[14] "La Leçon bien apprise" is an *imitatio* of a Boccaccian theme. Madame Violante gladly succumbs to the advances of M. Philippe Coetquis when Brother Jean Turelure shows her a human skull and tells her that she will soon come to that herself.[15] The bourgeois adultery of Madame Bergeret, banal and farcical, the "political" affair of Mme de Gromance from *L'Histoire contemporaine*, and the adulteries of Mme des Aubels in *La Révolte des anges* are characteristic of Francean *gauloiseries*, a mixture of comedy and libertinage.

If today the critics refer to France as "M. Voltaire", it is not only because of his sparkling and inexhaustible intelligence, his unquenchable irony, and his skepticism, but also because of his frivolous indulgence in light erotic subjects or in latent obscenities.[16] Although not

[13] See pp. 135-36 and p. 201.

[14] *O.C.*, IV, 177 q.s. See also below pp. 179, 192.

[15] *O.C.*, XIX, pp. 77-78.

[16] The term *gauloiserie* in this study is a combined feature: it may include eroticism or vulgarity with humor. Comical periphrase frequently disguises its frivolity or obcenity. Stewart (*op. cit.*, p. 258), points out that the lack of chastity of eighteenth century authors is a result of their anti-clericalism. He maintains that France's "pornography" and satire of chasity can also be explained by his anti-clerisalism rather than by his personal sensual appetites.

always the most refined or sophisticated literary technique, erotic license will always attract readers.[17]

In many ways France surpassed his master in ingenious understatements and periphrases which enabled him to integrate into his work many risqué details without violating the limits of *bon goût*. One might be tempted to add the "extreme" limits, since France, although hardly ever violating these limits by vulgarities unworthy of a writer of his caliber, fully exploited libertine topics. The gusto with which he satirizes Zola's lack of taste and his grave preoccupation with sex indicates that France appreciates the shock value of Zola's subject.

Mais le pire défaut de *La Terre*, c'est l'obscénité gratuite. Les paysans de M. Zola sont atteints de satyriasis. Tous les démons de la nuit, que redoutent les moines et qu'ils conjurent en chantant à vêpres les hymnes du bréviaire, assiègent jusqu'à l'aube le chevet des cultivateurs de Rognes. Ce malheureux village est plein d'incestes. Le travail des champs, loin d'y assoupir les sens, les exaspère. Dans tous les buissons un garçon de ferme presse "une fille odorante ainsi qu'une bête en folie".

Les aieules y sont violées, comme j'ai déjà eu le regret de vous le dire, par leurs petits-enfants.[18]

Perhaps the choicest *gauloiseries* in France's work can be found in the short stories *Les Sept Femmes de la Barbe-Bleue* and in some of the *Contes de Jacques Tournebroche*. The title of one of the stories in the first work illustrates the licentious trend of the whole collection: "Histoire de la Duchesse de Cigogne et de M. Boulingrin qui dormirent cent ans en compagnie de la Belle-au-Bois Dormant." In this case the interest lies not only in the erotic nature of the subject but in its presentation. The ambiguity, the grotesquely naive circumstances, the supernatural element which unexpectedly prolong the affair, the comical names, all are calculated to change the banal romance into a unique chapter in the history of frivolous loving.

In the title story of this collection, France rectifies the historical tradition by mockingly presenting Bluebeard not as a brutal killer but

[17] Greig (*op. cit.* p. 80), states in the chapter entitled "The Sexual, the Obscene and the Indecent": "There is no pretending that we do not enjoy the obscene and the indecent. Aand we laugh at them. But it is not to be hastily concluded that our enjoyment follows from our laughter. Our original pleasure in the obscene and the indecent is just our perennial pleasure in the sexual."

[18] *O.C.*, VI, p. 211.

as a meek victim of wedlock-hungry women. If it had not been for them, "this poor lord" might have stayed a widower. The following chronicle of Bluebeard's matrimonial miseries is marked by a striking concentration of *gauloiseries*, spiced with mischievous details.

Gigonne ne pensait plus qu'à paraître dans le monde, à se faire recevoir à la Cour, et à devenir la maîtresse du roi. N'y pouvant parvenir, elle sécha de dépit, et en prit une jaunisse dont elle mourut. La Barbe-Bleue, tout gémissant, lui éleva un tombeau magnifique.

Ce bon seigneur, abattu par une si constante adversité domestique, n'aurait peut-être plus choisi d'épouse; mais il fut lui-même choisi pour époux par demoiselle Blanche de Gibeaumex, fille d'un officier de cavalerie qui n'avait qu'une oreille; il disait avoir perdu l'autre au service du roi. Elle avait beaucoup d'esprit, dont elle se servit à tromper son mari. Elle le trompa avec tous les gentilshommes des environs. Elle y mettait tant d'adresse qu'elle le trompait dans son château et jusque sous ses yeux sans qu'il s'en aperçût. La pauvre Barbe-Bleue se doutait bien de quelque chose, mais il ne savait pas de quoi. Malheureusement pour elle, mettant toute son étude à tromper son mari, elle n'était pas assez attentive à tromper ses amants, ... Un jour, elle fut surprise, dans le cabinet des princesses infortunées, en compagnie d'un gentilhomme qu'elle aimait, par un gentilhomme qu'elle avait aimé et qui, dans un transport de jalousie, la perça de son épée. ... La pauvre Barbe-Bleue, apprenant d'un coup son abondant déshonneur et la fin tragique de sa femme, ne se consola pas. ... A la nouvelle qu'elle l'avait trompé avec constance et qu'elle ne le tromperait plus jamais, il ressentit une douleur et un trouble qui, loin de s'apaiser, redoublaient chaque jour de violence.[19]

The account of Bluebeard's first marriage contains many surprising features: irony, ironic understatement, buffoonery, aphoristic comments, stimulating digression, grotesque violence; but the licentious theme prevails and most of the other features help to emphasize it: for example, the ironic compassion of the adjectives "ce bon seigneur" or "La pauvre Barbe-Bleue" show this sexual sadist as the quarry of perverted feminine ambition, lechery and incredible simple-mindedness. The impersonal terms, "si constante adversité domestique" or "son abondant déshonneur", convince the reader that France is in fact indicating only a fragment of the victimized killer's troubles. The overstatement, "Elle y mettait tant d'adresse qu'elle le trompait ... jusque sous ses yeux sans qu'il s'en aperçût", is confronted for contrast with

[19] *O.C.*, XIX, pp. 139, 140.

an ironical understatement, "La pauvre Barbe-Bleue se doutait bien de quelque chose, mais il ne savait pas de quoi." The reader expects, but is still amused, that Blanche was not murdered by Bluebeard but by a lover, jealous of yet another of her lovers. This irony of fate emphasizes Blanche's frivolous obsession with sex. Her tragic end makes Bluebeard so seriously ill that the doctors fear his days are numbered. However, the afflicted lord is not going to die. The "serious" ailment threatening his life turns out to be just an unappeased sexual urge when the staff of doctors indicates its irrevocable therapy –another marriage. To avoid the bitter disappointment of his first experience the patient weds a simpleton. The ironic aphoristic contrast, "Ayant été trompé par une femme d'esprit, une sotte le rassurait", amuses by the grotesque absurd solution to the nobleman's odd tribulations. This statement, of course, promises further comical complication. Although he expects proof of the next wife's stupidity, the reader is nevertheless "surprised" by the farcical imbecility of Mlle de la Garandine and her elopement in Boccaccian style with a lewd monk. "This good man of God" introduces the archangel Gabriel, a parody of supernatural power. The seraph who, curiously enough, wants to offer Bluebeard's naive wife an unusual item of intimately feminine apparel, becomes an agent in seduction when his present opens the gate to Angèle's chastity, if any such exists.[20] There is entertainment in this farcical conflict

[20] *Ibid.*, pp. 140-41. "Les médecins, ayant employé divers médicaments sans effet, l'avertirent que le seul remède convenable à son mal était de prendre une jeune épouse. Alors il songea à sa petite cousine Angèle de la Garandine, ... ayant été trompé par une femme d'esprit, une sotte le rassurait. Il épousa Mlle de la Garandine et s'aperçut de la fausseté de ses prévisions. Angèle était bonne, Angèle l'aimait; elle n'était pas d'elle-même portée au mal, mais les moins habiles l'y induisaient facilement à toute heure. Il suffisait de lui dire: 'Faites ceci de peur des oripeaux; entrez ici de crainte que le loup-garou ne vous mange'; ou bien encore: 'Fermez les yeux et prenez ce petit remède'; et aussitôt l'innocente faisait, au gré des fripons qui voulaient d'elle ce qu'il était bien naturel d'en vouloir, car elle était jolie. M. de Montragoux, trompé et offensé par cette innocente autant et plus qu'il ne l'avait été par Blanche de Gibeaumex, avait en outre le malheur de le savoir, car Angèle était bien trop candide pour lui rien cacher. Elle lui disait: 'Monsieur, on m'a dit ceci; on m'a fait ceci: on m'a pris ceci; j'ai vu cela; j'a senti cela.' Et, par son ingénuité, elle faisait souffrir à ce pauvre seigneur des tourments inimaginables. Il les souffrait avec constance. Cependant il lui arrivait de dire à cette simple créature: 'Vous êtes une dinde!' et de lui donner des soufflets. Ces soufflets lui commencèrent une renommée de cruauté qui ne devait plus s'éteindre. Un moine mendiant,

between Mlle de la Garandine and Bluebeard and in its frivolous eroticism, marked throughout by a medieval crudity.

In "La Chemise", a story in the same collection, France surprises the reader by showing how King Christophe, fails in his search for erotic novelty:

La reine lui avait donné trois fils. Elle était laide, acariâtre, avare et stupide, mais le peuple, qui la savait délaissée et trompée par le roi, la poursuivait de louanges et d'hommages. Après avoir recherché une multitude de femmes de toutes les conditions, le roi se tenait le plus souvent auprès de Mme de la Poule, avec laquelle il avait des habitudes. En femmes il eut toujours aimé la nouveauté; mais une femme nouvelle n'était plus une nouveauté pour lui et la monotonie du changement lui pesait. De dépit, il retournait à Mme de la Poule et ce "déjà vu" qui lui était fastidieux chez celles qu'il voyait pour la première fois, il le supportait moins mal chez une vieille amie. Cependant elle l'ennuyait avec force et continuité. Parfois, excédé de ce qu'elle se montrât toujours fadement la même, il essayait de la varier par des déguisements et la faisait habiller en Tyrolienne, en Andalouse, en capucin, en capitaine de dragons, en religieuse, sans cesser un moment de la trouver insipide.[21]

Stimulation reaches its first and second climax in the paradoxes on the dead-end reached by the lustful monarch in his quest for new erotic adventures: "une femme nouvelle n'était plus une nouveauté" and "monotonie du changement". The Voltairean finale is the second high point. In resentment at his doctor's professional advice King Christophe demonstrates unexpected vigor:

Non seulement il ne fit plus rien de ce qu'ils lui ordonnaient, mais encore il prit grand soin d'observer au rebours leurs préscriptions: il demeurait étendu quand ils lui recommandaient l'excercice, s'agitait quand ils lui ordonnaient le repos, mangeait quand ils le mettaient à la diète, jeûnait quand ils préconisaient la suralimentation; et montrait à Mme de la Poule une ardeur si inusitée qu'elle n'en pouvait croire le témoignage de ses sens et pensait rêver.[22]

---

qui passait par les Guillettes, tandis que M. de Montragoux chassait la bécasse, trouva Mme Angèle qui cousait un jupon de poupée. Ce bon religieux, s'avisant qu'elle était aussi simple que belle, l'emmena sur son âne en lui faisant croire que l'ange Gabriel l'attendait dans un fourré du bois pour lui mettre des jarretières de perles. On croit que le loup la mangea, car on ne la revit oncques plus."

[21] *O.C.*, XIV, pp. 247-48.

[22] *Ibid.*, pp. 255-56.

Occasionally France violates the classical tradition of *bon goût* and introduces Rabelaisian vulgarities. The "Histoire de la Duchesse de la Cigogne et M. Boulingrin qui dormirent cent ans en compagnie de la Belle-au-Bois Dormant", mentioned above, is a frivolous parody of a fairy tale and some of its passages verge on pornography. One such episode, a lower form of *gauloiserie*, is M. Boulingrin's nocturnal adventure with three fairies. On his way to the castle of his amorous mistress, the Duchess of Cigogne, the courtier is surrounded by the three fairies, who dance around him with such provocative zeal that he collapses and asks for mercy. One of the fairies pleads for the aged lover, ambiguously stating his lustful intentions: "Mes sœurs, donnez congé à M. de Boulingrin qui va-t-au château baiser sa belle." A few steps further, the exhausted nobleman, who had not recognized the fairies, "maîtresses de destinées", meets three old women whose shriveled faces are like apples baked in ashes.

Leurs pieds nus allongeaient démesurément des doigts décharnés, semblables aux osselets d'une queue de bœuf ... elles ... lui envoyèrent leur mignon, leur amour, leur cœur, le couvrirent de caresses auxquelles il ne pouvait échapper, car, au premier mouvement qu'il faisait pour fuir, elles lui enfonçaient dans la chair les crochets aigus qui terminaient leurs mains.

– Qu'il est beau! qu'il est joli! soupiraient-elles.

Avec une longue frénésie elles le sollicitent à les aimer. Puis, voyant qu'elles ne parviennent point à ranimer ses sens glacés d'horreur, elles l'accablent d'invectives, le frappent à coups redoublés de leurs béquilles, le renversent à terre, le foulent aux pieds et, quand il est accablé, brisé, moulu, perclus de tous ses membres, la plus jeune, qui a bien quatre-vingts ans, s'accroupit sur lui, se trousse et l'arrose d'un liquide infect. Il en est aux trois quarts suffoqué; et tout aussitôt les deux autres, remplaçant la première, inodent le malheureux gentilhomme d'une eau tout aussi puante.[23]

Finally they leave him. The dazed Boulingrin rushes to his mistress. The duchess receives him coolly and shocks the reader with a down-to-earth diagnosis of the odor which emanates from the apparel of her overwrought Romeo. "Boulingrin, ... vous puez le pissat de chat."[24]

The frivolous themes are not limited to the two collections of short

[23] *O.C.*, XIX, p. 228.
[24] *Ibid.*, p. 229.

stories. The eighteenth century subjects, *La Rôtisserie de la Reine Pédauque*, *Les Opinions de M. Jérôme Coignard*, and *Les Dieux ont soif* are generously spiced with typical Voltairean libertinage often heightened by a naturalistic accent. An example is the rustically vulgar denouement of Desmahis's intended rendezvous with Juliette Hasard during a country excursion. When Desmahis comes to the loft where he planned to seduce Juliette, he finds there the sleeping Tronche, a Herculean farm maid. To his surprise, the intrepid hunter bags a sleepy elephant instead of a graceful gazelle.[25] Paradoxically, the reader is amused because the sleeping farm girl is not in the least surprised when she learns the purpose of the unexpected visit.[26] The episode reads like a risqué *chanson* not only because of the content but because of the numerous rhymes, assonances, and cadences, such as: chandelier - palier - la fille - un billet - priait - grenier; l'heure - graveur - (coula) couleur; rejoindre - chambre; Desmahis - se mit - au lit - nuit - eut - pieds nus; escalier - grenier - entre-baillée; fruit pourris - sur un lit, etc. Generally, however, the frivolity is much subtler in *Les Dieux ont soif* than in *Les Sept Femmes de la Barbe-Bleue*, and rather tends to reach a higher erotic level.

[25] See p. 200.

[26] *O.C.*, XX, pp. 139-140. "Quand vint l'heure de la retraite, Desmahis et la citoyenne Hasard, tenant à la main chacun son chandelier, se souhaitèrent le bonsoir sur le palier. Le graveur amoureux coula à la fille du marchand de couleurs un billet par lequel il la priait de le rejoindre, quand tout serait endormi, dans le grenier, qui se trouvait audessus de la chambre des citoyennes.

Prévoyant et sage, il avait dans la journée étudié les aîtres et exploré ce grenier, plein de bottes d'oignons, de fruits qui séchaient sous un essaim de guêpes, de coffres, de vieilles malles. Il y avait même vu un vieux lit de sangle boiteux et hors d'usage, à ce qu'il lui sembla, et une paillasse eventrée, où sautaient des puces. . . . Desmahis se mit au lit, mais, quand le silence de la nuit eut, comme une eau dormante, recouvert la maison, le graveur se leva et monta l'escalier de bois, qui se mit à craquer sous ses pieds nus. La porte du grenier était entre-baillée. Il en sortait une chaleur étouffante et des senteurs âcres de fruits pourris. Sur un lit de sangle boiteux, la Tronche dormait, la bouche ouverte, la chemise relevée, les jambes écartées. Elle était énorme. Traversant la lucarne, un rayon de lune baignait d'azur et d'argent sa peau qui, entre des écailles de crasse et des éclaboussures de purin, brillait de jeunesse et de fraîcheur. Desmahis se jeta sur elle; réveillée en sursaut, elle eut peur et cria; mais, dès qu'elle comprit ce qu'on lui voulait, rassurée, elle ne témoigna ni surprise ni contrariété et feignit d'être encore plongée dans un demi-sommeil qui, en lui ôtant la conscience des choses, lui permettait quelque sentiment . . ."

In most situations, Abbé Coignard is the mouthpiece of France's satire, irony, and skepticism, but sometimes he is reduced to the stature of a farcical hero. France paints the abbé's portrait as he is trying to seduce Catherine, the lacemaker.

... il lui tint des propos agréables. Il la loua d'avoir de l'esprit non seulement sur la langue, mais encore à la gorge et dans le reste de sa personne, et de sourire avec ses lèvres et ses joues, moins encore qu'avec toutes les fossettes et tous les jolis plis de sa chair, en sorte qu'on souffrait impatiemment les voiles qui empêchaient qu'on ne la vît sourire tout entière.

– Puisque enfin, disait-il, il faut pécher sur cettte terre, et que nul ne peut, sans superbe, se croire infaillible, c'est avec vous, mademoiselle, que je voudrais que la grâce divine me fît défaut de préférence, si toutefois tel pouvait être votre bon plaisir. J'y rencontrerais deux avantages précieux, à savoir: premièrement, de pécher avec une joie rare et des délices singulières; secondement, de trouver ensuite une excuse dans la puissance de vos charmes, car il est sans doute écrit au livre du Jugement que vos attraits sont irrésistibles. Cela doit être considéré. L'on voit des imprudents qui forniquent avec des femmes laides et mal faites. Ces malheureux, en travaillant de la sorte, risquent fort de perdre leur âme; car ils pèchent pour pécher, et leur faute laborieuse est pleine de malice. Tandis qu'une si belle peau que la vôtre, Catherine, est une excuse aux yeux de l'Éternel. Vos charmes allègent merveilleusement la faute, qui devient pardonnable, étant involontaire.[27]

Not only does the abbé's technique of seduction contrast with his unconventional theological reasoning but so does the whole situation: Catherine is disposed to yield to the abbé's excellent theological arguments for she also has a favor to ask. Her lover, Brother Ange, lost or embezzled an ass he borrowed from Abbé La Perruque. The owner of the animal intends to sue the dishonest monk through proper canonic channels and have him arrested, unless the monk pays an indemnity in the form of a dozen sermons. Catherine intimates that she would be pleased to let Mr. Coignard taste any delights a woman can offer if only he would write the sermons for the uninspired Abbé La Perruque on behalf of the equally uninspired Brother Ange. There is much farce in the strange economy of this unique trade: the lost ass equals a dozen sermons, equals a night of love with Catherine. But the moral premise of the equation irritates the generally unprejudiced, amorous cleric.

[27] *O.C.*, VIII, pp. 339-40. See also this study, pp. 82-5.

Coming to his senses, M. Coignard tells Catherine in no uncertain terms what he thinks of her lover. "Il est ignare, il est menteur et vous l'aimez. Ce sont là trois raisons pour qu'il me déplaise. Je vous laisse à juger, mademoiselle, laquelle des trois est la plus forte."[28] The fiery abbé does not even spare the charming Catherine in his attack.[29] His eloquent sarcasm enhances a situation which in itself is pure *gauloiserie.* The abbé's tête-a-tête with Catherine does not end satisfactorily for either of them. Realizing that her diplomatic mission has failed, Catherine uses threats instead of friendly persuasion. Finally, when the virtuous gossip, Mlle Lecœur, passes by on her way to the church for evening confession, Catherine starts to scream, wickedly accusing the poor man of God of accosting her. Her cries are heard not only by the bitter old spinster, who will spread an embellished version of the scene all over town, but even by M. Ménétrier, Jacques's father, who tends to consider every admirer of Catherine as a poacher on his own preserves. The portly Don Juan is, so to speak, between Scylla and Charibdis. The whole passage has the flavor of a mischievous *fabliau*, in which farce overshadows the satire and irony. The *gaulois* element alone would be much heavier, even banal, but the amalgamation with irony makes it exquisite.

In his attacks on the decadence of the French bourgeoisie and aristocracy, France spices his satire with farcical libertinage. Among the examples given of ambiguities in France's literary aesthetics is M. Roux's confession that he feels an atavistic urge to thrust his bayonet into the belly of the first comer.[30] Later, M. Bergeret's favorite student finds the opportunity of satisfying this same instinct symbolically with

[28] *Ibid.*, p. 342.

[29] *Ibid.*, p. 343. "Je ne m'effarouche pas, à l'exemple de monsieur Nicodème, pour une si petite affaire que de prendre du plaisir avec une jolie fille. Mais ce que je ne puis souffrir, c'est la bassesse de l'âme, c'est l'hypocrisie, c'est le mensonge et cette crasse ignorance, qui font de votre frère Ange un capucin accompli. Vous prenez dans son commerce, mademoiselle, une habitude de crapule qui vous ravale bien au-dessous de votre condition, laquelle est celle de fille galante. J'en sais les hontes et les misères; mais c'est un état bien supérieur à celui de capucin. Ce coquin vous déshonore, comme il déshonore jusqu'aux ruisseaux de la rue Saint-Jacques, en y trempant les pieds. Songez, mademoiselle, à toutes les vertus dont vous pourriez encore vous orner, dans votre incertain métier, et dont une seule peut-être vous ouvrirait un jour le paradis, si vous n'étiez soumise et assujettie à cette bête immonde."

[30] See p. 109.

a most cooperative victim, Mme Bergeret. The lovers are surprised *in flagranti* by M. Bergeret. Without saying a word, the husband picks up a publication on the stool and leaves as if he had not noticed the adultery on the sofa. Alone again in the *salon*, Mme Bergeret and her lover are uncertain if the absent-minded scholar saw their act of love. Therefore they try to re-enact the critical moment of M. Bergeret's entrance to check if he could have seen them from the door. Their desperate effort to assure themselves that nothing happened is a farcical epilogue to their adultery and at the same time a technically original return to the more serious aspects of the erotic theme.[31] Madame Bergeret's passionate adultery destroys her family life; in contrast, Madame de Gromance's calculated adultery, also described in the *Histoire contemporaine*, doesn't destroy anything, it is constructive: it advances the political career of her dull husband. It also furthers the political schemes of M. Panneton, a right-wing politician who knows how to combine duty with pleasure. Women play a significant role in his professional activities and Madame de Gromance is one of them. M. Panneton holds his political conferences in an apartment furnished with the reliable tools of his statemanship – an elaborate series of sofas – but the most delicate questions are invariably solved in his bedroom, decorated with two water colors by Baudouin, well-known painter of erotic scenes. In describing M. Panneton's collection of sofas, from the most puritanic to the most invitingly voluptuous, France sets the scene for the visit of Madame de Gromance with a flair for both comic and erotic stimulation.

[31] *O.C.*, XI, p. 314. "– Il ne nous a pas vus. J'en suis sûr. Il n'a regardé que le guéridon. ...

Madame Bergeret voulut s'en rendre compte. Elle alla se mettre contre la porte, tandis que M. Roux, répandu sur le canapé, figurait à lui seul le groupe des amants surpris.

L'expérience n'ayant pas paru concluante, ce fut ensuite le tour de M. Roux d'aller à la porte et celui de madame Bergeret de restituer la scène d'amour.

Ils procédèrent plusieurs fois de la même façon, ... Et M. Roux ne put faire cesser les incertitudes de madame Bergeret.

Alors, il s'écria, impatient:

– Eh bien! s'il nous a vus, c'est un fameux ...

Et il employa un mot que madame Bergeret connaissait mal, mais que, sur la mine, elle estima grossier, malséant et bassement injurieux. Elle sut mauvais gré à M. Roux de l'avoir prononcé."

En entrant, le regard, promené de droite à gauche, rencontrait d'abord un petit canapé de soie bleue, dont les bras à col de cygne rappelaient le temps où Bonaparte à Paris, comme autrefois Tibère à Rome, restaurait les mœurs; puis un autre canapé, moins étroit, en beauvais, avec des accotoirs de tapisserie; puis une duchesse en trois parties, garnie de soie; puis un petit sofa de bois, à la capucine, couvert de tapisserie de point à la turque; puis un grand sofa de bois doré, ... provenant de mademoiselle Damours; puis un vaste divan bas, ... Au delà il n'y avait plus qu'un amas chancelant de coussins moelleux, sur un divan oriental, très bas, qui, tout baigné d'une ombre rose, touchait à la chambre des Baudouin, à gauche ... Les plus pudiques allaient droit au petit canapé bleu et posaient leur main gantée sur le col de cygne. Il y avait même un haut fauteuil de velours de Gênes et de bois doré, trône autrefois d'une duchesse de Modène et de Parme, qui était pour les orgueilleuses. Les Parisiennes s'asseyaient tranquillement dans le canapé de beauvais. Les princesses étrangères marchaient d'ordinaire vers l'un ou l'autre sofa. Grâce à cette disposition judicieuse des meubles de conversation, Panneton savait tout de suite ce qui lui restait à faire.[32]

The literary embroidery suavely prefaces the demonstration of M. Panneton's ingenious political mechanism in action. In the subsequent seduction scene, the charming Madame de Gromance links serious political business with social obligations which are not after all so unpleasant. In Panneton's shrine, decorated with the two original Baudouins, she trades her charms for the promise of a future ambassadorial appointment for her husband. These two passages are typical Francean *gauloiseries*, combined with a touch of caricature and light satire.

Panneton ne lui déplaisait pas excessivement. Cet homme chauve avec des cheveux très noirs collés aux tempes, de gros yeux hors de la tête, un air d'amoureux apoplectique, lui donnait un peu envie de rire et contentait ce besoin de comique qu'elle avait dans l'amour. Sans doute elle eût préféré un superbe garçon, mais elle était encline à la gaieté facile, disposée à l'amusement qu'un homme procure par des plaisanteries un peu grasses et par une certaine laideur. Après un moment de gêne bien naturelle, elle sentit que ce ne serait pas horrible, ni même très ennuyeux.

Ce fut très bien. Le passage du beauvais à la duchesse et de la duchesse au grand sofa se fit convenablement. On jugea inutile de s'arrêter aux coussins orientaux et l'on passa dans la chambre des Baudouin.

Quand Clotilde songea à les regarder, la chambre était, comme ces tableaux du peintre érotique, toute jonchée de vêtements de femme et de linge fin.

[32] *O.C.*, XII, pp. 465-466.

– Ah! les voilà, vos Baudouin. Vous en avez deux.
– Parfaitement.
Il possédait le *Jardinier galant* et le *Carquois épuisé*, deux petites gouaches qu'il avait payées soixante mille francs pièce à la vente Godard, et qui lui revenaient beaucoup plus cher que cela par l'usage qu'il en faisait.[33]

The deft climactic arrangement of this text illustrates France's art of gradation and his ingenious blending of minor themes to achieve a major effect: from higher sofas to lower oriental divans, from the divans to the bedroom and to the parallel between reality and the frivolous paintings, and finally to the ambiguous "*Carquois épuisé*". Similar effects are achieved by the erotic adventures of the angel Arcade and Madame des Aubel in *La Révolte des anges*, with the additional stimulus of the supernatural element.[34] In *L'Ile des Pingouins*, France also mixes the supernatural with *gauloiserie*. The obliging Saint Orberose, answering the prayer of Madame Gaubert, changes Jean Violle, her young lover, into a charming young girl when M. Gaubert surprises them *in flagranti*. The beauty of the young maid so bewitches the cuckold that he in his turn commits adultery. The next day, after another metamorphosis, Jean Violle resumes his original form.[35]

France uses a gently frivolous tone to challenge the wishful thinking of a literary historian. In discussing the literary merits of the biography of Madame de La Fayette by Count d'Haussonville, France touches on the probability of an intimate relationship between Madame de La Fayette and the Duc de La Rochefoucauld. Counter to the then accepted theory, Haussonville established that Madame de La Fayete was not a widow and that her husband survived the duke. At the same time Haussonville refused to admit that the young Madame de La Fayette was intimate with the noble moralist. France lightly satirizes Haussonville's attitude.

Madame de La Fayette fut en réalité mariée pendant vingt-huit ans et elle n'était pas veuve quand elle souffrait les assiduités du duc. Madame de Sévigné ne s'en scandalisait nullement. M. d'Haussonville se montrerait

[33] *Ibid.*, pp. 467-468.
[34] *La Révolte des anges,* Ch. XXIX.
[35] *O.C.*, XVIII, pp. 392-394.

plus sévère. Il ne cache point que madame de la Fayette lui plairait moins si elle avait trahi la foi jadis promise à l'excellent gentilhomme qui chassait dans les forêts d'Auvergne pendant qu'elle écrivait des romans à Paris dans le petit cabinet couvert. Il la veut toute pure. Heureusement qu'il est sûr que sa liaison avec M. de la Rochefoucauld fut innocente. Elle aima le duc; elle en fut aimée; mais elle résista. Il le veut ainsi. Au fond, il n'en sait rien. Je n'en sais pas davantage, et, si je le contredisais, j'aurais pour moi la vraisemblance. Mais la politesse resterait de son côté et ce serait pour moi un grand désavantage. Aussi je veux tout ce qu'il veut. Mais je confesse qu'il me faut pour cela faire un grand effort sur ma raison. Madame de La Fayette avait vingt-cinq ans, le duc en avait quarante-six. On se demandera comment, de l'humeur qu'il était, elle put l'attacher sans se donner à lui. Il ne vivait que pour elle, et près d'elle. Il ne la quittait pas. Cela donne à penser, quoi qu'on veuille.[36]

This passage amuses and fulfills its critical purpose by constant interweaving of eroticism, irony, controversy and skilled diction, and by the climactic arrangement of these features. The two dramatic peaks in this passage are the résumé of Madame de La Fayette's intimate *collisio officiorum* and Haussonville's paraphrased apology, and France's immediate ironic comment on the veracity of Haussonville's conclusions. But the aesthetic fabric of France's controversy with the Count d'Haussonville has many other glittering threads: the ironic term which described the duke's courtship as "assiduities" which Madame de La Fayette had to "suffer"; a satirical hint that the celebrated writer was an adulterous wife with its shocking implication that adultery was commonplace in aristocratic circles; a contrast between Haussonville's prudishness and Madame de Sévigné's liberal attitude; the ironical uses of the adjective *excellent* to characterize the betrayed husband whose "excellence" is immediately summed up in the following relative clause; and ironical report of Haussonville's naive conflict with the accepted view of literary history; a reserved denial of Haussonville's conclusion followed immediately by ironic support of it; a new apology for Haussonville's opinion immediately followed by a new doubt; a persuasive argument that the romance between the countess and the Duke is highly probable; an insinuation that Haussonville's illusions about the secrets of the *petit cabinet couvert* did not prove anything, and in fact damaged Madame de La Fayette's reputation by reviving her husband.

[36] *O.C.*, VII, p. 657.

The *gauloiserie* does not always link the comical with erotic frivolity. In "Komm l'Atrébate", an obscure Celtic chief collaborates with the invading Romans as long as they do not interfere with his own and his tribe's simple interests. Later, when they occupy his former territory, he opposes their rule, and in one instance manifests with a persuasively *gaulois* barbarism his contempt for the Roman cult. Disguised, Komm steals into the town built by the Romans on his former territory and views the Roman architecture decorated with mythological scenes which he does not understand. He feels an impulse to offend the power and the religion which destroyed his home. "Reconnaissant, debout, sur son socle de marbre, la déesse Rome, la tête coiffée du casque et le bras étendu pour commander aux peuples, il accomplit devant elle, avec une intention injurieuse, la plus ignoble des fonctions naturelles."[37] The surprise of contrast here is at two levels: the actual contrast between Komm's blasphemy and the marble pedestal and statue, and the abstract contrast between the chieftain's primitive contempt and the extreme reverence of those who worship the goddess.

The wide scope of erotic themes in literature makes it difficult for a writer to be original on the subject, yet France succeeded. In the hey-day of naturalism he enriched the erotic literature of his era by his revival and parody of ancient and mediaeval romances. His traditional treatment of love is much closer to Boccaccio, to the writers of the *fabliaux* and to Voltaire than to the naturalists, whose clinical approach to any subject imposes its own aesthetic limitation. France did not share the contempt of his contemporaries for mythology, fables and miracles, but, on the other hand, he did not limit himself to literary parody and adaptation. His love affair with Madame Caillavet inspired an urgent analysis of modern emotional conflicts and a significant portrait of an emancipated woman.

The scholars who censor France's scepticism and the excess of his ironic temper also usually declare his quest of *volupté* to be detrimental to art. Dargan divides the students of Francean sensualism into three categories: "Three attitudes are possible before such avowals. There are those who defend them as proceeding from the inevitable interlacing of art with *la volupté*; those who condemn them severely, as indicative of general disintegration; and those who, without prejudice,

[37] *O.C.*, XIII, p. 52.

simply accept them as part of the mixture that was Anatole."[38] Guehenno's opinion "il n'est point d'art sans concupiscence" represents the supporters of France's hedonism.[39] The censors are either the "clerics" who, like Klein and Bethleem, "find in his neopaganism, his sensual impiety, the hall-marks of a modern Antichrist",[40] or the moralists like Cerf who expounds in his study the "degeneration theory, or vice as corroding the soul of the artist".[41] Among the "unprejudiced" Dargan includes Lewis Galantière, who finds that France's work invites "a most interesting study of the cerebral voluptuary, [of] imaginative hedonism".[42] Any critic's approach to art ultimately reflects in part his own philosophical, moral and sexual attitudes. A puritan inevitably views the merits of the Dantean veneration of woman or the Gidean apotheosis of homosexual friendship in an entirely different light than an individualist who accepts unconventional instincts and tastes as natural. Thus, the Francean hedonism cannot be morally acceptable to an orthodox Christian of any denomination, and it is probable that such a critic's moral evaluation will influence his "aesthetic" verdict. On the other hand, the critic who feels that Christian sexual morals are obsolete may find France's treatment of love refreshing. The artist will appeal to him as a pioneer of a desirable erotic emancipation of modern man. Aesthetically and historically, of course, the moral and social angles are of secondary importance. To a humanist and aesthete, France's return to the ancient concept of love is more in harmony with tradition than the Christian worship of chastity. Like Epicurus and Lucretius, like Condillac and Voltaire, France is an apostle of sensualism. The simple and uninhibited drive of Francean love springs naturally from his cult of joy and beauty. He is unique in his artistic resurrection of the ancient ἡδονή, the divorce of Eros and sin, the revival of the charming erotic climate of the eighteenth century, the elegant alliance of *bon goût* and license. France's erotic paganism is not the revolt of an intellectual materialist versed in modern psychoanalysis, but the attitude of a free and civilized man.

38 Dargan, *op. cit.*, p. 564.
39 *Ibid.*, p. 565.
40 *Ibid.* Dargan's footnote not retained.
41 *Ibid.*
42 *Ibid.*

VIII

THE SUPERNATURAL AND UTOPIAN ELEMENTS

France has strong aesthetic reasons for resurrecting the gods, demigods, and other mythical beings of ancient literature, and, since he so often finds inspiration in the miracles and bizarre adventures of the medieval saints, he cannot do without angels, demons, and the devil as well. The wish to penetrate into the sphere of the absolute and the unknown is a universal human desire and a wise author will try to satisfy it. France quotes Baron Gleichen in *L'Hypnotisme dans la littérature* and wholeheartedly agrees with him:

Le penchant pour le merveilleux, ... inné à tous les hommes, ... mon goût particulier pour les impossibilités, l'inquiétude de mon scepticisme habituel, mon mépris pour ce que nous savons et mon respect pour ce que nous ignorons, voilà les mobiles qui m'ont engagé à voyager ... dans les espaces imaginaires. Aucun de mes voyages ne m'a fait autant de plaisir; ... Je suis comme le baron de Gleichen: je veux qu'on m'amuse et je crois qu'il n'y a pas de bonheur sans illusion.[1]

Whether presented seriously or in parody, supernatural topics relieve the monotony of realism. "Nous ne croyons pas non plus aux diableries dont le moyen âge était plein. Les moines vécurent jusqu'au XVe siècle dans un sortilège perpétuel. Ils assistaient à des miracles simples et naifs, mais qui du moins rompaient la lourde monotonie de leur existence."[2] France's ironical implication that miraculous phenomena are absurdities often increases the stimulation produced by the supernatural element itself. Christian dogma and its fundamental notion of a single God in three persons is for France one of these absurdities. The passage quoted from "La Légende des Saintes Oliverie et Libe-

[1] *O.C.*, VI, pp. 115-116.
[2] *Ibid.*

rette" is typical of the Francean treatment of the Holy Trinity: he uses one comical paradox to show that this miraculous monism is metaphysically as profound as the pagan fables.[3] Like Voltaire, France resents the Christian idea of an almighty, omnipresent, omniscient Creator who is supreme good but who at the same time implies evil in his own creation. He challenges the theological definition of this power in the discussion between the atheist Brotteaux and Père Longuemare:

Epicure a dit: "Ou Dieu veut empêcher le mal et ne le peut, ou il le peut et ne le veut, ou il ne le peut ni ne le veut, ou il le veut et le peut. S'il le veut et ne le peut, il est impuissant; s'il le peut et ne le veut, il est pervers; s'il ne le peut ni le veut, il est impuissant et pervers; s'il le veut et le peut, que ne le fait-il", mon Père? [4]

Through Epicurus and Brotteaux France expresses astonishment that men, knowing absolutely nothing about God but merely believing in his uncertain existence, yet presume to define him in such detail. This discrepancy may challenge the believer or corroborate the skeptic's doubts. But, be that as it may, speculation on the creative forces which shaped him has always stimulated man's natural curiosity. France knows that man tries to catch a glimpse of the absolute whenever he can, even if it is presented tongue-in-cheek. And there is always a latent fear of offending the omnipotent creator, about whose existence or non-existence he cannot be sure.

In France's eyes, the Christian theology and the religious intolerance of Judaism, whose concept of a jealous God inspired the Christian doctrine of love, are regrettable influences in our spiritual culture.[5] They led to new barbarism and unprecedented fanaticism; they inhibited not only physical freedom but freedom of thought and extinguished the Promethean torch for more than a thousand years. France satirizes what strikes him as Judeo-Christian obscurantism in *La Révolte des anges.* The Judeo-Christian God, Iadalbaoth, is a tyrant who made man in his own image: a jealous, violent, greedy, quarrel-

[3] See p. 63.
[4] *O.C.*, XX, p. 185. Walton (*op. cit.*, p. 218) points out that Brotteaux, although a confirmed reader of Lucretius, attributes the statement to Epicurus.
[5] See *Le Révolte des anges,* Ch. XVIII, the symbolism of "Le Saint Satyre" or various remarks in "Le Procurateur de Judée". The same theme is repeated in many other works.

some, lustful enemy of the arts and beauty. It is true that modern man has expelled from his mind this mediocre demiurge, but this will not help him unless he listens to the friendly demons who teach the whole truth, namely Dionysos, Apollo, and the Muses. Lucifer, the fallen Promethean seraph, the curious lover of freedom and beauty, finds much more grace in France's eyes. France's serious plea for Dreyfus against French society, for Pilate and Julien Apostate against the fanatic Jews and Christians; his ironic defense of Bluebeard against historical tradition, of defeated paganism against established and self-righteous Christianity, of the devil against God – such advocacy provides excellent aesthetic excitement.[6] These opinions shock those who accept what our convention establishes as good, humble, pious, and right. France's Satan is comparable to that of Milton: he is not a repulsive, horned and tailed monster with goat hooves, but a serene sovereign as beautiful as an ancient Apollo, as charming as Dionysos, as courageous and as loving as Prometheus. His handsome appearance can break a woman's heart and inspire eternal love, as in "La Dame de Vérone".[7] In a medieval setting of the "Humaine tragédie", Satan may resemble a theologian versed in scholastic philosophy or a loving, wise, and beautiful angel:

> Et Satan répliqua: "Tous les biens sont de chair et se goûtent par la chair. Et cela, Epicure l'a enseigné et Horace le satirique l'a mis dans ses chants." ... le saint homme Giovanni soupira: "Seigneur, je ne vous entends point." ... Et Satan dit encore au saint homme Giovanni: "As-tu le bonheur? Si tu as le bonheur, je ne prévaudrai pas contre toi. ... Pourquoi tenter cet homme? Il est heureux." Mais frère Giovanni soupira: "Seigneur, je suis moins heureux depuis que je vous écoute. Et vos discours me troublent." En entendant ces paroles, Satan rejeta son bâton pastoral, sa mitre et sa chape. Et il parut nu. Il était noir et plus beau que le plus beau des anges. Il sourit avec douceur, et dit au saint homme: "Rassure-toi, mon ami. Je suis le mauvais esprit." [8]

The angel's probing is not the temptation of the snake, trying to seduce by the promise of unknown bliss, but an incitement to independent speculation, showing man the Promethean path towards the light. His mythological incarnation inspires not hatred, but a tragic sympathy,

[6] See pp. 129-30.
[7] *O.C.*, X, p. 109 q.s.
[8] *O.C.*, X, pp. 152-153.

since man shares his aspiration as well as his punishment.

Et Giovanni contempla son compagnon, beau comme le jour et la nuit. Et il lui dit: "C'est par toi que je souffre, et je t'aime. Je t'aime parce que tu es ma misère et mon orgueil, ma joie et ma douleur, la splendeur et la cruauté des choses, parce que tu es le désir et la pensée, et parce que tu m'as rendu semblable à toi. ... Et je t'aime pour tout le mal que tu m'as fait. Je t'aime parce que tu m'as perdu." [9]

Man shares the aspirations as well as the damnation of the friendly Prometheus.

France, the Hellenist, does not hesitate to introduce also a buffoonish caricature of the medieval devil: with evident delight he dramatizes the monk Schnoudi's conflict with the devil, basing his description on E. Amélineau's *Vie de Schnoudi*.[10] France implies that the non-existent demon which had haunted primitive man influenced Christian doctrine, the creed of modern man. France's contradictory versions of Lucifer provide rare literary entertainment in an era of monumental social novels obsessed with grave social problems of contemporary humanity.

A keen reader of hagiographical literature, France projects the

[9] *Ibid.*, p. 211.

[10] *O.C.*, VII, p. 135. "Un jour, ... comme, assis dans la chambre sépulcrale, il tressait des cordes, le Tentateur lui apparut sous la forme d'un homme de Dieu. 'Salut, ô beau jeune homme', lui dit-il; 'le Seigneur m'a envoyé vers toi pour te consoler. Renonce désormais aux travaux de la piété, quitte l'aride désert; redescends vers la campagne riante et va manger ton pain en compagnie de tes frères.' A ses paroles, Schnoudi connut qui était devant lui. Il lui dit: 'Si tu es venu pour me consoler, étends la main et prie le Seigneur Jésus.' En entendant le nom de Jésus, Satan (car c'était lui-même) reprit sa forme véritable, qui est celle d'un bouc cornu. Et le saint lui passa autour du cou une des cordes qu'il venait de tresser. Le diable fut saisi d'une telle épouvante, qu'il en oublia qu'il était immortel.

– Je t'en prie, dit-il à Schnoudi, ne me fais pas périr avant le terme de ma vie.

Schnoudi lui fit entendre ces paroles menaçantes:

– Par les prières des saints, si tu reviens ici, je t'exilerai à Babylone de Chaldée, jusqu'au jour du Jugement.

Et il lâcha Satan, qui s'enfuit couvert de confusion.

On peut être surpris tout d'abord que Schnoudi, qui tenait le diable en son pouvoir, l'ait laissé aller. Mais le diable, à tout considérer, est aussi nécessaire que Dieu lui-même à la vertu des saints; car, sans les épreuves et les tentations, leur vie serait privée de tout mérite. Toutefois il n'est pas certain que Schnoudi ait agi par cette considération."

pioneer era of the Christian cult into his own literary setting. His favorite method is to dramatize in literary form the clash between paganism and the young Christian cult. Alvida Ahlstrom explains France's interest in this particular subject matter as resulting from his philosophical inclinations and his interest in history.[11] To Ahlstrom's supposition may be added another explanation: France the artist may be attracted to such themes more than France the philosopher, because they are a richer source of aesthetic stimulation than the favorite contemporary themes of the realists and the naturalists. Many a Christian reader, seeing the conflict between Christianity and paganism through France's eyes, is surprised to find himself regretting the victory of a drab cult over the poetic mythology of the Greeks.

The mythologies of both cults supply France with heroes entirely different from the Romantic and realistic Sorels, Javerts and Bovarys, and their psychological conflicts. Many of the new Francean characters were parodies of the exotic Salammbô and/or the St. Anthony tortured in the torrid North African sands. All their miraculous adventures and accomplishments, all their private meetings with God, the devil, the Virgin, with satyrs and nymphs, are re-enacted with a blasphemous twist, often reaching the level of sublime irony, by the mischievous *régisseur*, France. France's own attitude to such subjects and his reasons for indulging in them are made evident in his *Vie de Jeanne d'Arc.* In this historical monograph, France dissipates religious myths relative not only to Joan but also to other saints. He questions and comments with gusto on the veracity of Joan's mystical adventures and the whole work is an attempt to explain the circumstances which favored the

[11] Ahlstrom, *op. cit.*, pp. 44, 48. "Si ce mélange de paganisme au christianisme dans l'art médiéval intéresse Anatole France, c'est qu'il y voit l'évolution ininterrompue des idées. Il y voit l'écho ou la répétition, ... La mythologie paienne et polythéiste semble se répéter dans la symbolique chrétienne. ... Et ainsi les deux religions se trouvent mêlées par la juxtaposition de leurs monuments, symbole du mélange qui se fit des croyances. France se plaît à chercher les restes du paganisme dans le christianisme, ... et à voir comment ces survivances parfois sont combattues par les nouvelles croyances et parfois se mêlent à elles. Il explique en partie par le mysticisme naturel à l'homme la possibilité de ce mélange ... : car l'homme ... ne change pas beaucoup. La confusion du culte ancien avec le culte moderne ... est un objet d'étude qui captivait France ... dans ses féeries pascales, de ce doux paganisme qui l'enlace, au fond de nos campagnes, comme le lierre et la ronce embrassent une croix de pierre." Ahlstrom's notes have not been retained. See also this study p. 212.

political rise of Joan. The sarcasm directed at the saints, who allegedly visited her as ambassadors of God in order to meddle in international medieval policy, is echoed in France's fiction. Saint Catherine of Alexandria excited France's curiosity, both in *Vie de Jeanne d'Arc* and in his *Histoire contemporaine*, for two main reasons: her colorful biography was filled with miraculous fables and in all probability she never existed. In one of their typical conversations, Abbé Lantaigne and M. Bergeret discuss Jeanne d'Arc's mystic visions of the Greek Saint, accompanied by Saint Michael and Saint Marguerite. The sceptical scholar teases the theologian by his reference to the research of a learned seventeenth century historian who concluded that Catherine was merely a literary heroine of an inferior Greek novel.[12] Paraphrasing Voragine's *La Légende dorée*,[13] France tells with relish the story of this royal princess versed in the arts and in silk weaving.

La beauté de son corps resplendissait, mais son âme demeurait plongée dans les ténèbres de l'idolâtrie. Plusieurs barons de l'empire la recherchaient en mariage; elle les dédaignait et disait: "Trouvez-moi un époux qui soit sage, beau, noble et riche." Or, pendant son sommeil, elle eut une vision. Le Vierge Marie lui apparut tenant l'Enfant Jésus dans ses bras et dit: "Cathérine, veux-tu prendre celui-ci pour ton époux? Et vous, mon très doux fils, voulez-vous avoir cette vierge pour épouse?" L'Enfant Jésus repondit: "Ma mère, je ne la veux point; éloignez-la plutôt de vous, parce qu'elle est idolâtre. Mais si elle consent à se faire baptiser, je lui promets de mettre à son doigt l'anneau nuptial."

Désireuse d'épouser le Roi des cieux, Cathérine alla demander le saint baptême à l'ermite Ananias, qui vivait en Arménie, dans la montagne Nègre. Peu de jours après, comme elle priait dans sa chambre, elle vit venir Jésus-Christ au milieu d'un chœur nombreux d'anges, de saints et de saintes. Il s'approcha d'elle et lui mit au doigt son anneau. Et Cathérine connut seulement alors que ces noces étaient des noces spirituelles.[14]

In unmasking the false saint, France does not omit a single miraculous detail of Catherine's marriage to the Son of God arranged so obligingly by his Holy Mother. Delight and scepticism are further aroused by grotesque contrasts, the parody of divine courtship, the sly use of ecclesiastic rhetoric, the farcical name evoking *ananas*, the mischievous

[12] *O.C.*, XI, p. 102.
[13] Jacques de Voragine, *Légende dorée* (légende de sainte Marguerite), Douhet, *Dictionnaire des Légendes*, pp. 824-36.
[14] *O.C.*, XV, p. 112.

repetition of the geographical error of the legend, which placed *la montagne Nègre* (Montenegro) in Armenia. Catherine's marriage is exposed to tragedy when another powerful suitor lays vigorous siege to her; the pagan emperor, Maxentius, having executed his wife for daring to reproach his cruelty, offers a last chance to the martyr, but even in the face of death Catherine remains faithful to her celestial husband:

Puisque, par tes arts magiques, tu as fait périr l'impératrice, si tu te repens, tu seras maintenant la première dans mon palais. Aujourd'hui donc, sacrifie aux dieux, ou tu auras la tête coupée. Elle répondit: "Fais ce que tu as résolu, afin que je prenne place dans la troupe virginale qui accompagne l'Anneau de Dieu." L'empereur la condamna à être décapitée. Et lorsqu'on l'eut menée ... au lieu du supplice, elle leva les yeux au ciel et dit: "Jésus, espoir et salut des fidèles, gloire et beauté des vierges, je te prie d'accorder que quiconque m'invoquera en souvenir de mon martyre sera exaucé, soit au moment de sa mort, soit dans les périls où il pourra se trouver."

Et une voix du ciel lui répondit:

– Viens, mon épouse chérie; la porte du ciel t'est ouverte. Je promets les secours d'en haut à ceux qui m'invoqueront par ton intercession.

Du col tranché de la vierge il coula du lait au lieu de sang.[15]

Like in the scholarly résumé of the miracles in this legend[16] the supernatural element in France's work is rarely an isolated feature; his parodies of the legends, abound in farcical, ironical, or bizarre effects, in archaisms and in primitive rhymes.[17]

Only rarely are Christian miracles treated with the relative gravity of "Le Jongleur de Notre Dame". To please the Holy Virgin, in the

[15] *Ibid.*, pp. 117-18.

[16] France's references do not indicate that he is aware of other miracles mentoined in other versions of the legend: for example, in the Czech fourteenth century version, which undoubtedly is as authentic as the one by Jacques de Voragine, the intrepid martyr is whipped so mercilessly that her body shines like a rainbow, the seven colors of which symbolize the seven knightly virtues.

[17] Similar parodies of the supernatural features in the Christian cult are the main source of aesthetic stimulation in "Laeta-Acilia", *Thaïs*, "Amycus Célestin", "La Légende des Saintes Oliverie et Libérette", "Sainte Euphrosine", "Scolastica", "Le Saint Satyre", "Histoire du bienheureux Longis et de la bienheureuse Onoflette", Histoire de Saint Gualaric ou Valéry", 'Histoire des trois chevaliers d'Eppes et de la belle Ismérie", Histoire de saint Adjutor", *L'Ile des Pingouins; La Révolte des anges,* and in many digressive passages of other works.

only way he can, the juggler demonstrates his skill in front of the altar. The monks are shocked by this unprecedented blasphemy. When they try to expel him from the chapel, the Virgin descends from the altar and wipes the juggler's forehead. The amazed monks prostrate themselves before this miraculous vision. "Alors le prieur, se prosternant le visage contre la dalle, récita ces paroles: 'Heureux les simples, car ils verront Dieu!' 'Amen!' répondirent le anciens en baisant la terre."[18] If France does not parody the miracle in this theme, he may have good reason: he suggests that a humble performer who provides joy pleases God more than the monks who mortify and smother any spark of joy God gave man. France treats the miracle seriously in "Caution", if we disregard the frame, and also in "La Messe d'ombres".[19]

France rarely satirizes the Graeco-Roman cult and the pagan deities in the same spirit as he does those of Christianity. Even if they are mocked, their mere presence usually evokes the charming atmosphere of the mythical past. They introduce the theme of beauty and joy which no religious fanaticism, no austere, mystical doctrine and no elaborate cult can affect or destroy. In the "Saint Satyre" and in *La Révolte des anges* France glorified the pagan cult of natural beauty, untouched by the doctrine of original sin.[20] Moreover, he points out that paganism charms Western man despite his Christianization.

Mais, hélas! direz-vous, ils ont tué les petits génies. . . . saint Valéry a fait mourir la nymphe de la fontaine. C'est pitié.

– Oui, ce serait une grande pitié. Mais cessez de vous attrister. Je vous le dis tout bas: les doux démons qu'il chassait d'un arbre entraient dans un autre. Les génies, les nymphes et les fées . . . ne meurent jamais.[21]

The pagan phenomena appeal to man's humble respect for the inexplicable creative and vital forces of nature. The Greek deities never shock in France's work, they charm by their freedom, beauty, and joy.

[18] *O.C.*, V, p. 298.

[19] Ahlstrom, *op. cit.*, indicates in detail which medieval themes, all containing the supernatural element, are imitated or assimilated in France's work. Besides mentioning such supernatural beings as God, the devil, and the Saints (p. 76) she thoroughly outlines the occurrence of Hell (p. 139) and of the macabre element (pp. 42-43).

[20] See pp. 151-53, 163.

[21] *O.C.*, X, p. 435.

When the aged Homer has the first premonition that his pilgrimage might be ended by Apollo's arrows, he offers his sacrifice to Léto's son in a most unusual way:

Il remplit sa coupe d'eau fraîche, et, comme il était pieux il en versa quelques gouttes devant l'autel, avant de boire. Il adorait les dieux immortels qui ne connaissent ni la souffrance ni la mort, tandis que sur la terre se succèdent les générations misérables des hommes. Alors il fut saisi d'épouvante et il redouta les flèches du fils de Léto. Accablé de maux et chargé d'ans, il aimait la lumière du jour et craignait de mourir. C'est pourquoi il eut une bonne pensée. Il inclina le tronc flexible d'un ormeau et, le ramenant à lui, suspendit la coupe d'argile à la cime du jeune arbre qui, se redressant, porta vers le large ciel l'offrande du Vieillard.[22]

What a vehement prayer for life! What a naively captivating way of reaching God! The bard's sacrifice may stir our melancholy and our hunger for vigorous, meaningful poetry in the cult of modern man.

Fra Mino, the prior of Santa Fiore, rules in a monastery whose chapel had been built above the ruins of an ancient temple. In it is the tomb of Saint Satyre, similar to an ancient pagan sarcophagus. One day, in the surrounding grove, *Fra* Mino sees the graceful nymphs and the satyrs, symbolic of an immortal, free beauty which Christianity was unable to stifle.[23] Puzzled by their presence in the old shrine itself, the prior tries to solve the mystery by studying ancient texts and even magic. His heresy reflects the scope of his desperation, but ironically, the plunge into spiritual darkness will enable him to see the light. Fatigued by his nocturnal reading, he leaves his cell and seeks refreshment in the slowly awakening forest. The dawn disperses all the uncertainty of vain research. The vital breath of nature shivers in every leaf and the reader feels that the young sun will cast light on all mysteries. The moment of revelation is near.

The path which will lead him out of darkness is steep but charming. Its playful gaiety is suggested by the musical assonances and rhymes, sentier - montueux - mariées - oliviers - pieds.

Il prit le sentier montueux qui, cheminant parmi les vignes mariées aux ormeaux, va vers un bois de myrtes et d'oliviers, sacré jadis aux Romains. Les pieds dans l'herbe humide, le front rafraîchi par la rosée qui s'égout-

[22] *O.C.*, XIII, p. 5.
[23] See note 20.

tait à la pointe des viornes, fra Mino marchait depuis longtemps dans la forêt, quand il découvrit une source sur laquelle les tamaris balançaient mollement leur feuillage léger et le duvet de leurs grappes roses.[24]

The beauty of living nature embraces and bewitches him. The text also echoes the nocturnal reading which in darkness seemed to be so frustrating, but which may have provided the solution of the mystery; mythological beauty and the cadence of ancient poetry resound from such "lines" as:

bois de myrtes et d'oliviers (8)
sacré jadis aux Romains. (7)
Les pieds dans l'herbe humide (6)
(le)
front rafraîchi par la rosée qui s'égouttait (12)
à la point(e) des viornes, ... (6)

A feeling of liberating freshness is suggested by the coolness of the wet morning grass and the dew evaporating from the tops of the viburni. The senses are awakened and soothed. The monk's vanishing bewilderment is parodied sympathetically in a short rhymed passage. As he strives to grasp the significance of the texts he studied during the night, the conviction grows that they will ultimately reveal the meaning of his earlier meeting with the attractive revenants of the groves.

... sens qu'il importe
de découvrir soit par illumination
soudaine, soit en faisant une application
exacte des règles de la scolastique
et j'estime que dans ce cas particulier
les poètes que j'ai étudiés
à Bologne, tels qu'Horace, le satirique,
et Stace ...[25]

After lowering the lyrical mood by crude rhymes and the "rules of medieval scholasticism", France lets it soar in pagan style: a satyr appears from nowhere and after preluding on his *syrinx*, begins to sing:

... il leva les yeux et s'aperçut qu'il n'était pas seul. Adossé au tronc caverneux d'une yeuse antique, un vieillard regardait le ciel à travers le

[24] *O.C.*, X, pp. 22-23.
[25] *Ibid.*

feuillage et souriait. A son front chenu pointaient des cornes émoussées. ... Sur ces cuisses une laine épaisse traînait jusqu'à ses pieds fourchus. Il appuya sur ses lèvres une flûte de roseaux, ... Puis il chanta d'une voix à peine distincte:

> Elle fuyait, rieuse,
> Mordant aux raisins d'or
> Mais je sus bien l'atteindre,
> Et mes dents écrasèrent
> La grappe sur sa bouche ...[26]

Besides imitating the ancient Graeco-Roman and Judeo-Christian myths, France dramatizes a purely Judaic myth which combines the supernatural with the excitement of the erotic: Lilith, the first wife of Adam, gave life to immortal feminine beings before Adam's fall in the arms of Eve. This Talmudic legend inspired the short story, "La Fille de Lilith",[27] and many passages in *La Rôtisserie de la reine Pédauque*. M. d'Astarac, a cabalist, tries to establish contact with the *ewig weiblich Salamandres*, and Jacques Tournebroche tastes the delights of paradise in the arms of a "daughter of Lilith". An erotic relationship with a luminous *Salamandre* is presented as not only extremely gratifying but entirely possible for any man willing to renounce contact with the human daughters of Eve.

The revival of mythology is an auxiliary but integral technique in the Francean conflicts between paganism and Christianity, but this is not the exclusive aesthetic function of the supernatural element. It is also a logical ingredient of the author's Utopian visions. There are various short utopian passages scattered in France's work, but in *L'Ile des Pingouins*, *La Révolte des anges* and "Par la porte de corne ou par la porte d'ivoire" the utopian element predominates. In each case the utopian constituents spring from different factors. The short story paints a society transformed by technological progress and by the moral and economic collapse of Western civilization. Its hero, Hippolyte Dufresne, is mysteriously transported to the Paris of 2270, and has the opportunity of seeing the French capital during the era of European Federation. He meets people whose political and social order, style of living, and language differ considerably from those of the late nineteenth and early twentieth centuries. He views his own

[26] *Ibid.*, p. 24.
[27] See pp. 163-64, 202.

period from a distant utopian perspective and is struck by the enormous degree of mechanization, by the disappearance of ugly cities, including Paris, and the complete residential decentralization made possible by air travel.[28] Business, courts, army, alcoholism, and money have been abolished.[29] Women are completely emancipated and the distinctions between the two sexes less pronounced. A new and somewhat asexual woman develops a type of feminine eunuch comparable to a worker bee and thus productivity is increased without undue growth of the population. Books are gradually being replaced by films.[30] Defense is in the hands of one small bespectacled soldier who can destroy an army of half a million invaders by pressing one of the keys on his keyboard.[31] The only subversive elements in the new society are the scientists who advocate anarchy, claiming that humanity will not be happy unless it reaches the stage of spontaneous harmony which will follow only after the complete destruction of civilization.[32] Later, the hero listens to the narration of European history between his time and 2270. He learns that European capitalism has collapsed, except for the economic systems of England and Russia. The latter, in the Francean utopia written in 1905, has remained a theocratic tyranny.[33] The first collectivist state in the new post-capitalistic era is France and not Germany, which had been thought to be the best prepared for social progress.[34] The democratic ideals, *Liberté*, *Egalité*, *Fraternité*, are absurd to the new generations.[35]

[28] *O.C.*, XIII, pp. 522-523.
[29] *Ibid.*, p. 525.
[30] *Ibid.*, pp. 544-45.
[31] *Ibid.*, p. 547.
[32] *Ibid.*, p. 548. See also Levaillant's comment (*op. cit.*, p. 622): "... c'est Darwin et Wells, autant et plus que le socialisme, qui inspirent les grand thèmes de *Sur la Pierre Blanche*." And also (*ibid.*, p. 623): "Voilà bien le point. ... Pour ne laisser place qu'à nature, France a supprimé de sa cité idéale les notions politiques abstraites qui, exigeant trop de l'homme, lui servent en fin de compte de masque: 'il faut subordonner la société à la nature et non, comme on l'a fait trop longtemps, la nature à la société.' " (Levaillant's note not retained.)
[33] *Ibid.*, p. 531.
[34] *Ibid.*, p. 533.
[35] *Ibid.*, pp. 541-542. "La liberté ne peut pas être dans la société, puisqu'elle n'est pas dans la nature. Il n'y a pas d'animal libre. ... L'idée d'égalité est moins raisonnable encore, et elle est fâcheuse en ce qu'elle suppose un faux idéal. Nous n'avons pas à rechercher si les hommes sont égaux entre eux. Nous

Although the utopian women no longer even have Christian names and seem to find the "capitalistic" method of courtship savage, and in spite of their weird biological propensity, the elementary factors of life remain the same. Dufresne awakes just as he is about to prove it, and realizes that his utopia was a dream.[36]

This utopia is a literary prophesy which stimulates the reader's curiosity about the future. He wonders if the changes he expects parallel those the author foretells – amusing and surprising innovations in the style of living and a different scale of values. And, when other aesthetic features are mixed with the utopian element, the reader's stimulation is that much greater.

A long utopian fragment in *M. Bergeret à Paris* is inspired by the same socialist vision of human society as "Par la porte de corne ou par la porte d'ivoire." However, M. Bergeret has no illusions about a rapid evolution for the better. Man is not good by nature and the rise from his original barbarism is slow. Human justice is uncertain, man's kindness is precarious and he will continue to resort to violence for some time to come. "Je crois que le règne de la violence durera longtemps encore, que longtemps les peuples s'entre-déchireront pour des raisons frivoles."[37] But things are not quite hopeless: ". . . les hommes sont moins féroces quand ils sont moins misérables, . . . les progrès de l'industrie déterminent à la longue quelque adoucissement dans les mœurs, et je tiens d'un botaniste que l'aubépine transportée d'un terrain sec en un sol gras y change ses épines en fleurs."[38] In his utopia, man will get what he earns and begging will disappear.[39] But evil will not be defeated because evil and pain are necessary: "Le mal est nécessaire. . . . La souffrance est sœur de la joie . . ."[40] Man will perhaps be liberated from heavy work. Private enterprise will vanish, not as

devons veiller à ce que chacun fournisse tout ce qu'il peut donner et reçoive tout ce dont il a besoin. Quant à la fraternité, nous savons trop comment les frères ont traité les frères pendant des siècles. Nous ne disons pas que les hommes sont mauvais. Nous ne disons pas qu'ils sont bons. Ils sont ce qu'ils sont. Mais ils vivent en paix quand ils n'ont plus de cause de se battre."

[36] *Ibid.*, p. 552.
[37] *O.C.*, XII, pp. 443-444.
[38] *Ibid.*, p. 444.
[39] *Ibid.*, pp. 444-45, 448.
[40] *Ibid.*, p. 446. See also above p. 124 and n. 28.

the result of revolution but rather as the result of the gradual enlightenment of the capitalists. The State will be abolished and identified with all the social services.[41]

L'Ile des Pingouins, a satire on the ancient, medieval, and modern history of France, presents an entirely different utopia. The utopian setting is provided by the odd missionary activities of St. Mael: one day this holy navigator lands on the shore of an island, where he sees the dim outlines of some beings crowded on the rocky ledges. Blinded by the eternal snows, he takes them for people and thus christens a colony of penguins. His apostolic *faux pas* arouses a heated theological controversy in Paradise. Finally St. Mael is given a special dispensation to convert the ornithological congregation not only to Christianity but also to humanity, validating the misused sacrament of baptism. The six subsequent books of the novel describe the historical evolution of this utopian island populated by a new race of mankind, and satirize the progress of French history. The last book, "Les Temps futurs", contains an ironic vision of the future degeneration and collapse of the penguin capitalistic society.[42] In the first part of the novel, the utopian elements are farcical; in the central part of the work, they provide a vehicle for satire; only at the end, in the denunciation of capitalistic society, does the utopian element become the main source of aesthetic enjoyment. The gloomy future predicted for Western society makes the reader aware of the fatal trends in our civilization but his concern never becomes anxiety, because the satirical utopia emphasizes the comical or grotesque aspects of the coming social cataclysm.

La Révolte des anges, which blends comical reality with supernatural elements, could be called a theological utopia. An anarchistic group of immortal fallen angels, who live incognito in a tolerant, somewhat libertine Parisian milieu, quietly prepares a coup against the dictator of the universe, Jahve. Lucifer, the enlightened and wise leader of this militant group, lives his eternity in a sublime inferno on the lofty terraces of the Himalayas. France describes Lucifer's "shangri-la" toward the end of the novel, when five of the rebels journey to an

[41] *Ibid.*, pp. 448, 450.
[42] *O.C.*, XVIII, p. 393. See also above p. 100.

audience with their leader.[43] The utopian hell has a serenely mythological beauty. Satan receives the delegation of friendly revolutionaries like Tityrus in the Virgilian eclogue.[44] The exotic details, rhythmical prose, and euphonius effects of these passages add their own aesthetic stimulation to that of the utopian element.

Unlike most utopias, *La Révolte des anges* is inspired neither by technological progress nor by an ideal of social justice, but rather by the eternal teleological conflicts of pagan, Judaic, and Christian myths. Satan's wise reluctance to seize power from the hands of the ambitious and bigoted Iahveh at the end of the novel reveals the nature of France's utopia – a return to the ideal of joy and beauty.

Compagnons, dit le grand archange, non; ne conquérons pas le ciel. C'est assez de le pouvoir. La guerre engendre la guerre et la victoire, la défaite.

Dieu vaincu deviendra Satan, Satan vainqueur deviendra Dieu. Puissent les destins m'épargner ce sort épouvantable! J'aime l'enfer qui a formé mon génie, j'aime la terre où j'ai fait quelque bien, ... Maintenant, grâce à nous, le vieux Dieu est dépossédé de son empire terrestre et tout ce qui pense sur ce globe le dédaigne ou l'ignore. Mais qu'importe que les hommes ne soient plus soumis à Ialdabaoth si l'esprit d'Ialdabaoth est encore en eux, s'ils sont à sa ressemblance, jaloux, violents, querelleurs, cupides, ennemis des arts et de la beauté; qu'importe qu'ils aient rejeté le Démiurge féroce, s'ils n'écoutent point les démons amis qui enseignent toute vérité, Dionysos, Apollon et les Muses. Quant à nous, esprits célestes, démons sublimes, nous avons détruit Ialdabaoth, notre tyran, si nous avons détruit en nous l'ignorance et la peur.[45]

France's skepticism and his sympathetic parody of mythological deities seems to result in a blend of agnosticism and pagan pantheism. Perhaps there may exist some creative forces so far unknown but

[43] *O.C.*, XXII, p. 397. "Ayant gravi les sept hautes terrasses qui montent de la berge du Gange jusqu'aux temples ensevelis dans les lianes, les cinq anges atteignirent par des allées effacées le jardin sauvage plein de grappes parfumées et de singes rieurs, au fond duquel ils trouvèrent Celui qu'ils étaient venus chercher. L'archange s'accoudait à des coussins noirs brodés de flammes d'or. Sous ses pieds des lions et des gazelles reposaient. Enroulés aux arbres, des serpents domestiques tournaient vers lui leurs yeux amis."

[44] *Ibid.*, p. 398. " ... je savais le sujet de votre visite. Des corbeilles de fruits et des rayons de miel vous attendent à l'ombre de ce grand arbre. Le soleil est prêt de descendre dans les eaux roses du fleuve sacré. Quand vous aurez mangé, vous dormirez agréablement dans ce jardin où règnent l'intelligence et la volupté depuis que j'en ai chassé l'esprit du vieux Démiurge."

[45] *Ibid.*, p. 322. See also above pp. 33-4.

manifested in nature. These forces lend us our subjectivity, our speculative power, our genius, and they perpetuate the regeneration, the dynamism and all the tragic as well as poetic conflicts in nature. They are the divine metabolism, they are life and death, they are the creators of the beauty which inspires us and brings joy to life. Of course, these forces are perhaps not omnipotent, omniscient, omnipresent, absolute and eternal Good. Levaillant defines France's position toward the Judeo-Christian God as follows: "Quant au Dieu infini, transcendant, absolu, placé par les gnostiques au-dessus du démiurge usurpateur et grossier, France le supprime: rien n'existe au-dessus de la création mauvaise, tout se passe dans le domaine de la finitude, . . ."[46] France is not as sure as Nietzsche or Marx that God is dead, should be dead, or that he does not exist. Is it because he is a sentimental bourgeois who lacks the courage to face a completely godless life, or because his humanism and his wisdom make him resent the intransigent and sterile certainty of the revolutionaries? The answer will be left forever to speculation.

The *chef d'œuvre* in which he defined his goal of life is not artistically flawless. It is digressive and abundantly padded with farce and *gauloiserie*. But for its unique subject matter, for its unorthodox treatment of moral and spiritual problems, and for its poetry, this utopia will always rank among the most significant modern European novels. It is France's major achievement that he added to the Divine and Human comedies his *comédie angélique*.

[46] Levaillant, *op. cit.*, p. 797; Levaillant's note not retained.

IX

BIZARRERIE

Miracles, bloodshed, adultery or farce, the " abnormal", in fact, tends to be more exciting than what is considered to be "normal". The "normal" may indeed catch the reader's interest, but the author has to reveal it in an unusual light. Deviations from the normal surprise or charm; contrasts with the dull routine of life arouse interest. France speaks of the inborn human thirst for the unaccustomed in one of his literary causeries: "Il nous faut du nouveau. On nous dit: 'Que voulez-vous?' Et nous répondons: 'Je veux autre chose' ".[1] Man restlessly seeks *autre chose* in science, in politics, in women. Even if France finds that life is essentially the same today as it was three thousand years ago, he tries to amuse at least by variations on the commonplace, thus offering an illusion of *autre chose*, – something different, something unusual, something special, which will always entertain.

Bizarre, exotic, historical or shocking topics attract precisely because they are such an *autre chose*. The instinct they awaken is usually curiosity. If the bizarre is shrouded in mystery, it provokes fear; shocking incongruity inspires disgust. As in all aesthetic enjoyment, these reactions result from a contrast – in this case, the contrast between the strange and the normal. No general evaluation of France's art can be complete without an analysis of the *bizarreries* which decorate his prose. They are the logical complement of the typical Francean hero – the old man, with an invariably thorough knowledge of history, philosophy and the arts, who hovers around like a tragi-comic Greek chorus, commenting with delight on every imaginable discrepancy, and making continual reference to obscure precedents. His humanist erudition is an inexhaustible fountain of France's *pessimisme jouisseur*

[1] *O.C.*, VI, pp. 111-112.

as well as of *bizarreries*. Heroes such as Bonnard, Boni, Bergeret, or Abbé Coignard, are not bizarre in themselves, but each of them has a bizarre streak. Their sophisticated interests and opinions are invariably whimsical, unexpected, sometimes bizarre and often shocking.

Their scholarly taste for *bizarrerie* is as typical as their cynicism.

France's *roman livresque, Le Crime de Sylvestre Bonnard*, is a typical early *bizarrerie*. The adventures of the elderly medievalist, Bonnard, who devoted his life to the study of unknown manuscripts, arouse interest precisely because of the quaint bibliographical revelations. The reader meets the archivist in his modest residence as he praises his cat, Hamilcar, for protecting his precious medieval manuscripts, including *Acta Sanctorum*, from the greed of the rats. The scholar's placid reading is interrupted by the arrival of a little book peddler with the grotesque name of Coccoz. Their conversation on peculiar books emphasizes the bizarre environment of the scholar. Later, after he returns to his obscure catalogue, he suddenly becomes excited over an unexpected reference to an ancient manuscript of a French translation of the *Legenda Aurea.* His agitation reaches a climax when he discovers that the manuscript contains several legends not recorded in any known manuscript of Jacques de Voragine's work. The reader concerned with the prosaic, practical aspects of life, is amazed that someone should get so excited over an obscure collection of old legends. Yet, at the same time he may well share Bonnard's thrill in discovering a "buried treasure". A subtle suspense mounts until the unwrapping of the memorable Christmas *bûche* sent to M. Bonnard by Countess Trépof [-Coccoz], when it turns out that the Christmas "treat" is a case filled with Parma violets and the precious manuscript of the *Légende dorée* the scholar had been seeking so stubbornly.[2]

Imagination, subtle theological speculation and verbal wit are characteristic of Abbé Coignard's bizarre streak. His contemplation on the heresy of a person who forces his dog to observe Lent illustrates his indulgence in theological *bizarrerie.*

Ma sainte mère n'eût point souffert que Miraut, notre gardien, rongeât un os le vendredi saint. En vain, M. l'abbé Coignard lui représentait-il ... qu'en bonne justice Miraut, qui n'avait point de part aux sacrés mystères

[2] *O.C.*, II, pp. 334-335.

de la rédemption, n'en devait point souffrir dans sa pitance. ... Une telle pratique, ma bonne dame, va droit à la plus épouvantable des hérésies. Elle ne tend pas à moins qu'à soutenir que Jésus-Christ est mort pour les chiens. ... Il se peut, répondit ma mère. Mais, si Miraut faisait gras le vendredi saint je m'imaginerais qu'il est juif ...[3]

The argument is comical but it also provokes interest in a fine point of Christian doctrine.

Bizarre pedantry is satirized in "M. Pigeonneau". Summing up his life work, the hero confesses with modest pride:

J'ai voué, comme on sait, ma vie entière à l'archéologie égyptienne. ... Mes travaux n'ont pas été stériles. Je dirai, sans me flatter, que mon *Mémoire sur un manche de miroir égyptien, du musée du Louvre*, peut encore être consulté avec fruit, ... Quant à l'étude assez volumineuse que j'ai consacrée postérieurement à l'un des poids de bronze trouvés, en 1851, dans les feuilles du Sérapéon, j'aurais mauvaise grâce à n'en penser aucun bien, puisqu'elle m'ouvrit les portes de l'Institut.

Encouragé par l'accueil flatteur ... je fus tenté, un moment, d'embrasser dans un travail d'ensemble les poids et mesures en usage à Alexandrie sous le règne de Ptolemée Aulète (80-52). Mais je reconnus bientôt qu'un sujet si général ne peut être traité par un véritable érudit, et que la science sérieuse ne saurait l'aborder sans risquer de se compromettre dans toutes sortes d'aventures.[4]

France is far from being a materialist who approves only research that is economically useful, but he enjoys poking fun at the book worm who is unable to see the limits of his study from a higher, humanistic perspective. He mocks the over-specialization which prevents him from contributing to intellectual or spiritual culture. Here the bizarre enhances the satire.

Historical and exotic *bizarreries*, stylized with a glittering impressionist technique, have an irresistible appeal. The unsuccessful courtship of the wise, black Balthasar suited France's taste for the unusual. The opening of this ancient Afro-Oriental romance is characteristic of the exotic historicism in France's early work.

En ce temps-là, Balthasar, que les Grecs ont nommé Saracin, régnait en Ethiopie. Il était noir, mais beau de visage. ... La troisième année de son régne, qui était la vingt-deuxième de son âge, il alla rendre visite à Balkis,

[3] *O.C.*, VIII, pp. 369-370.
[4] *O.C.*, IV, pp. 157-158.

reine de Saba. Le mage Sembobitis et l'eunuque Menkéra l'accompagnaient. Il était suivi de soixante-quinze chameaux, portant du cinnamome, de la myrrhe, de la poudre d'or et les dents d'éléphant. Pendant qu'ils cheminaient, Sembobitis lui enseignait tant l'influence des planètes que les vertus des pierres, et Menkéra lui chantait des chansons liturgiques; mais il ne les écoutait pas et il s'amusait à voir les petits chacals assis sur leur derrière, . . .[5]

The grotesque royal tour, in the days just before Christ's birth, intrigues the reader, and provokes several sensual illusions. He sees the royal caravan silhouetted against brilliant African skies. He hears the pious eunuch's liturgic solo. He smells the aroma of spices. He imagines the ancient lesson in petrography and astrology offered by the learned Sembobitis to the king. The *couleur locale* in the themes drawn from early Christian history and from the medieval conflicts between Christianity and paganism is the result of the same technique. Paphnuce, the fanatic hermit of *Thaïs*, lives among the cenobites and Anchorite ascetics. Their Spartan vegetarianism, their dwellings in graves and their "master-pieces of penitence" stimulate the curious reader.[6] Paphnuce seeks mystical extasy by living on the top of an ancient column for many days and nights under the Egyptian sun and in the demon-filled darkness, but later, to please God, he finds shelter in a grave.[7] Religious *bizarreries* are integrated with idyllic, comic or tragic topics: "Amycus et Célestin" is a serene apotheosis of the peaceful co-existence of a satyr and a tolerant monk inspired by Christian love; "Scolastica", an *imitatio* of Grégoire de Tours, parodies the weird matrimonial chastity in the pagan-Christian marriage of Scolastica and Injurious; *Fra* Giovanni, the humble St. Francis-like hero of the "Humaine tragédie", does not hesitate to give all his clothes

[5] *O.C.*, IV, p. 123.

[6] *O.C.*, V, pp. 5, 6. "Il y avait aussi, tout au bord du fleuve, des maisons où les cénobites, renfermés chacun dans une étroite cellule, ne se réunissaient qu'afin de mieux goûter la solitude.

Anachorètes et cénobites vivaient dans l'abstinence, ne prenant de nourriture qu'après le coucher du soleil, mangeant pour tout repas leur pain avec un peu de sel et d'hysope. Quelques-uns, s'enfonçant dans les sables, faisaient leur asile d'une caverne ou d'un tombeau et menaient une vie encore plus singulière.

Tous . . . portaient de cilice et la cuculle, dormaient sur la terre nue après de longues veilles, . . . et, pour tout dire, accomplissaient chaque jour les chefs-d'œuvre de la pénitence."

[7] *Ibid.*, pp. 167-87.

to the poor in the winter for the love of God; naked except for his Franciscan girdle, he crosses the town amidst the snowball barrage of mocking children.[8]

A grotesque echo of the tragic *Fra* Giovanni is the unforgettable modern apostle, Choulette of *Le Lys rouge*. Upon meeting the impeccably groomed *mondaine*, Thérèse Martin-Bellème, and her conservative companion, Mme Marmet, this Christian pacifist-anarchist shocks the two ladies with his travelling bag, made from a musty old carpet. He apologizes for almost missing the train because of having to attend mass in his beloved church. His apology leads to a discussion on the *cingulum*. While explaining the string he wears around his waist as a sign of poverty, Choulette carves the symbol of human misery on the handle of his walking stick. Misery later becomes the *Pietà* and finally the Virgin. He also writes a quatrain to be carved in a spiral on the cane.[9] In this caricature of the modern prophet there is an odd blend of *bizarrerie*, controversial views, and contrasting, apparently incompatible qualities. Choulette unites ascetic mysticism with hedonistic but radical anarchism, and a vagabond's roguishness with a sublime saintlines rare in the materialistic society.[10]

La Rôtisserie de la Reine Pédauque is rich in a different kind of peculiarity. Its mysterious hero, M. d'Astarac, and his strange staff – the learned, intolerant Mosaide, M. Coignard and his understudy, Jacques Tournebroche – try to verify certain passages of the Koran, Talmud, and obscure Alexandrian texts. M. d'Astarac immediately betrays his oddity. Anyone trying to corner a Salamander in a restaurant fireplace on Christmas Eve must be an eccentric and is bound to excite the guests with his strange outcry.[11] The reader is attracted by the *bizarrerie*, but principally wants to follow the eccentric into the sphere of magic. The Salamander hunt, with its striking accent on the supernatural, climaxes the novel, but the general historical setting and many descriptive details of the novel rely more on the bizarre. There is an ominous poetry, for example in M. Coignard's and Jacques' pilgrimage to the weird *château* of M. d'Astarac.

[8] *O.C.*, X, p. 119.
[9] *O.C.*, IX, p. 151.
[10] Many religious *bizarreries* can be found in other short stories, in *Les Noces Corinthiennes* and in *L'Ile des Pingouins*.
[11] See pp. 146-48.

Le lendemain, nous cheminions de bonne heure, mon maître et moi, sur la route de Saint-Germain. La neige qui couvrait la terre, sous la lumière rousse du ciel, rendait l'air muet et sourd. La route était déserte. Nous marchions dans de larges sillons de roues, entre des murs de potagers, des palissades chancelantes et des maisons basses dont les fenêtres nous regardaient d'un œil louche. Puis, ayant laissé derrière nous deux ou trois masures de terre et de paille à demi écroulées, nous vîmes, au milieu d'une plaine désolée, la croix des Sablons. A cinquante pas au delà commençait un parc très vaste, clos par un mur en ruines. Ce mur était percé d'une petite porte verte dont le marteau représentait une figure horrible, un doigt sur la bouche. Nous la reconnûmes facilement pour celle que le philosophe nous avait décrite et nous soulevâmes le marteau.[12]

The eerie solitude and silence, the coat of soft snow which muffles every sound, the coldness, the decrepit architecture, the bizarre door-knocker, – all suggest mystery.

Generally, *bizarrerie* lies in the remote and the distant. It thrives in the mysterious atmosphere of Kabala, in dusty stacks of old libraries and in unknown collections. But nature itself is not always "natural". Perhaps, like man, it has its own whimsical hunger for the unexpected, an *autre chose*, and to satisfy it endows its own creatures with peculiar gifts. Citizen Pelleport, health officer, designates the Herculean beauty, La Tronche, as a physical *bizarrerie*:

... ce n'est pas une fille, ... c'est deux filles. Comprenez que je parle littéralement. Surpris du volume énorme de sa charpente osseuse, je l'ai examinée et me suis aperçu qu'elle avait la plupart des os en double: à chaque cuisse, deux fémurs soudés ensemble; ... Ce sont, à mon sens, deux jumelles étroitement associées ou, pour mieux dire, fondues ensemble ... Ces gens-ci l'appellent "la Tronche." Ils devraient dire "les Tronches": elles sont deux. La nature a de ces bizarreries ...[13]

Apart from major bizarre subjects in France's work there are hundreds of strange details blended with lyrical, tragic, shocking, supernatural or comical elements. Although seemingly insignificant, such a detail

[12] *O.C.*, VIII, pp. 51, 52. The bizarre in this passage is integrated with lyrical element: the accumulation of the dark *ou*'s and *o*'s strikes a deep, austere note (route, couvrait, sous, rousse, sourd, nous, roues) and emphasizes along with many rhymes and assonances the poetry of mystery (le lendemain – Saint-Germain; cheminions – marchions – sillons – maisons – des Sablons; terre – lumière – l'air; sourd – rous; écroulées – désolée and the more distant murmasure and louche – bouche).

[13] *O.C.*, XX, p. 135. See also above p. 170, esp. n. 26.

may catch the reader's attention like an unusually designed piece of jewelry, placed with care on an exquisite garment. In describing the environment of Euripides, which may have inspired much in his immortal works, France mentions in one breath the oddly exotic adornment used by elegant Greeks of Euripides' era and the irrational temperament of some anonymous women in ancient Hellas.

Ce petit rocher de Cécrops fut longtemps rude, couvert d'idoles raides et peintes, qui souriaient mystérieusement. Là vivaient des hommes à la fois grossiers et magnifiques, qui portaient des cigales d'or dans leurs longs cheveux nattés, et tout un peuple de matelots nourri d'ail et de chansons. Les femmes, encore sauvages, déchiraient sur la place publique les messagers des désastres.[14]

For all we know, Euripides himself may never have used such an exotic pin on his braid; perhaps he did not even wear a braid. Perhaps a mob of females attacked a bearer of bad tidings only once in Greek history. Still, the golden grasshopper in men's braids and the lynching of messengers of bad news, especially twenty-five centuries ago, is for the curious reader both enjoyable and unforgettable.

The pomp of Doña Maria's wedding in the mentioned *Histoire de Doña Maria d'Avalos et de Don Fabricio, duc d'Andria* is a dazzling, exotic bacchanale.

Douze chars, trainés par des chevaux recouverts d'écailles, de plumes ou de fourrures, de manière à figurer dragons, griffons, lions, lynx, panthères, licornes, promenaient dans la ville des hommes et des femmes nus, dorés tout en plein, qui représentaient les divinités de l'Olympe, descendues sur la terre pour célébrer les noces vénosiennes. On voyait dans un de ces chars un jeune garçon ailé qui foulait aux pieds trois vieilles d'une laideur dégoûtante. Une tablette élevée au-dessus du char portrait cette devise: L'AMOUR VAINQUEUR DES PARQUES.[15]

The allegory of the uninhibited love-play and sunny, pagan bliss ahead for the duke and his bride, is hardly compatible with the matrimonial delights reluctantly sanctioned by the chaste Christian cult.[16] The reader is amused by the farce and his imagination is caught by the exotic Greco-Oriental grandeur.

[14] *O.C.*, VI, p. 457.
[15] *O.C.*, X, p. 237.
[16] Thomas Mann, *op cit.*, p. 249. " . . . gute Rasse, ein . . . , sauberer Mann. Er durfte um sie werben, durfte sie anschauen, . . . – sie zum christlichen Weib

He laughs first at the farcical staging of what will turn out to be a bitter truth. Only after reading the whole story does he realize the full irony of what had appeared to be just a bizarre detail. The prophecy will be fulfilled – love will win, but its "victory" will also be tragic victory of the Parcae.[17] This passage shows how France concentrates in a minor *bizarrerie* several aesthetic features: eroticism, farce, exoticism and grave irony.

Similar importance attaches to the love amulet in "La Fille de Lilith", that Ary receives from the wife of a good friend. It is a cypress leaf covered with Oriental writing. Ary's former teacher, the learned Abbé Safrac, later identifies the inscription as a Persian prayer which reads: "Mon Dieu, promettez-moi la mort, afin que je goûte la vie. Mon Dieu, donnez-moi le remords, afin que je trouve le plaisir. Mon Dieu, faites-moi l'égale des filles d'Eve!"[18] The amulet expresses the idea behind the whole story, which runs surprisingly counter to our own instincts with its paradoxical praise of death.[19] The dead leaf and the prayer on it are pathetic reminders that even immortality can be as absurd and tragic as our own short life.

Bizarre features may also shock the reader's sense of decency, as, for instance, the anecdote on Baudelaire's morbid *gourmandise*. Satirizing Baudelaire's taste for the tasteless, France exploits the poet's satanic humour.

> Il a ... des manies odieuses; ... il grimace comme un vieux macaque. Il affectait dans sa personne une sorte de dandyisme satanique qui semble aujourd'hui assez ridicule. Il mettait sa joie à déplaire et son orgueil à paraître odieux. Cela est pitoyable et sa légende, ... abonde en traits de mauvais goût.
>
> – Avez-vous mangé de la cervelle de petit enfant? disait-il un jour à

---

zu begehren, wie wir Theologen sagen, mit berechtigtem Stolz darauf, daß wir dem Teufel die fleischliche Vermischung weggepascht haben, indem wir ein Sakrament, das Sakrament der christlichen Ehe draus machten. Sehr komisch eigentlich, diese Kaperung des Natürlich-Sündhaften für das Sakrosankte durch die bloße Voranstellung des Wortes 'christlich', – wodurch sich ja im Grunde nichts ändert. ..."

[17] See pp. 135-36 and 164.

[18] *O.C.*, IV, p. 193. See also above pp. 163-64, 189.

[19] Aesthetically the passage is intensified by the double antitheses, mort – vie and remords – plaisir; euphonious effects such as the series of grave vowels, promettez-moi la mort, donnez-moi le remords; by the rhyme and the assonances.

un honnête fonctionnaire. Mangez-en; cela ressemble à des cerneaux et c'est excellent.

Une autre fois, ... il commença un récit en ces termes:

– Après avoir assassiné mon pauvre père ...

En admettant, ... que ces historiettes ne soient par réellement vraies, elles ont le tour baudelairien ... Tout cela n'est pas douteux, mais il faut dire aussi que Baudelaire était poète.

J'ajouterai que c'était un poète très chrétien. On a découvert dans ses poèmes des immoralités neuves et une dépravation singulière. C'est le flatter et c'est flatter son temps.[20]

By alluding to such a bizarre menu and to suggested patricide France achieves a double purpose. In a few lines he deftly caricatures Baudelaire, censuring him tolerantly for his eccentricities, but enough to register disapproval. However, while dissociating himself from the repulsive aspect of the humor, France still makes full use of it; he reinforces the effect of the anecdotic perversities by passing them off as flattery of the Christian poet. In sum, babybrains à la Baudelaire are quite a morsel for the imagination. Were it not the joke of an eccentric gourmet, the subject would shock more; still the reader can visualize the reaction of a correct civil servant to this kind of morbid humor. "Le Miracle du grand Saint Nicolas" also relies for effect on mock shock. France points out that none of the biographers of St. Nicolas mentions the resurrection of three children chopped to pieces by an innkeeper and marinated for seven years, as reported in an ancient ballad. To compensate for this oversight, he dwells on all the crude details of the bizarre crime, satirizing in the biographies of the revived children the blasphemous consequences of the miracle.

Revelations of scandalous opportunism and turpitude in his society may arouse the same indignation mixed with contemptuous laughter. M. Mazure's exposé of the vulgar sins of socially prominent families, their ancestors' opportunism and bizarre crimes unearthed from dusty archives, may well shock the living generations.[21] France revels in all

[20] *O.C.*, VII, pp. 32-33.

[21] *O.C.*, XI, pp. 285-87. – ... j'ai déniché le dossier des Gromance, qui appartiennent à la petite noblesse de la région. Il y a une demoiselle Cécile de Gromance qui se fit faire en 1815 un enfant par un Cosaque. Ce sera un joli sujet d'article pour une feuille locale. .... Mazure avait trouvé, dans les archives, un Terremondre qui, terroriste et président du club des Sans-Culottes dans sa ville en 1793, avait changé ses prénoms de Nicolas-Eustache en ceux de

bizarre records of our civilization, no matter whether found in the archives or in obscure collections of miracles. He amuses himself as well as his readers by his description of queer hobbies and by his satire on the worship of relics fostered in the Roman Catholic church. Baron Denon's passion appealed to France, as he showed in a *causerie* of the same name:

Possédant un beau reliquaire du XVe siècle dépouillé sans doute pendant la Terreur, il l'avait enrichi de reliques nouvelles dont aucune ne provenait du corps d'un bien-heureux. ... Il était né trop tôt pour goûter, en dilettante, comme Chateaubriand, les chefs-d'œuvre de la pénitence. Son profane reliquaire contenant un peu de la cendre d'Héloise, recueillie dans le tombeau du Paraclet; une parcelle de ce beau corps d'Inès de Castro, qu'un royal amant fit exhumer pour le parer du diadème; quelques brins de la moustache grise de Henri IV, des os de Molière et de La Fontaine, une dent de Voltaire, une mèche des cheveux de l'héroique Desaix, une goutte du sang de Napoléon, recueillie à Longwood.[22]

The problematic value and heterogenous nature of these morbid collector's items stimulate the reader's curiosity and his taste for the grotesque.[23] Meditating on the satisfaction man draws from his personal achievements, the critic of *Le Temps* says: "... je n'ai connu en ce monde que deux hommes heureux de leur œuvre: l'un est un vieux colonel, auteur d'un catalogue de médailles; l'autre, un garçon de bureau, qui fit avec des bouchons un petit modèle de l'église de la Madeleine."[24]

A combination of two minor elements, not necessarily bizarre in

---

Marat-Peuplier. Et Mazure s'était hâté de fournir à son collègue de la Société d'archéologie, M. Jean de Terremondre, monarchiste rallié et clérical, des notes sur cet aïeul oublié, Marat-Peuplier Terremondre, auteur d'un hymne à sainte Guillotine. .... la famille Quatrebarbe, qui sort de deux chauffeurs, un homme et une femme, pendus à un arbre de la côte Duroc, sous le Consulat, par les habitants eux-mêmes. Et l'on rencontrait encore, aux environs de 1860, des vieillards qui se rappelaient avoir vu, dans leur enfance, sous la branche d'un chêne, une forme humaine autour de laquelle flottait une longue chevelure noire, dont s'effrayaient les chevaux.

– Elle resta pendue trois ans, s'écria l'archiviste, et c'est la propre grand'mère d'Hyacinthe Quatrebarbe, l'architecte diocésain!

[22] *O.C.*, VII, pp. 166-67.

[23] Stylistic effects integrated into this passage, are the assonanced and rhymed series: reliquaire – diadème – Molière – La Fontaine – Voltaire; possédant – sans – pendant – dilettante – Chateaubriand – amant – dent – sang; une goute – Longwood.

[24] *O.C.*, VI, pp. 354-55.

themselves, may result in a distinct *bizarrerie*, as, for instance, the contradictory traits in Pierre Nozière's grandfather:

... M. Hippolyte Nozière, commis principal au ministère de la Justice, ... jouait de la flûte de six à neuf heures du matin et de cinq à huit heures du soir. ... Mon grand-père Nozière est l'auteur d'une *Statistique des Prisons*, Paris, Imprimerie royale, 1817-19, 2 vol. in-40; et *Filles de Momus, chansons nouvelles*, Paris, chez l'auteur, 1821, in-18.[25]

An unexpected action may yield a surprise similar to that created by *bizarrerie*. Many of the analyzed features were, of course, unexpected: Murder is an unexpected development in the negotiations between Groult and Reuline in *Jocaste*,[26] yet the chief stimulation in this incident remains violence. Desmahis's discovery of the elephantine Tronche sprawled on a bed in the attic, where he planned his rendezvous with the Citoyenne Hasard, was an unexpected turn of events, but the *gauloiserie* is at least as significant in this passage as the unexpected element.[27]

Typical literary examples of unexpected events are the contrived finales in classical comedies, involving the sudden reappearance of long-lost relatives, inheritance of fortune and title, or cases of mistaken identity; Pangloss's miraculous yet perfectly natural survivals from a series of "mortal" blows, including his execution; Chabert's burial alive in a mass military grave, or the unexpected twists in modern detective stories. Such actions have an aesthetic value, even if the author makes the reader "expect the unexpected" for instance the continual survivals of Pangloss.

Parodying the moralistic fairy tale about the shirt of the happy man, France confronts the unhappy king Christophe with a happy dreamer, who declares that nothing can increase his bliss. The monarch then tries to buy the dreamer's "happy shirt".

– Un mot encore, monsieur. Vous pouvez me sauver. Je ...
– On n'est sauvé qu'en me prenant pour exemple. Vous devez me quitter ici. Adieu!

Et l'inconnu, ... s'élança dans le bois ... Christophe, sans vouloir rien entendre, le poursuivit: au moment de pénétrer dans le taillis, il entendit un coup de feu, s'avança, écarta les branches et vit le jeune homme

[25] *O.C.*, III, pp. 266.
[26] See p. 170 and n. 26.
[27] See p. 170.

heureux couché dans l'herbe, la tempe percée d'une balle et tenant encore son revolver dans la main droite.

A cette vue, le roi tomba évanoui.[28]

The reader, familiar with the imitated fairy tale and used to the comical tone of France's narrative, expects a farcical obstacle to the purchase. But the tragedy inherent in the discovered happiness takes him by surprise. The happy man's suicide is a bizarre satire of the Greek wisdom that the darling of the gods dies young.[29]

Madame de Luzy hides the persecuted philosopher, Planchonnet, in her bed. When the national guardsmen search her bedroom, she and another man, who came to confess his love for her, pose as surprised lovers in the bed, while the scholarly fugitive chokes under the mattress. Although blended with a threat of violence and a touch of eroticism, Madame de Luzy's ruse is a typical case of surprise produced by unexpected action.[30]

The contrived, unexpected finale typical of medieval legends is parodied in the "Sainte Euphrosine". After Euphrosine's mysterious disappearance, her father Romulus and her prospective husband Longin search for her in vain. In despair they seek peace in a monastery. Without realizing it, they are reunited there with Euphrosine when the jubilant Brother Smaragde, gatekeeper of the male institution, receives and screens them. Longin never learns that Brother Smaragde is Euphrosine; it will be revealed to him only in Paradise.[31]

France uses the unexpected action as he does the supernatural and the miraculous, mockingly but with a canny realization of its aesthetic effect. Sudden but sufficiently convincing artificialities as well as *bizarreries* are standard techniques of France's art of surprise. His flair for contrast and his alert but suave alternation of themes, combined with his Ciceronian sense of proportion, enable him to draw fully, and without any aesthetic harm, on that reservoir of *bizarreries*, his own humanist background. His taste for the bizarre is one of his instinctive qualities.[32] But the technique itself depends entirely on his unusual

[28] *O.C.*, XIX, p. 317.
[29] Hon hoi theoi filousin apothneskei neos.
[30] *O.C.*, V, pp. 420-425.
[31] *O.C.*, V, pp. 272-275.
[32] See pp. 22-23.

familiarity with the many remote fields of learning to which he alludes so often and so specifically. Evaluating the depth and scope of France's interests, Stapfer points out that it is not a potpourri of anecdotes absorbed by a whimsical amateur of history, but the broad knowledge of a rare modern polyhistor. An avid reader of Darwin and Haeckel, France knows about the genesis of the universe, earth and life as much as one can expect from an "honnête homme". He is thoroughly familiar with the history of art, with historical collections, with all styles and periods of architecture. He has mastered the jargon of bookdealers, bookbinders, hunters, beggars, heraldry, archivists, gun collectors, and automobilists.

> Il est ferré comme un juriste sur les questions d'impôt ecclésiastique et de main morte, sur les encycliques des papes, sur les lois du 28 décembre 1880 en du 29 décembre 1884. Il n'a garde de confondre une custode avec un ciboire. Dans une discussion entre un médecin et quelques gens d'étude sur les anomalies physiques, telles qu'une denture anormale, qui prédisposent certains individus aux troubles moraux et au crime, il s'amuse à nous rappeler, . . . que Mithridate avait une sœur tenue pour magnanime par son grand frère et qui eut en effet un trépas héroique, bien que la nature lui eût fait le vilain cadeau d'une double rangée de dents à chaque machoire.[33]

However, many quaint items discovered in historical writings and haphazardly integrated in a polished narrative do not produce art. They remain a mere junkyard of literary *bizarreries*, piled up by a pseudo-humanist. But Francean *bizarreries* are seldom sterile. They frequently lend color and plasticity to his thought and a touch of the transcendental to his stylizations of life. Thus he manages to convert even the abnormal mandible of Mithridate's sister into a glittering fragment in the mosaic of his wisdom.[34] *Bizarrerie*, like his wit or his poetic style, is a pertinent substance of France's art and Epicurean humanism.

[33] Stapfer, *op. cit.*, pp. 159-160.

[34] *Ibid.*, p. 160 "Assurément, un grand liseur peut avoir logé dans sa mémoire ce commérage de quelque vieux conteur de balivernes, – Aulu-Gelle ou Plutarque, – sans être un érudit. Assurément aussi, Anatole France n'a pas commencé son propre conte avec le dessein arrêté de nous entretenir, à un certain endroit, de la mâchoire d'une sœur de Mithridate. Mais c'est justement cette liberté flottante des souvenirs, c'est l'aisance parfaite d'un curieux qui a tout lu et trouve, à point nommé, des exemples inattendus et plaisants pour illustrer sa pensée, – que cette 'mâchoire' fait ressortir."

X

FRANCEAN *IMITATIO*

Often France's topics and stylistic features are adaptations or imitations of various literary precedents. Like most of his literary techniques, the art of adaptation reflects France's traditionalism. *Imitatio* is one of the basic techniques of the ancient literary *métier* that France admired and emulated. As an imitator, no truly French *homme de lettres* can ignore his national literary tradition since, in quality, it matches the ancient heritage. Therefore France cannot limit himself merely to the *imitatio* of the Greco-Latin and Italian writers. Stylistically he must imitate above all the French classics. As for subject matter, France seeks inspiration both in the ancient and in the medieval tradition; and, as he admires the age of Voltaire, he also finds his themes and stylistic precedents in eighteenth century literature. But, although France has more classical examples to draw from, his treatment of adopted topics differs little from Petrarch's *imitatio* as described in Hermann Gmelin's study, *Das Prinzip der Imitatio in den Romanischen Literaturen der Renaissance*.[1] Like the Italian imitator France was

[1] Hermann Gmelin, *Das Prinzip der Imitatio in den romanischen Literaturen der Renaissance* (Erlangen, *Romanische Forschungen* Vol. XLVI, 1932), pp. 98-100. "Das Ausschlaggebende aber war, daß in jenem Lande der Trobadors sein Ohr an den Weisen ihrer Lieder geschult ward, und daß er Petrarca nun darauf verfiel, die lateinischen Autoren zum erstenmal auch mit jenem musikalischen Sinn der Trobadors zu lesen und sich an der klanglichen Schönheit der ciceronianischen Sprache zu berauschen ... Diese musikalische Einfühlung und Feinhörigkeit hat sein ganzes Verhältnis zur antiken Literatur und ... auch den Charakter seiner Imitatio bestimmt. Dazu kommt nun noch, daß er die Befriedigung seines tief religiösen Gefühls, das ihn bald die Sitten von Avignon und die ganze damalige Kirche gering achten ließ, an den hohen Idealen der Antike und an dem geistigen Umgang mit ihren großen Menschen glaubte befriedigen zu können. Dieser Glaube hat ihm die Kraft gegeben, so viele ihrer

brought up in a humanist tradition, and like him he resents, though perhaps for different reasons, the Christian cult, and favors paganism and the ancient culture. Woolsey points out in his study what a fountain of inspiration France found in antiquity.[2]

France is the first to recognize his debt to society, to its culture and all the authors from whom he borrows ideas or whose style he imitates.

On ne prend pas assez garde qu'un écrivain, fût-il très original, emprunte plus qu'il n'invente. La langue qu'il parle ne lui appartient pas; la forme dans laquelle il coule sa pensée, ode, comédie, conte, n'a pas été créée par lui; il ne possède en propre ni la syntaxe ni sa prosodie. Sa pensée même lui est soufflée de toutes parts. Il a reçu les couleurs; il n'apporte que les nuances . . . nos œuvres sont loin d'être toutes à nous. Elles croissent en nous, mais leurs racines sont partout dans le sol nourricier. Avouons donc que nous devons beaucoup à tout le monde.[3]

Gestalten wiederzugeleben und das Wissen um ihre Werke, ihr Leben, ihre Gesellschaft und ihre Kunst wieder zu erneuern. Aus diesen beiden Wurzeln, einer dichterischen und einer religiös-ethischen, ist der Humanismus Petrarcas erwachsen.

Das Sicheinleben in die antikel Autoren hat die ganze Lebens- und Empfindungsweise Petrarcas bestimmt. Während Dante seinem Virgil noch als einem gottgesandten Führer ehrfurchtsvoll gegenüberstand, hat Petrarca die antiken Geister unbedenklich in seine private Sphäre gerückt, mit ihnen einen täglichen imaginären Umgang gepflogen und ihre Handlungen und Gedanken diskutiert und nachgeahmt."

[2] Pierce Edgar Woolsey, "Greek and Latin Influence in the Work of Anatole France", (unpublished doctoral dissertation Cornell University, Ithaca, N.Y. 1932. Abstract, p. 6. "For Jules Lemaître he is 'l'extrême fleur du génie latin,' and in similar vein, Michaut . . . remarks: 'Nul auteur, peut-être, n'a plus répété les anciens.' " More recently Levaillant (*op. cit.*, p. 823), sums up the influence of a vital cultural heritage on France's world outlook and on his art. "France a beaucoup imité: l'imagination reste chez lui tributaire de la lecture. La tension créatrice se manifeste presque toujours à l'occasion d'un rapport entre ce qu'il sait pour l'avoir lu, et ce qu'il sent pour l'avoir vécu. Création de culture, et non pas expression directe d'une personnalité donnée, d'une nature toute faite, son œuvre est le fruit d'une élaboration volontaire à partir d'un héritage. Mais il y a un drame du livre chez France . . . L'œuvre se tisse alors au lieu de rencontre, au point d'échange entre le livre et la vie. Malgré le risque d'imitation qui est celui de toute culture, son œuvre demeure porteuse d'une expérience originale. Même si 'l'univers' d'Anatole France manque du relief suffisant, ou de la densité imaginative nécessaire, pour qu'une analyse synchronique à elle seule en rende compte, on ne peut lui dénier les caractères singuliers qui conditionnent un sens personnel."

[3] *O.C.*, VI, pp. 512, 513.

France has much sympathy with the creative tribulation that faced the ancient bards. In his portraits of Homer he imagines the difficulties relating to the Homeric *imitatio*; the wandering poet must conceal his original contributions to the ancient sagas and myths he sang. When asked by his host, Mégès, if his recital describes the true adventures of Achilles and Ulysses, the old man answers:

> Ce que je sais de ces héros, je le tiens de mon père, qui l'avait appris des Muses elles-mêmes, car autrefois les Muses immortelles visitaient, dans les antres et les bois, les chanteurs divins. Je ne mêlerai point de mensonges aux antiques récits.[4]

No one among Mégès' guests would have been interested in an original chant. Although he relied on the literary heritage, Homer was a poet, but he had to conceal the fruit of his own creative genius from his patrons: "Il composait lui-même des chants presque tout entiers. Mais il n'avouait pas qu'ils étaient son ouvrage de peur qu'on y trouvât à redire."[5] There is a delightful paradox here for a modern writer who, in his own way, imitates and invents as Homer did, but tends to keep his sources secret, as everyone expects him to produce something totally unprecedented; and modern critics, who put a high premium on "originality", are quite often ready to charge contemporary bards with plagiarism. This does not seem to bother France. After all, Boileau, the preceptor of the French Parnassus, recommends *imitatio* as a legitimate creative procedure: "Entre ces deux excès la route est difficile. / Suivez, pour la trouver, Théocrite et Virgile"[6] or: "Imitons de Marot l'élégant badinage."[7] He cites Tibullus and Ovid as models for lyrical poets.[8]

The scope of France's imitations has been amply documented in many longer studies and articles. Woolsey establishes the density of classical references and imitations; France apparently refers to the

[4] *O.C.*, XIII, p. 18.
[5] *Ibid.*
[6] Boileau, *op. cit.*, Chant II, vv. 53-54.
[7] *Ibid.*, Ch. I, v. 56.
[8] *Ibid.*, Ch. IV, vv. 111-114.

"Ce n'était pas jadis sur ce ton ridicule
Qu'amour dictait les vers que soupirait Tibulle,
Ou que, du tendre Ovide animant les doux sons,
Il donnait de son art les charmantes leçons."

Greek authors 629 times, to Latin masters 673 times, and to mythological subjects 757 times.[9] Walton analyzes and illustrates the influence of the Greek world on France's thought and art. France indirectly draws from antiquity through Racine, whose tragedies and style offer so many lessons in masterful *imitatio.* Des Hons examines in detail Racine's influence on France and amply illustrates the density and variety of Racinian echoes in France's subject matter and style.[10] Des Hons finds that Racine's influence is the most remarkable aesthetic trait of France's wit. The scholar's commentary on the literary relationship certainly resembles Petrarch's inspiration and working technique.

[9] Woolsey, *op. cit.*, abstract, p. 5. "He has alluded to Virgil and his poems fifty times in excess of his nearest rival, Homer."

[10] Des Hons, *op. cit.*, pp. 26-27: "Racine, dans sa *Phèdre,* a donné à l'expression des troubles élémentaires de l'amour une forme que le Maître tient pour définitive et ne croit pouvoir mieux faire que d'adapter à son propre texte aussi fidèlement que celui-ci s'y prête:

Je le vis, *je rougis, je pâlis* à sa vue;
Un trouble s'éleva dans mon âme éperdue;
Mes yeux ne voyaient plus, je ne pouvais parler ... (*Phèdre*)

... la voix mordante et les mouvements insidieux de cette créature *me jetèrent dans un trouble inconnu. Je pâlis, je rougis, mes yeux se voilèrent, ma langue sécha dans ma bouche, je ne pouvais* me mouvoir. (*La Révolte des Anges*) *Je rougis, je pâlis, ... il me fut impossible de parler.* (*Balthasar*) Hélène *avait la gorge sèche, ... ses yeux ne voyaient plus* ... (*Jocaste*) Elle le regarda tandis qu'il parlait et elle vit qu'il était beau. Soudain ... elle *devint verte comme l'herbe; ... un nuage descendit sur ses paupières. ... sa langue s'était subitement desséchée dans sa bouche; un tumulte effrayant s'élevait dans sa tête.* Tout à coup *son regard se voila* et il ne vit plus devant lui qu'un nuage épais. (*Thaïs*), or: *ibid.*, pp. 183-84: "Non, non, le temps n'est plus que Néron, jeune encore, Me renvoyait les vœux d'une cour qui l'adore ... Et que, derrière un voile, *invisible et présente,* J'étais de ce grand corps l'âme toute puissante. (*Britannicus*) *Invisible* aux païens, il était *présent* à la fois dans toutes les assemblées des chrétiens ... (*Thaïs*) Les mères athéniennes craignaient Némésis, cette déesse toujours *présente,* jamais *visible* ... (*Le Livre de mon Ami*) ... Si [dans les écrits des métaphysiciens] l'on mettait en lumière le sens primitif et concret, qui demeure *invisible et présent* sous le sens abstrait et nouveau, on trouverait des idées bien étranges et parfois peut-être instructives. (*Le Jardin d'Épicure*) L'association de ces deux termes est si étroite dans l'esprit d'Anatole France, que l'antonyme même de l'un y appelle aussitôt l'autre, ou l'antonyme de cet autre: ... tous les saints, tous les anges parleraient en vers ... Ils seraient *visibles et présents* ... (*La Vie littéraire*) ... mademoiselle Lefort, *visible,* mais *absente.* (*De Livre de mon Ami*)" The critic's paginal references were not retained.

Peu à peu et de plus en plus étroitement, il se rattache à cette tradition grecque et latine hors de laquelle il professe bientôt "qu'il n'est qu'erreur et que trouble". Et Jean Racine lui en apparaissant comme le plus parfait symbole, il le pratique avec amour. Le sachant par cœur, il le relit encore, "lui demande presque chaque jour le secret des justes pensées et des paroles limpides", et, de cet incessant commerce, résulte chez le Maître, entre son propre génie et celui du poète, par *imprégnation* mentale, force attractive de leurs *affinités* naturelles, une étroite combinaison, un pur alliage classique, sur quoi toute influence décomposante, qu'elle souffle du romantisme, du naturalisme, de l'exotisme ou du symbolisme, demeure sans effet.[11]

France's frame of reference actually embraces all the periods, and his art is pervaded with other equally significant influences. Assessing the role of medieval culture in France's art and inspiration, Alvida Ahlstrom uses the same term as Des Hons: "... les œuvres d'Anatole France témoignent d'un vif intérêt pour l'art médiéval. Il est comme *imprégné* de la vue des monuments de cet âge, et des images en viennent souvent sous sa plume, en métaphores dont la fréquence est remarquable."[12] She identifies many medieval sources. She sets side by side the texts of *Scolastica* and the *Histoire des Francs* by Grégoire de Tours, and, quoting France, she outlines the extent of the borrowing.

Grégoire de Tours a fourni la matière d'un des contes d'Anatole France, qui indique lui-même la source de cette *Histoire des Amants d'Auvergne* ou *Scolastica*, comme il l'appelle en la mettant dans un recueil de contes: "Je la rapporte à peu de chose près comme elle est dans Grégoire de Tours, qui l'a prise sans doute à quelque hagiographe plus ancien."[13]

In other instances the *imitatio* is very short. The cited biblical "Acel-dama" – *prix du sang* –[14] is a typical example. Floyd Zulli Jr. points out that the statement from the opening of *Le Lys rouge*, "Amour et gentil cœur sont une même chose", is "a compliment of imitation bestowed by France on Dante". It is the Dantean "Amore e'l cor gentil sono una cosa".[15] France treats his later sources just as he does

[11] Des Hons, *op. cit.*, p. 278.
[12] Ahlstrom, *op. cit.*, pp. 30, 31. Italics are mine.
[13] *Ibid.*, p. 56. See also p. 183, n. 11.
[14] See Ch. V, n. 64.
[15] "Anatole France and Dante" Modern Language Notes. Vol. LXIX, June 1954, No. 6, p. 420 *Dante Vita Nuova,* Ch. XX v. 1 of the opening sonnet.

the ancient and medieval texts. Sometimes he adapts major portions of specific works; sometimes he merely borrows an idea. In such case an accurate diagnosis of *imitatio* may present some difficulties, especially where the subjects are parallel but independent. For example, Ryland discusses the literary pilgrimage of the flying bed in France's "Joyeux Buffalmacco". In spite of a motto cited from Vasari's *Vite de' più eccellenti pittori*, Ryland claims that France has borrowed the subject from "Le Président mystifié", one of the twenty-six unpublished short stories by the Marquis de Sade he discovered around 1880. The Marquis, in his turn, imitated Gatien de Courtilz de Sandras' *Mémoires de M. d'Artagnan*, which also inspired Dumas.[16] Although most improbable, the source indicated by Ryland may have played a limited role in France's inspiration.[17]

Sareil rectifies the older critical generalizations which tend to overestimate France's debt to Voltaire. The critic states that, in spite of his astonishing knowledge of Voltaire's work, France does not derive his subjects from it. Voltaire is his master, but France's similar technique and tone indicate a similar temperamental and philosophical make-up rather than *imitatio*.[18] Like any ingenious spokesman of his race, France assimilates in his art many striking influences. To the literary

[16] Hobart Ryland, "Anatole France, le Marquis de Sade, et Courtilz de Sandras", *Kentucky Foreign Language Quarterly*, IV, p. 200-04.

[17] In one of his notes Sareil (*op. cit.*, p. 26, n. 11) challenges Ryland's conclusion that "Buffalmacco's" precedent is not "Le président mystifié" but Vasari, whom other critics and France designate as his source.

[18] Sareil, *op. cit.*, p. 432. "S'il y a ressemblance c'est par cette démolition systématique et réjouie de tout ce qui d'ordinaire est considéré comme respectable: le style voltairien consiste en une accumulation de catastrophes traitées gaiement ... Voilà donc tout ce que France a emprunté à Voltaire dans quelques unes de ses meilleures œuvres: le ton. Mais ce qu'il a trouvé en lui, et qui, est bien plus important même si on ne peut exactement le mesurer, c'est un modèle et un symbole. Voltaire est pour France un maître. . Après un siècle et demi, il a trouvé un successeur. ... le maître et le disciple me paraissent dignes l'un de l'autre."

Generally, the *imitatio* of the specific eighteenth century topics seem to be inspired by more obscure authors. For example, Léon Carias ("Quelques sources d'Anatole France", *La Grande Revue,* December 25, 1912 pp. 725-37), tracing the origin of the Salamanders and of M. d'Astarac, compares Père Ant. Androl's *Les Génies assistans et Gnomes irreconciliables ou suite au Comte de Gabalis* with a passage in *La Rôtisserie.* The dependence on Androl's text is quite evident. See also Bancquart, *op. cit.*, pp. 238 q.s.

models and ancestors of France already mentioned one could add Marot, Rabelais, Ronsard, Montaigne, Molière, La Fontaine, Montesquieu, Diderot, Leconte de Lisle, Verlaine.

To add the *couleur locale* to his prose France integrates folk songs, epitaphs or bizarre epigraphs, sometimes merely to achieve a striking contrast between prose and song, between libertinage and pedantry. In the conversation between Abbé Coignard and the libertine nobleman, M. d'Anquétil, France sets against the obscure details of ancient history an ambiguous, risqué chanson:

> – Je me fiche de votre Zozime, répondit M. d'Anquétil ... Je m'en fiche comme le Roi de sa première maîtresse.
>
> Et il chanta:
>
> Pour dresser un jeune courrier
> Et l'affermir sur l'étrier
> Il lui fallait une routière,
> Laire lan laire.
>
> – Qu'est-ce que ce Zozime?
>
> – Zozime, monsieur, répondit l'abbé, Zozime de Panopolis, était un savant grec ... qui composa des traités sur l'art spagirique.[19]

An obscure *chanson* with grotesquely primitive rhymes is integrated in a digressive anecdote in the same novel to drive home the bitter moral lesson given to the *rôtisseur* Quoniam by the generous and influential lover of his wife. Suspecting his Mariette when she appears "parée comme une chasse", Quoniam surprises them *in flagranti.* But this does not reform his marriage; the lover has the husband arrested and sent to Mississippi. Thus the *rôtisseur* and the reader learn that "un mari sage et commode // n'ouvre les yeux qu'à demi", and that "il vaut mieux être à la mode, // que de voir Mississipi".[20] The evocation of the song "Ce sont les dragons qui viennent // Maman sauvons nous."[21] introduces the brief character sketch of Bluebeard's brother-in-law, Cosme de Lespoisse, a vicious hussar, who far exceeds the reputation attributed to the dragoons. In fact it would be impossible to find any other such "grand paillard, écornifleur" and "bas coquin"[22] in the two regiments of His Majesty. Woolsey sums up and

[19] *O.C.*, VIII, p. 165.
[20] *Ibid.*, pp. 210-11.
[21] *O.C.*, XIX, p. 146.
[22] *Ibid.*

comments on Latin inscriptions and on epitaphs used as mottoes or directly integrated in the text:

Of the Latin epitaphs mentioned by Anatole France in his books, the one which probably meant most to him was that prepared by Boileau for Racine, situated in the church of Saint-Etienne-du-Mont. Here the aged scholar resorted now and then to commune with the spirit of the great poet of classical France. The first line of the eulogy France quotes in *l'Histoire Comique*: "Hic jacet nobilis vir Johannes Racine." [23]

Such references are effective only if they are amalgamated with the main theme. If the interpolated subject is not fully integrated, the aesthetic significance of the *imitatio* becomes dubious. For example, in *Le Chat maigre* M. Godet Laterasse, tutor of Remi Sainte-Lucie, introduces, apropos of nothing, the beginning of Chapter XVII of Book XIII of Tacitus' *Annales*:

. . . il entrait haletant dans la chambre de son élève et s'écriait:
– Piochons le Tacite! Courage!
Il disait avec emphase: *Nox eadem Britannici necem atque rogum conjunxit.* Puis il s'embarrassait dans quelques difficultés grammaticales et s'en tirait par des considérations très vagues sur le grand écrivain qui marque d'un fer rouge, disait-il, le front des tyrans.
La leçon aisi terminée, il se levait . . .[24]

The reader's curiosity is immediately "excited" by such a quotation but the excitement vanishes as soon as he discovers that the Latin text does not have any deeper bearing on the content. Any quotation would do; none at all would be best. In his later works France imitates more judiciously and his art of *imitatio* becomes a source of rare and varied themes.

A complete and accurate identification of all an author's sources is essential in a historical assessment of his art. In an aesthetic analysis, although a thorough historical knowledge of the author's life, work and sources is important, the accent is necessarily on his artistic treatment of the material. In his borrowings and imitations France most often seeks stylistic or topical inspiration, either to help him reach poetic heights or to provide bizarre forgotten themes for modern

[23] Woolsey, *op. cit.*, p. 59.
[24] *O.C.*, II, p. 179.

parody. Miss Ahlstrom's very extensive comparison of France's "Scolastica" and the text of Gregoire de Tours is a perfect example of a parodied legend. The first part exemplifies the extensive use of *imitatio rerum* as well as *verborum*; his *pointe* is a case of satirical *dissimulatio* or of *extensio*.[25]

In "Le Gab d'Olivier", an adaptation of the *Pèlerinage de Charlemagne*, France depends much less on the original than in "Scolastica". The miracles described in the *Pèlerinage* lend themselves ideally to a typical Francean parody. Returning from his pilgrimage to the Holy Land, bringing home to France some exquisite relics, the emperor Charlemagne and his entourage of twelve peers pay a visit to King Hugo of Constantinople. They are royally received and after the banquet the King accommodates them in a dormitory, the arched ceiling of which is supported by a column. Before retiring, the imperial guests entertain themselves by making fantastic boasts, ridiculing and disparaging their host, his family, and his knights.

In France's version, the Emperor opens the boasting contest, just as he does in the *Pèlerinage*.

> E dist carlem̄ ben dei auant gabber
> Li reis hugun li forz nen ad nul bacheler
> De tute sa maine qi tant seit fort mēbre
> Ait uestu dous haubers & dous hames fermeet
> Si seit sur un destrer curant suiurnet
> Li reis me prestet sa espee al poin dor adubet
> Si ferrai sur les heaumus u il erēt plus chers
> Trancherai les haubercs & les heaumes gēmez
> Le feutre od la sele del destrer suiurnez
> Le branc en t're si io le les aler
> Ia nē ert mes receuz par nul hume charnel
> Tresq; il seit pleine haunste de t're desteret . . .[26]

Economy and dramatic pace are undeniable merits of France's *imitatio rerum*.

– Qu'on m'amène à cheval et tout armé le meilleur chevalier du roi Hugon. Je lèverai mon épée et l'abattrai sur lui d'une telle force qu'elle fendra heaume, haubert, selle et cheval, et que la lame s'ira enfoncer d'un pied sous terre.[27]

[25] Gmelin, *op. cit.*, p. 357.
[26] *Le Pèlerinage de Charlemagne,* Anna J. Cooper, ed. (Paris, La Lure, 1925).
[27] *O.C.*, XIX, p. 6.

When all peers have finished, the column in the middle of the room opens and King Hugon walks out.

Cette colonne était creuse et disposée de telle sorte qu'un homme pût s'y cacher à l'aise pour tout voir et tout entendre. C'est ce que ne savaient point Charlemagne et les douze comtes. Aussi furent-ils bien surpris d'en voir sortir le roi de Constantinople. Il était pâle de colère, ses yeux étincelaient.

Il dit d'une voix terrible:

– C'est donc ainsi que vous reconnaissez l'hospitalité que je vous donne, hôtes discourtois? Voilà une heure que vous m'offensez par vos vanteries insolentes. Or, sachez-le, sire et chevaliers, si demain vous n'accomplissez tous vos gabs, je vous ferai couper la tête.[28]

In the original poem, "li reis hugun li forz" does not spy personally but: "en la cābre desuz un pun marbrin // desuz cauez si ad un hume mis".[29] Only when the Emperor and his knights finish their boasting and fall asleep does the spy leave to inform the King:

> Quant li cūte unt gabet si sen st' ēdormit
> Li eschut ist de cambre q' trestut ad oit
> Vint al us de la cābre u li reis hug' gist . . . [30]

In the imitated epos the boasts are fulfilled in a different sequence and the King never gives Charlemagne the chance to fulfill his *gab*. Three examples of the knights' superhuman valor convince him that any further challenge to his guests and to their divine relics would not be wise. But in France's parody Hugon does not hesitate to sacrifice his best knight just to test Charlemagne's skill and strength. When the Emperor complains that his rival is late, Hugon orders his best warrior to meet Charlemagne. The same economy and irony dominate in the description of Charlemagne's swordmanship. "Hugon le manda. Il vint. C'était un chevalier d'une haute taille et bien armé. Le bon Empereur le coupa en deux, comme il l'avait dit."[31] The title alone of France's adaptation indicates an essential shift in emphasis in the treated theme. In spite of the calculated eroticism of Olivier's bet,[32]

[28] *Ibid.*, p. 11.
[29] *Pèlerinage, ed. cit.*, vv. 437-440.
[30] *Ibid.*, vv. 618-620.
[31] *O.C.*, XIX, p. 14.
[32] *Pèlerinage, ed. cit.*, vv. 484-489.

the anonymous epos tends to magnify the miraculous power of the relics the Emperor is bringing from Jerusalem. France, however, makes Olivier's offer to gratify the Royal Princess one hundred times within a single night the focal point of his adaptation. While treating the remaining twelve "bets" as economically as the Emperor's *gab*, France extends Olivier's boast. He endows the medieval knight with the rudiments of humanistic upbringing and with taste and *esprit*; invited by the Emperor to present his *gab*, Olivier first recalls an ancient precedent.

– Mon fils, lui dit-il, ne voulez-vous point gaber aussi?
– Volontiers, sire, répondit Olivier. Connaissez-vous Hercules de Grèce?
– On m'en a fait quelques discours, dit Charlemagne. C'était une idole des mécréants, à la manière du faux dieu Mahom.
– Non point, sire, dit Olivier. Hercules de Grèce fut chevalier chez les paiens et roi de quelque royaume. Il était homme bon et bien formé de tous ses membres. S'étant rendu à la cour d'un empereur qui avait cinquante filles pucelles, il les épousa toutes la même nuit, si bien que le lendemain matin elles se trouvèrent toutes femmes bien satisfaites et instruites. Car il n'avait fait injure à aucune. Or, s'il vous plaît, sire, je ferai mon gab à l'exemple d'Hercules de Grèce.[33]

At this point the *gabeur* inspired by Greek mythology is interrupted and the subsequent repartee between Charlemagne and Olivier introduces the details of the libertine *gab*.

– Gardez-vous-en, mon fils Olivier, s'écria l'Empereur. Ce serait péché. Je pensais bien que ce roi Hercules était un Sarrasin.
– Sire, reprit Olivier, sachez que je compte faire dans le même temps, avec un seule pucelle, ce que Hercules de Grèce fit avec cinquante. Et cette pucelle sera princesse Hélène, fille du roi Hugon.
– A la bonne heure! dit Charlemagne. Ce sera agir honnêtement et de façon chrétienne. Mais vous avez eu tort, mon fils, de mettre les cinquante pucelles du roi Hercules dans votre affaire, où, quand le diable y serait, je n'en vois qu'une.
– Sire, répondit doucement Olivier, il n'y en a qu'une à la vérité. Mais elle recevra de moi telle satisfaction que, si je nombre les témoignages de mon amour, on verra le lendemain matin cinquante croix au mur. C'est là mon gab.[34]

[33] *O.C.*, XIX, p. 8.
[34] *Ibid.*, pp. 8-11.

In the source the Princess, afraid of excess, collaborates with the gallant knight, who satisfies her only thirty times in exchange for a promise that she will tell her royal father that the bet was fulfilled to the letter.[35] In the modern version Olivier is not given the chance to fulfill his *gab* first. His achievement is reserved for the finale. France mischievously rectifies the moral flaw of the legend: prior to the proof of his vigor, the chaste Christian pilgrim has to be married to the Princess Hélène to avoid sin.[36] Thus France converts an episode of a religious epos into a subtle Boccaccian farce. The gloating King is sure he will see his new son-in-law beheaded, but the Princess disappoints him by confessing the *gab* to be fulfilled.[37] Another deviation from the source is Charlemagne's skeptical question addressed to Olivier's happy spouse and her natural answer.

Mais confiez-moi cela en grand secret: Avez-vous dit la vérité?
Elle répondit:
– Sire, Olivier ... m'a distraite par tant de gentillesses et de mignardises, que je n'ai point songé à compter. Il n'y a pas songé davantage.[38]

The previous analysis of France's poetic technique points out the Francean echoes of dactylic prosody, of pastoral lyricism and of the primitive rhyming of the legends. He stimulates his own tragic pathos by an intimate contact with Racine's tragedies and with the Greek myths.

In *Les Dieux ont soif*, France foreshadows Evariste Gamelin's destiny by suggesting the similarity between him and Orestes.[39] To emphasize the parallel France invents a situation which allows him to integrate in his text a longer quotation from Euripides' *Orestes* and a socialite, Louise Masché de Rochemaure, bedizened in an impressive hat, comes to ask the painter the favour of introducing her to Marat. In passing, she notices Evariste's paintings and the satirical sketch of

[35] *Pèlerinage, ed. cit.*, vv. 703-731.
[36] *O.C.*, XIX, p. 15.
[37] *Ibid.*
[38] *Ibid.*, p. 16.
[39] Walton, *op. cit.*, p. 275. "In *Les Dieux ont soif,* Evariste Gamelin fulfils his destiny like a Greek tragic hero of Sophoclean proportions." See also an extensive interpretation in Levaillant's *op. cit.*, p. 761, q.s.

the social climber is interrupted. The reader's attention is focused on a striking painting of *Oreste veillé par Electra sa sœur*. The *mondaine* expresses interest in the reclining man whose mouth is covered with the foam of madness. The artist, in explaining the subject, recalls the scene of Euripides' tragedy which inspired his canvas:

– Le sujet ... est tiré de l'*Oreste* d'Euripide. J'avais lu, dans une traduction déjà ancienne ... une scène qui m'avait frappé d'admiration; celle où la jeune Electre, soulevant son frère sur son lit de douleur, essuie l'écume qui lui souille la bouche, ... et prie ce frère chéri d'écouter ce qu'elle lui va dire dans le silence des Furies ... En lisant ... je sentais comme un brouillard qui me voilait les formes grecques. ... Je m'imaginais le texte original plus nerveux et ... j'allai prier monsieur Gail, ... de m'expliquer cette, scène mot à mot. ... Ainsi, Electre dit à Oreste: "Frère chéri, que ton sommeil m'a causé de joie! Veux-tu que je t'aide à te soulever?" Et Oreste répond: "Oui, aide-moi, prends-moi, et essuie ces restes d'écume attachés autour de ma bouche et de mes yeux. Mets ta poitrine contre la mienne et écarte de mon visage ma chevelure emmêlée: car elle me cache les yeux ..." Tout plein de cette poésie si jeune et si vive, de ces expressions naives et fortes, j'esquissai le tableau que vous voyez, citoyenne.[40]

Carried away by the lyrical pathos of his subject and encouraged by his visitor, Gamelin recalls Hennequin's masterful interpretation of the myth:

Oreste nous émeut encore plus dans sa tristesse que dans ses fureurs. Quelle destinée que la sienne! C'est par piété filiale, par obéissance à des ordres sacrés qu'il a commis ce crime dont les Dieux doivent l'absoudre, mais que les hommes ne pardonneront jamais. Pour venger la justice outragée, il a renié la nature, il s'est fait inhumain, il s'est arraché les entrailles. Il reste fier sous le poids de son horrible at vertueux forfait.[41]

This *imitatio* is not an incidental detail but a carefully chosen mold for the whole theme. It enables France to leap suddenly from caricature to the heights of tragedy. Its digressive nature is not an imperfection; it elevates the central conflict to a myth; it becomes the bowstring which sends the "arrow of desire" toward the tragic clouds. Orestes' quest for justice and his crime become those of Gamelin, and the

[40] *O.C.*, XX, pp. 86-87.
[41] *Ibid.*, p. 87.

painter's sympathy for the mythological hero becomes the *leitmotif* of the novel.

Also in *Les Dieux ont soif*, Brotteaux, awaiting his execution in jail, seeks stoic consolation in reading his Lucretius Carus. The *imitatio* opens the vast perspective of death and eternity, but its serenity creates a soothing counter-point to the anxiety and the frustration of the prisoners.[42] All multiple aspects of Francean *imitatio* reveal that ancient medieval classical and modern literary traditions, in fact the occidental culture in the broadest sense, form France's frame of reference.

Any effort to reduce it to insignificant dimensions would seem to be a critical contrivance. Walton challenges the conclusions of Cerf, who interprets France's imitations of the Ancients, not as "Atticism" or "classicism", but as "Alexandrianism", and who sees in them decadent artistic manifestations of a degenerate genius.[43]

> Was France an Alexandrian in his taste for such evocations? Certainly not when, with his artistic gift for external effects, he preferred to probe the moral truth of ancient life rather than dwell on the surface of things. He did not view Greek culture from the standpoint of petty imitation, which characterized the men of the Mousaion with all their learning. Greece to him was a form of the life of the human mind, not a set of artistic formulae, wise though he was in such matters.[44]

This re-evaluation is significant, not only because it is based on a very broad knowledge of the Greek culture and France's work, but because

[42] *Ibid.*, pp. 241-42. "Quand germinal ramena les jours clairs, Brotteaux, qui était voluptueux, descendit plusieurs fois par jour dans la cour qui donnait sur le quartier des femmes, ... Une grille séparait les deux quartiers; mais les barreaux n'en étaient pas assez rapprochés pour empêcher les mains de se joindre et les bouches de s'unir. Sous la nuit indulgente, des couples s'y pressaient.

Alors Brotteaux, discrètement se refugiait dans l'escalier et, assis sur une marche, tirait de la poche ... son petit Lucrèce, et lisait, à la lueur d'une lanterne, quelques maximes sévèrement consolatrices: '*Sic ubi non erimus* ... Quand nous aurons cessé de vivre, rien ne pourra nous émouvoir, non pas même le ciel, la terre et la mer confondant leurs débris ...' " See also pp. 26 and 160-61.

[43] Cerf, *op. cit.*, pp. 259-86.

[44] Walton, *op. cit.*, p. 273.

it marks a different trend in Francean criticism.[45] It substantiates the high value Stapfer placed on Francean *autre chose*[46] of which *imitatio* is an important aspect.

[45] More recently, Levaillant (*op. cit.*, p. 804-5) evaluates France's aesthetic assimilation of antiquity and its transformation into art. "Le très long récit de Nectaire s'attarde sur l'hellénisme, quand Satan parmi les hommes a pris la forme de Dionysos, premier auteur de la science et de la joie. Hellénisme de routine? Bien sûr, si l'on considère seulement les poncifs parnassiens d'une Hellade édénique qui encombrent le chant de Nectaire. Rien, dans cet éloge de Dionysos, sur les aspects tragiques de la pensée grecque; rien, même, sur la tragédie en tant que forme d'art. Du Ménard, du Chénier de convention, alors que Nietzche et ses commentateurs avaient fait connaître le côté nocturne de l'enthousiasme dionysiaque." But the same critic hastens to add that Nectaire's flute offers more than a shallow, idealized version of antiquity (*ibid.*, p. 805): "Nectaire n'est pas seulement celui qui enseigne les plaisirs simples de Dionysos: un autre jour sa flûte chante aussi la brièveté de l'univers, la mort inévitable de la terre, du soleil et des astres; sans angoisse, avec une sérénité qui accepte le néant, Nectaire apprend aux hommes à vivre en accord avec la nature. La Grèce qu'il décrit n'est faite que d'harmonie et de sagesse, parce qu'après s'être lassé de l'absurde, France exprime son besoin de retrouver une certaine participation à l'ensemble des choses: ... Contrairement à la vérité cette dernière Grèce de France ne connaît ni tensions ni conflits: ... les dieux ne sont pour lui qu'un facteur d'intégration entre les hommes, la société et la nature. La culture de la Grèce selon lui ne sépare pas la notion du divin de celle de l'homme, ... Seule tension qui subsiste: la curiosité intellectuelle, dépouillée de toute forme du tragique intérieur aux passions. Ainsi l'esprit seul conserve le droit à l'inquiétude créatrice: c'est une sagesse humaniste ouverte sur la connaissance relative, une sagesse qui ne tient plus compte de l'éternel. .... Mais cette naturalisation de l'homme resterait superficielle, si ne l'accompagnait la découverte de la beauté.

[46] See p. 90 of this study.

CONCLUSION *

France's thought is dynamic. His work reflects many shades of *pessimisme jouisseur*, yet his lifelong wisdom, for all its evolution and range is homogeneous. Like Epicure, he thinks that the goal of life is pleasure, and his art reflects this hedonistic belief. Pleasure is not merely sensual; it is the many-sided experience of all human faculties. Francean pleasure implies agreeable sensual stimulation, intellectual inspiration, and the spiritual enjoyment provoked by human love, pity, and irony, which he says is the joy of wisdom; Francean pleasure implies heroic pathos which springs from man's awareness of his own tragic destiny. Art offers to man's imagination the same range of sensual and spiritual enjoyment. Its practical goal is to give pleasure; its ideal goal is the creation of beauty, which to France is the purest form of joy. He believes that the aesthetic enjoyment a writer offers should not require any excessive effort, intellectual or spiritual, from the reader. "A mon sens, le poète ou le conteur, pour être tout à fait galant homme, évitera de causer la moindre peine, de créer la moindre difficulté à son lecteur. Pour faire sagement il n'exigera point l'attention; il la surprendra."

There are various ways of surprising the reader and of stimulating his imagination. The main thing is to offer him something he does not know or which he does not expect, thus satisfying his inborn hunger for novelty and change. France writes: "il nous faut du nouveau. On nous dit: 'Que voulez-vous?' Et nous répondons: 'Je veux autre chose.' " In France's work is an abundance of "autre chose". This *autre chose* surprises the reader's imagination and, through it, stimulates his intellectual and sensual and intuitive faculties. Such an aesthetic value has many significant topical and formal aspects. For

* Only the citations not quoted previously are footnoted.

this reason, any general critical evaluation which tries to prove that one or two "dominant" qualities of France's art or of his temperament are particular "keys" to his art is open to the charge of over-simplification. This study has attempted to specify and analyze features of style and content that are typical of France's art and that are rooted in his natural inclinations, his acquired personal and intellectual tastes, his practical philosophy and professed aesthetic principles. Emphasizing France's style, a relatively less studied area of his art, this work explains some of the techniques behind the magic conversion of subject matter into an aesthetic value. Various excerpts show the force of surprise in an obscure, rare, exotic, obsolete, or slangy term, or a *mot juste*, and, at the same time their importance in *couleur locale*, in subtle characterization, or in the mood of the text. France exploits all the traditional figures of speech to dramatize his subject matter, oxymorons, antitheses, numerous periphrases, understatements, euphemisms, hyperbole, metaphors, similes, and other less common rhetorical effects. These are welcome "deviations" from gray lexical or syntactic normalcy. The same can be said of the aphorism and the florid sentence. The musicality of France's prose is another rich source of aesthetic enjoyment. Extensive illustrations show France's use of rhythm, rhyme, harmony, assonances, and sonorous euphonies. In some instances, his prose is so pervaded with rhythm that it is possible to arrange it into one or more versions of free verse.

To express a mythical atmosphere in rhythmical terms, France creates an illusion of ancient metric prosody, in particular, dactylic hexameters. France also imitates the primitive rhymes and assonances of hagiographic literature in his parodies of the medieval legends. Often, to emphasize the pagan-Christian conflicts he is so fond of dramatizing, France parallels his topical contrasts with metrical contrasts: the pagan elements are expressed in harmonious *vers libres* which vaguely echo the dactyls; the Christian and medieval topics are stylized by primitive rhymes and assonances. Of course, France did not limit his use of rhythm and rhyme to the legends; he applied them in most of his works.

Veiling the subject in poetry is one of France's subtle skills. The harsh realities of life disappear; everything is suffused with a timeless charm or mysterious gloom. The lyrical effects in France's prose depend on a refined combination of poetic subject and exceptional stylistic skill. Radiant visions of mythical life as in "Amycus Célestin", "Le Saint Satyre", "Le Chanteur de Kymé", or in *La Révolte des anges*, are typical examples of this alliance of lyrical style and matter. The Greco-Roman past is not the only source of France's rich lyrical inspiration. He finds poetry everywhere: in the arid sands of Africa, along the snowy road which leads to the ominous gate of M. d'Astarac's lonely mansion, in Brotteaux's attic, facing the night skies over revolutionary France, or under the elm tree where M. Bergeret meditates about the futility of life. France is able to grasp and make permanent the poetry of each situation. Blanck, who pays little attention to Des Hons's findings and no attention to Becker and who concludes that France's stylistic skill is *Plauderstil*, seems nearly deaf to the rhythm of his prose; he does not analyze rhymes and euphonies in France's prose at all, and thus weakens his own conclusions.

Most critics of France's style emphasize his extraordinary stylistic ease, but France himself points out that such ease is usually an illusion. He compares a good style to a sun ray: its complex nature is revealed only if it is resolved into a spectrum. His own style ideally exemplifies his thesis. It is clear, precise, concise, and it projects the subject matter in elegant contours and shades. His rhymes, assonances, alliterations, and numerous euphonies give his prose a pleasing melody and his rhythms give it graceful cadence. France's art of expression was inspired by the finest influences in the French tradition: La Fontaine's charming free verse, the disciplined lyricism of Racine, Voltaire's elegant art of satirical understatement and the musicality of Verlainean diction. France does not resent all symbolist precepts. He combines Ciceronian lucidity with a musical diction worthy of any disciple of Mallarmé. An analysis of his diction and rhythmical, euphonious prose leaves little doubt that his extraordinary stylistic brilliance alone makes him a classic. The discipline of his diction, syntax and poetic technique is not always so evident in his composition. Yet the frequent charge of critics that France's works are poorly composed is not fully justified. The critics tend to forget that his short stories and essays, which represent a substantial part of his work, are generally well constructed. His novels are digressive and composed in the tradition of great *prosateurs* such as Rabelais, Cervantes, Lesage, Voltaire, Fielding,

Dickens or Gogol. Yet, like them, France turns this weakness to a relative advantage. His art of suave digression, comparable to that of Horace or La Fontaine, can stimulate like any other aesthetic feature. It is characteristic of him to use a short digressive subordinate clause for comical or unusual effects. France also weaves into his text countless digressive anecdotes, citations, and major interpolations. Some of them are detrimental to his art, others add aesthetic charm. Unity and economy of form is not an infallible dogma; it can occasionally be violated to advantage. The aesthetic glow of digression may stimulate the *connoisseur* and divert the average reader. Cerf's effort to diminish the artistic value of France's work because of its imperfect composition seems to be too dogmatic: many masterpieces of world literature are not well constructed, yet this flaw is not detrimental either to their significance or to their lasting popularity. Cerf's apodictic maxims, such as "Structure is a framework of drama" or "where there is no life there is no drama and no need of structure", cannot be considered fully substantiated critical arguments which could permanently negate the value of France's art. Besides, Cerf failed to prove persuasively that there was no drama and life in works such as *Jocaste*, *Les Désirs de Jean Servien*, "Balthasar", *Thaïs*, "Le Jongleur de Notre Dame", *Le Lys rouge*, "L'humaine tragédie", "Le Chanteur de Kymé", "Komm l'Atrébate", *L'Histoire comique*, *L'Histoire contemporaine*, "Crainquebille", *Les Dieux ont soif*, or *La Révolte des anges*; he also failed to prove that there was no structure in many of France's short stories and essays.

In spite of the vicissitudes of critical fashion, France will always rate with Shaw as the greatest satirist of his era, and with Rabelais, Molière and Voltaire as one of the greatest French wits. Much of this reputation depends on the excellence of his style, which is a faithful servant of his humor. Humor, irony in particular, is paramount in France's art. Some critics would hesitate to consider humor an aesthetic value. "... car l'humoriste est ... le contraire d'un artiste par l'espèce de perversité avec laquelle il se plaît à détruire la beauté de son propre ouvrage ..."[1] says Stapfer, who with the same breath expresses surprise and admiration that humor does not destroy the striking artistry

[1] Stapfer, the cited article, p. 240.

of France's literary achievements. Like Stapfer, Cerf and Chevalier dismiss irony as a doubtful artistic blessing but, unlike Stapfer, conclude that irony prevented France from reaching the heights which his great talent and genius could have attained.

This analysis considers humor as one of many aspects of art. It seems inaccurate to reduce the aesthetics of masterpieces such as *Thaïs*, "Balthasar", "Le Jongleur de Notre Dame", "Le Procurateur de Judée", "Le Saint Satyre", "Le Chanteur de Kymé", *Les Dieux ont soif*, and *La Révolte des anges* to irony alone. Besides, France's irony itself has diverse facets and effects. It can express many different attitudes: sympathy and gratitude, sardonic contempt and hatred, gentle blame, mischievous or melancholy joy. It may playfully draw a benign caricature or etch an acid satire. Grave and sublime irony, vehicles of France's significant themes, usually contain a latent paradox and do not always provoke laughter.

Although less significant in France's art than his irony, the second aspect of humor, farce, is by no means rare. His early novel, *Le Chat maigre*, is mainly farcical, and so is his collection of licentious short stories, *Les Sept Femmes de la Barbe-Bleue.* One finds highly farcical short stories in all his collections and long farcical passages are blended with irony and *gauloiseries* in all his major novels. Farce is not necessarily a low form of art, it is often sublime, especially when it is elevated to the metaphysical level.

Closely related to irony, are the many ambiguities, paradoxes, contradictions, and contrasts. These features, just as deservedly as irony, could be regarded as the "key" to France's art. Although less pervasive than pure irony, they are a constant ingredient in France's prose and create a variety of effects – many are comical and licentious, others are symbolic and, like irony, often express a higher universal meaning.

France's contradictions and paradoxes provide perhaps the sharpest spice of aesthetic surprise; they give an unmistakable tang to his prose. They often outgrow their aphoristic form and, like symbolism or grave irony, may suggest a universal meaning or reveal an unknown spiritual perspective. Thus the extended paradox is raised to a paradoxical controversy, or to major conflict. France, the skeptic and polemist, likes to dwell on the hidden discords in social and ethical conventions, general beliefs or philosophical and religious doctrines. These controversial ideas are disseminated through the typical Francean heroes, learned scholars, and wise men such as Bonnard, Nicias, Coignard, M. d'Astarac, Choulette, Bergeret, Doctor Trublet, and Brotteaux. The sagacious satyrs, fallen angels, and Satan are frequent challengers of Christian moral and social standards. *La Révolte des anges* dramatizes the most significant of France's paradoxical controversies. It formulates his pagan creed and expresses his profound sympathy for the underdog, Satan. Satan is not the supreme evil in France's view but a Promethean Lucifer, a friendly titan, who worships the two mythical charioteers, Apollo and Dionysos. France also depicts the clash between Christianity and paganism in several short stories, never failing to present paganism as a more charming and more natural cult.

Violent and tragic conflicts, described with shocking naturalistic detail in *Jocaste, Les Désirs de Jean Servien,* or *Les Dieux ont soif,* give readers "les frissons délicieux d'une piété tempérée et d'une terreur passagère".[2] Other conflicts, such as those in *La Rôtisserie de la Reine Pédauque* or "Komm l'Atrébate", are tragi-comical, while violence in parodies such as "Le Gab d'Olivier" or "Les Sept Femmes de la Barbe-Bleue" is pure farce.

Some of the violent topics may stimulate not by violence alone but by the heroism, bravery, or adventures related to such violence. Komm l'Atrébate's colorful adventures behind the enemy lines, the subject of "La Muiron", or Nectaire's song about the angels' mutiny, exemplify this type of stimulation. But physical courage, raw valor and heroic adventures are rare elements in France's work, because his favorite heroes are intellectuals with a propensity for humanistic speculations.

The moral indignation provoked by the non-violent, shocking topics is very similar to that excited by violence; it is merely less intense. For instance, the absurd execution of Jean Servien excites the same feelings as Abbé Lantaigne's apparently gross injustice to Piedagnel. As in the case of violent subjects, the general tone of the shocking, non-violent topics provokes either pathos, if the treatment is serious, or laughter, if it is comical.

France stimulates the reader by eroticism and *gauloiserie* in almost all his works. He has a sensual and hedonistic conception of love. In

[2] *O.C.*, XXI, p. 8.

this respect his erotic subjects are in the tradition of Ovid, Boccaccio, La Fontaine, and the *galant* literature of the eighteenth century. Without considering his early poetic work, it may be said that *Jocaste*, *Thais*, *Le Lys rouge*, *Histoire comique*, and *Les Dieux ont soif* contain France's serious love themes. The first novel is a subdued caricature of the Greek myth in a modern bourgeois setting. In *Thaïs*, France accuses Christianity of degrading to the level of sin the most obvious manifestation of love and of having stifled the most precious values in life: joy, charm and beauty. The third work dramatizes some aspects of the author's and Madame de Caillavet's love affair. France's empirical conclusion, that a profound, but jealous and intolerant, passion inevitably destroys itself, is reflected in *Le Lys rouge*, a nineteenth century version of the ancient *odi et amo*. *L'Histoire comique* describes the mysterious power of a fateful legacy sealed and enforced by the suicide of a jealous lover. Jealous love is one of the Erinyes which persecutes Gamelin, the eighteenth century Orestes.

Some of France's minor works are gems in the erotical literature of the nineteenth and twentieth centuries. The love play of the satyrs and nymphs in the "Saint Satyre", written in rhymed and rhythmical prose, dramatizes sensual, pagan eroticism, free of the slightest implication of sin. "La Fille de Lilith" tries to imagine the passion and ecstasies inspired by the supernatural, immortal daughters of Adam and his first wife, Lilith.

Libertinage characterizes the erotical themes in *La Rôtisserie de la Reine Pédauque*, and the *Contes de Jacques Tournebroche*; *gauloiserie* is the main feature of aesthetic stimulation in *Les Sept Femmes de la Barbe-Bleue*. The satirical tetralogy, *L'Histoire contemporaine*, as well as *L'Ile des Pingouins* and *La Révolte des anges* are full of *gauloiserie*. If the critics call France "M. Voltaire", they refer not only to his satirical genius but also to his hedonistic and libertine approach to love and sex.

France frequently stimulates less definite urges than the undeniable animal instincts of sex, fear and pugnacity. One of these is man's attraction towards the unknown. This curiosity is stimulated most intensely by the supernatural element: miracles and supernatural beings have always aroused human curiosity. A skeptic such as France would hardly take miracles, ghosts, angels and devils seriously, but they are one of his favorite topical ingredients. Walton, referring to France's skepticism, talks about his distaste for the miraculous.[3] France certainly satirizes the miraculous, but the term "distaste" does not seem to characterize France's attitude. France does not believe in the miracle, but the idea of it constantly amuses and attracts him. One might say that France has a taste for the supernatural, in spite of his irreverence toward it. This interest of the skeptic in the supernatural is one of the paradoxes in France's wisdom and in his art. It is reflected in the first comment made by the farcical hero, M. Boulingrin, when he awakes after a miraculous centennial sleep: "Rien n'est qui ne soit naturel."[4] France treats the supernatural element in three ways: he conceives it seriously, he uses it symbolically, or he treats it as a fraud and a source of parody. An example of France's rare serious treatment of the supernatural element would be "Le Jongleur de Notre Dame". Used as symbols, supernatural beings may represent the inexplicable physical and spiritual conflicts in life or its unknown creative forces. The surprise produced by these beings is sometimes enhanced by the paradoxical presentation of Satan as Prometheus, who loves man and suffers for him, and Jahve as a jealous parvenu who has no sense of beauty. But most frequently, the pagan and Judeo-Christian deities and saints are the targets of France's parody. The reader cannot help but be amused when France dramatizes these deities as our ancestors may have imagined them and as contemporary theologians, attached to religious traditions, persist in representing them to modern "believers". In a skeptical, materialistic age which "believes" only in what is natural and explicable by science, the supernatural subjects break the monotony of things. Supernatural and utopian elements form a substantial part of the subject matter in "La Fille de Lilith", *Thaïs, L'Etui de Nacre, La Rôtisserie de la Reine Pédauque, Le Puits de Sainte Claire,* "Par la porte de corne ou par la porte d'ivoire", *Les Contes de Jacques Tournebroche, Les Sept Femmes de la Barbe-Bleue, L'Ile des Pingouins,* and *La Révolte des anges.* In *La Vie littéraire,* France devotes a great deal of attention to supernatural topics: "L'Hypnotisme dans la littérature – Marfa", "Le Grand Saint Antoine", "Roman et Magie", "Un Moine égyptien", "Mysticisme et science", and others.

[3] Walton, *op. cit.,* 310.
[4] *O.C.*, XIX, p. 241.

It is irrelevant whether France believes in supernatural phenomena or whether he satirizes them. The fact that he treats supernatural and utopian topics so often, in an era of naturalistic and psychological novels, indicates that in his choice of subject matter France relies on the classical tradition, in which supernatural topics are a desirable source of aesthetic pleasure.

France's parodies of the old legends dealing with the supernatural keep the original exotic or historical setting. Both the exotic and the historical are typical aspects of what is designated in this study as *bizarrerie.* This term includes subjects striking for their oddness or strangeness. In general, *bizarrerie* contributes to the topical richness so characteristic of France's style, in the wider sense of the word. It illustrates, most unexpectedly, France's general ideas. In some instances, the *bizarrerie* borders on the controversial; in other cases it has a purely decorative function. France's controversial or comical heroes such as Tudesco, Bonnard, Coignard, Pigeonneau, or Bergeret, have a bizarre streak which usually originates in their humanism and in their unconventional social code. The minor *bizarreries* are decorative. Most of France's works include either a bizarre theme or at least a bizarre hero. Bizarre scenes and topics are especially evident in *Le Chat maigre, Le Crime de Sylvestre Bonnard, Thaïs, La Rôtisserie de la Reine Pédauque, Les Dieux ont soif, L'Ile des Pingouins, La Révolte des anges*, and in most of the short stories. France's bizarre heroes include Paphnuce, Marquis Tudesco, Choulette, and many characters from *L'Ile des Pingouins* and, from the short stories, heroes ranging from M. Pigeonneau to the Grand Saint Nicolas.

Aesthetic incongruities gain part of their effect from being "unexpected", but they excite chiefly by some rare or unusual quality, such as a sudden contrast or conflict, a supernatural element, humor, or eroticism. Occasionally, however, one finds in France's prose instances where unexpectedness is the main source of surprise, as in the description of the Christmas *bûche* which turns out to be a case containing flowers and a valuable manuscript, the suicide of a "most happy" man or the ruse of Mme Luzy. However, France exploits this type of feature moderately: too extensive a use would make it seem contrived. Many poetic passages and rare historical or literary allusions are consummate imitations of classical authors of all eras. Modern art and critics look with suspicion at *imitatio*, a technique which seemingly verges on plagiarism. But France disregards this attitude, taking ample advantage of the technique used by the ancient and Renaissance masters. The imitated topics and style broaden the frame of his artistic reference. They are not aesthetic ballast but a source of contrasts and decorations unusual in the literature of our materialist age. The most convincing justification of this technique is the fact that *imitatio* organically integrates France's life work into the realm of the *ars longa*, into a humanist tradition, which shaped all those he admired and which taught him how to speculate and how to write.

Like his Epicurean *Weltanschauung* and like his style and wit, France's life-long contact with classical literature strengthens both the formal and the spiritual cohesion of the whole work. His style and wit account for a great deal of structural unity; they assimilate and reconcile many discrepancies, but alone they could never account for an entirely harmonious synthesis of all aesthetic factors. To achieve this, the author has to express a coherent wisdom which can interpret, or at least face, any aspect of life.

Contrary to Cerf, who accuses France of having no teleology, and contrary to Chevalier, who accuses him of being unable to achieve a satisfactory major synthesis, this study has attempted to show that France had speculated intensely about the goal of life, had found it for himself, and conceived his own great synthesis. France has his goal of life, his great truth-joy. All his contemplations and all his efforts are subordinated to this Epicurean ideal. France's joy is composed of many joys: beauty, love, freedom, justice, pain and evil. Such a joy, which manages to reconcile the incompatible values of life, can be as worthy an ideal as Cerf's virile devotion to some other unspecified goal. In many ways, such a goal is much more universal and transcendent than the various specific ideologies preached by crusading artists of the present. France himself is a socialist but his socialism is integrated in a *Weltanschauung* which would not be acceptable or even comprehensible to some of the more doctrinaire or *engagé* intellectuals. Showing humanity the path of beauty towards the sublime joys of life is worthier than promoting the practical political goals of any government or movement. The really great humanists of all eras were rarely political lackeys. As for the lack of gravity of which the two critics (among others) accuse France, it remains to be proved that, if a writer regards the serious problems of life with an ironic smile, his judgments on these problems are in any way inferior to those pronounced with humorless gravity. One has a right to ask which of two equally qualified thinkers makes a more valuable contribution – the one with illusions about his conclusions, who thinks he has grasped the universal truth, or the one who doubts, with some justification, the veracity of his own and his colleagues' judgments.

It was suggested that it is time to have a fresh look, not only at France's art itself, but also at some of the generally accepted views of Francean critics. Although one cannot ignore the general trend of the criticism, one should not hesitate to assess the quality of the aesthetic speculations which constitute the trend. Without ascribing the paraphrased objections to any specific source, Bancquart sums up what seems to be the general climate of opinion among many French critics. She implies that the anonymous resentment of France's art is partially perpetuated by politically or moralistically oriented critics and by "Neoromantics" who accuse France's "reheated" humanism of solving the problems not from inside with intense conviction but superficially from outside and with a rational Voltairean detachment.

On lit toujours de ses œuvres; mais on ne lit guère que ses souvenirs d'enfance, *Thaïs, Le Rôtisserie de la Reine Pédauque, Les Dieux ont soif.* Aussi n'a-t-on de lui qu'une connaissance limitée. Il n'est pas toujours de bon ton d'attacher à l'écrivain une grande importance, même si l'on prend plaisir à le lire. Les uns admirent qu'il ait écrit dans une langue pure et harmonieuse, qui semble aux autres le comble de l'artifice et de la convention. Sa pensée choque parfois par son irrévérence, parfois semble déplorablement banale. Certains lui font grief d'avoir attaqué Mallarmé et les symbolistes, certains d'avoir été anticlérical.

On l'accuse parfoit d'avoir soutenu des idéologies "de gauche," parfois de n'être jamais allé jusqu'à l'engagement politique. Des reproches plus sérieux, parce qu'ils vont au cœur le l'œuvre, lui sont adressés: France n'a jamais créé puissamment; il pratique une sorte d'humanisme recuit, désormais insupportable! il est disert, mais non pénétrant, ne parle pas de manière à toucher, reste à l'extérieur des sentiments et des problèmes. Académicien, vedette d'un salon, tel il apparaît dans sa vie et dans son œuvre.[5]

[5] Bancquart, *op. cit.* p. 9. See also Levaillant (*op. cit.*, p. 823): "La désaffection des lecteurs d'aujourd'hui s'explique en quelque mesure parce que France paraît

Such views are not surprising. The experimenting pioneers of new aesthetic trends, inspired primarily by the symbolist cult of obscurity and the inexpressible, logically resent France's lucid Atticism: like a lighthouse beam, it pierces the darkness of absurdity, it is not swallowed by the night, it discovers there beauty and joy. As for the nationalists and Catholics, it would be a miracle, indeed, if most of them, like Charles Maurras,[6] managed to overcome their antipathy for the pagan *freigeist*. For Maurras it was less difficult, as he was *Romain* rather than *catholique*. In spite of France's political affiliation, the Marxists have not any reason to see in him an apostle of their creed either. If officially applauded, the Epicurian heresy of this left intellectual could even undermine from inside the very foundations of the

d'abord un écrivain de connaissance et non un traducteur d'expériences. A cette œuvre qu'on dit de plain pied, qu'on dit faite de culture et de goût plus que de création vraie, on reproche de ne pas comporter d'ombres, d'ignorer le mystère et l'imprévu de n'être liée à aucun secret." Carter Jefferson's historical study *Anatole France: The Politics of Skepticism* (New Brunswick, N. J., Rutgers University Press 1965), pp. 239-34, outlines the scope of France's political individualism (the conservative; the anarchist; the crusader; the socialist; the "Bolshevik"). He explains why, politically speaking, an intellectual like France is not a desirable fellow traveller of any political movement which enforces party discipline and professes infallibility of the party apparatus and of its doctrine. "Developed by Montaigne and Rabelais, carried on by such luminaries as Voltaire and Renan, the tradition of skeptical humanism has never been popular with zealots. It is conservative in its caution, yet conservatives distrust it because it dares to question. It is liberal in its humanitarianism, but apostles of change seldom like to be reminded that they may be wrong. France's defense of that tradition has won him many enemies. Before he died he was under attack from critics of the Right as a traitor to his nation, ... The old attacks continued after his death. He was even blamed for his country's defeat in World War II. Jean Dutourd, A Gaullist intellectual, writing in 1957 of the 'sniveling humanitarianism of the Moderate Left', identified that wicked doctrine with the 'paltry Bergeret who talks smoothly to us of freedom and justice but who has done everything to disarm France.' The Left has been only a little more friendly. An obituary that appeared in *La Vie ouvrière* a few days after France died gave him credit for sympathizing with the workers but said that his lack of a doctrine made him weak and vacillating. Marcel Cachin, writing in *l'Humanité* at about the same time, said much the same thing. More recently, in a highly laudatory anniversary article published in 1954, *l'Humanité* rehabilitated France by the simple expedient of speaking of him as if he had been a dedicated orthodox Communist. Socialists have generally been kinder when they bothered with France at all, but their criticism has been quite superficial. ... This is the century of the doctrinaire, and skepticism is in bad odor."

[6] Ch. Maurras, *Anatole France poètique et poète* (Paris, Plon, 1934).

doctrine more successfully than a frontal attack by the liberal and capitalist ranks. The orthodox Marxists had, and have even today, the best of reasons for forgetting *citoyen* France. In fact, those guarding the dogmatic purity of the communist masses will always be wise to discourage any interest in the late comrade's subversive speculations. Where would his artistic "rehabilitation" lead?

The scholars who have criticized France *sine ira et studio* substantiated their verdicts more convincingly than some of France's younger *confrères*. But if one does not count the criticisms of Johannet[7] and other lesser Catholic critics, who attacked France's anticlericalism, there are only five scholars, Gottschalk, Cerf, Chevalier, Giraud and Blanck, who in major studies condemn France. Among these, only Cerf's condemnation is unreserved, but at the same time it is debatable because of its dogmatism and lack of evidence. Chevalier contradicts his own negative verdict by asking, at the very end of his conclusions, "Must we not admit him [France] to the gallant company of Boccaccio, and Erasmus and Chaucer and Rabelais and Montaigne?" Henri Peyre sums up the fundamental objections of contemporary scholarly critics to France's art in the review of Jean Sareil's recent study, *Anatole France et Voltaire*. Peyre calls France a "dilettante choyé par le succès."[8] Among the main reasons for this condemnation are France's lack of tragic sense, "que la mode aujourd'hui nous fait parader . . ."[9] and his adherence to tradition and his limited aesthetic horizons. Peyre blames France for not having understood his contemporaries, Baudelaire, Rimbaud, Nietzsche, and Mallarmé, and for remaining unaffected by their thought and aesthetic efforts. Nor, apparently, did France understand Zola and the younger generation, Gide, Claudel, Cézanne. Finally, Peyre concludes by saying:

Mais alors que Bergson, Sorel, Nietzsche, Jaurès lui-même créaient de l'avenir, France, érudit, antiquaire, conservateur dans son goût et même dans son style (n'en déplaise à M. Sareil) regardait obstinément vers le passé, sans toujours infuser à ce passé, à Montaigne, Voltaire, à Racine,

[7] René Johannet, *Anatole France, est-il un grand écrivain?* (Paris, Plon, 1925).
[8] Henri Peyre, "Sareil, Jean. *Anatole France et Voltaire*" (book review), *The French Review*, Vol. XXXV No. 3 (January 1962), p. 336.
[9] *Ibid.*, p. 335.

à Chénier ou au Parnasse, une vie nouvelle. Le verdict un peu sévère de la postérité n'est somme toute qu'à demi injuste.[10]

In other words, there is some justice in the negative judgments of Francean critics; but on the same basis one may conclude that some of these judgments are unjust and exaggerated. Peyre's last sentence could apply even to his own judgments: the term "dilettante" has many connotations and Peyre obviously does not use it in the same sense as Annette Antoniu in her study, *Anatole France, critique littéraire*, in which it is not a derogatory term.[11] Other critics may find that France, deeply with all his irony contemplated enough about the future and the metaphysical problems which preoccupied Nietzsche and his generation. One may draw a striking parallel between Nietzsche's Zarathustra, who preaches that God is dead and that the Promethean *Übermensch* is coming, and France's Satan, who advocates man's spiritual revolt against God and his return to Apollo, Dionysos, and the Muses. One could also compare some aspects of Baudelairean and Francean Satanism.[12] Some comments on Baudelaire in *La Vie*

[10] *Ibid.*, p. 336.

[11] Annette Antoniu, *Anatole France critique littéraire* (Paris Boivin, 1929), pp. 90-91), outlines the attitude of "dilettantes" in her discussion on Renan's *Dialogues Philosophiques,* which ushered in the era of "dillettantism". "Renan ne renia pas ses convictions de jeunesse, il resta toujours philologue et historien passioné – donc savant et par définition même, partisan de la science – mais en dehors de son activité d'érudit, sa pensée devint profondément sceptique. Dans une atmosphère encore chargée de scientisme, il osa soutenir l'idée d'un doute universel. ... Néanmoins, ce doute n'aboutit pas à la suppression du raisonnement et de la recherche scientifique ... l'homme continuera à demander à la nature et à la vie l'explication de leur mystère, ... se sont des problèmes auxquels on pense toujours, même en sachant bien qu'on ne les résoudra jamais. ... Seulement, comme il ne croit plus à une vérité absolue, la spéculation philosophique devient pour lui un simple jeu de l'esprit, un amusement de la pensée. Il renonce aussi à tout dogmatisme et à tout fanatisme." Another connotation of the term implies a certain superficiality of erudition and a shallow nonchalance in the choice, treatment, and solution of literary subjects. Precisely this second connotation seems to be implied in the term, "dilettante choyé par le succès". See also Dargan (*op. cit.*), who cites Souday, pp. 374-5, and Levaillant who cites, Bourget, Moreau, Seailles, Klein, Saulner and Renan. (*op. cit.*, pp. 191-192).

[12] J. P. Wickesham, ("Anatole France", *Pennsylvania University Lectures,* 1914-15, pp. 99-125), points out the similarity between France's and Carducci's sympathy for Lucifer: " ... Lucifer is the personification of science, progress and the human intellect, as pictured in Carducci's hymn to Satan."

littéraire indicate that France was quite aware of Baudelaire's significance. There are some similarities between Jaurès's and France's political engagement. The fact, that he did not make his art a servant of any political doctrine is a merit rather than drawback. The parallel between the Francean man from "L'Humainc tragédie" and Camus's Sisyphean heroes has already been mentioned.[13]

What Peyre calls "le sens tragique que la mode aujourd'hui nous fait parader" is not likely to remain an eternal fashion. New, brighter aesthetic perspectives may open. Readers and critics may tire of socially and psychoanalytically oriented art and return to humanism, to aesthetic tradition and to beauty. If this happens, France's star may rise once again.

[13] See this study, Ch. V., p. 120. See also Levaillant's conclusion (*op. cit.*, p. 832): "Albert Camus n'était pas loin d'un humanisme ainsi compris."

BIBLIOGRAPHY

A. WORKS BY ANATOLE FRANCE

Œuvres Complètes illustrées. (Paris, Calmann-Lévy. 1925-1935), I-XXV, edited by L. Carias and G. Le Prat. (Each volume ends with a "Bibliographie" compiled by M. Carias.)

Tome I.
7-119: *Alfred de Vigny*
127-413: *Poésies*
127-182: *Les Poèmes dorés*
185-246: *Idylles et Légendes*
249-361: *Les Noces corinthiennes*
363-397: *Leuconoë*
Etc.

Tome II.
3-134: *Jocaste*
137-262: *Le Chat maigre*
267-508: *Le Crime de Sylvestre Bonnard, Membre de l'Institut*

Tome III.
3-179: *Les Désirs de Jean Servien*
185-439: *Le Livre de mon ami*

Tome IV.
5-118: *Nos Enfants*
123-352: *Balthasar:*
123-148: "Balthasar"
151-153: "Le Réséda du Curé"
157-174: "M. Pigeonneau"
177-193: "La Fille de Lilith"
197-212: "Laeta Acilia"
215-226: "L'Œuf rouge"
229-352: "Abeille"

Tome V.
5-213: *Thaïs*
219-463: *L'Étui de nacre:*

219-238: "Le Procurateur de Judée"
241-246: "Amycus et Célestin"
249-259: "La Légende des Saintes Oliverie et Liberette"
263-276: "Sainte Euphrosine"
279-283: "Scolastica"
287-298: "Le Jongleur de Notre-Dame"
301-308: "La Messe des Ombres"
311-324: "Leslie Wood"
327-335: "Gestas"
339-350: "Le Manuscrit d'un médecin de village"
353-397: "Mémoires d'un Volontaire"
401-412: "L'Aube"
415-425: "Madame de Luzy"
429-432: "La Mort Accordée"
435-441: "Anecdote de Floréal An II"
445-453: "Le Petit Soldat de plomb"
457-463: "La Perquisition"

Tome VI.

3-662: *La Vie littéraire*
13-521: *Première Série:*
13- 19: "Hamlet à la Comédie-Française"
20- 24: "Sérénus"
25- 33: "La réception de M. Léon Say à l'Académie Française"
34- 42: "M. Alexandre Dumas moraliste"
43- 51: La jeune fille d'autrefois et la jeune fille d'aujourd'hui"
52- 61: "M. Guy de Maupassant et les conteurs français"
62- 73: "Le journal de Benjamin Constant"
74- 82: "Un roman et un ordre du jour. – Le cavalier Miseray"
83- 91: "A propos du *Journal des Goncourt*"
92-101: "M. Leconte de Lisle à l'Académie Française"
102-110: "Sur le Quai Malaquais. – M. Alexander Dumas et son discours"
111-123: "L'Hypnotisme dans la littérature. – Marfa"
124-134: "Le prince de Bismarck"
135-143: "Balzac"
144-154: "François Coppée. – Frédéric Plessis"
155-163: "Marie Bashkirtseff"
164-172: "Les Fous dans la littérature"
173-184: "Le chevalier de Florian: les félibres à la fête de sceaux"
185-196: "A propos de l'inauguration de la statue d'Armand Carrel à Rouen"
197-203: "Louis de Ronchaud, souvenirs"
204-214: "La terre"
215-228: "M. Thiers historien"
229-238: "Correspondence de Marie-Louise"
239-250: "La reine Catherine"
251-259: "Pour le latin"
260-267: "Propos de rentrée: La terre et la langue"
268-279: "M. Becq de Fouquières"
280-285: "M. Cuvillier-Fleury"

286-291: "M. Ernest Renan, historien des origines"
292-299: "La vertu en France"
300-307: "George Sand et l'idéalisme dans l'art"
308-314: "Mensonges, par M. Paul Bourget"
315-321: "L'amour exotique. – Madame Chrysanthème"
335-662: *Deuxième Série*
335-342: "M. Alexandre Dumas Fils"
343-349: " 'Les jouets d'enfants,' par M. Camille Lemonnier"
350-358: "Gustave Flaubert"
359-365: "M. Guy de Maupassant"
366-375: "*Le Bonheur,* par Sully-Prudhomme"
376-385: "Mérimée"
384-391: "Hors de la littérature"
392-400: "Bibliophilie"
401-408: "Les criminels"
409-417: "La mort et les petits dieux"
418-425: "La Grande encyclopédie"
426-427: "M. Henri Meilhac à l'Académie Française"
428-436: "Un poète oublié: Saint-Cyr de Rayssac"
437-445: "Les torts de l'histoire"
446-454: "Sur le scepticisme"
455-463: "Euripide"
464-468: "Les marionnettes de M. Signoret"
469-486: "La mère et la fille: *Madame de Sabran et Madame de Custine,* par M. A. Bardoux"
487-492: "M. Jules Lemaître"
493-503: "1814"
504-514: "Demain"
515-525: "M. Charles Morice"
526-537: "Le grand Saint Antoine"
538-545: "Anthologie"
546-548: "La sagesse de Gyp: *Les séducteurs, Mademoiselle Loulou*"
559-569: "Anthologie"
570-579: "M. Gaston Paris et la littérature française au moyen âge"
580-587: "Lexique"
588-594: "La pureté de M. Zola"
595-602: *La Tempête*
603-608: "*La tresse blonde,* par Gilbert-Augustin Thierry"
609-617: "*Brave fille,* par Fermand Calmettes"
618-624: "*Histoire du peuple d'Israël,* Tome II, par Ernest Renan"
625-630: "L'éloquence de la tribune. – Le sénat"
631-638: "Roman et magie"
639-645: "M. Octave Feuillet: *Le divorce de Juliette*"
646-662: "Jeanne d'Arc et la poésie. – Vallerand de la Varanne. – M. Ernest Prarond"

Tome VII.

3-717: *La Vie littéraire*
15-379: *Troisième Série*
15- 22: "Pourquoi sommes-nous tristes?"

23- 31: "Hrotswitha aux marionnettes"
32- 39: "Charles Baudelaire"
40- 47: "Rabelais"
48- 55: "Barbey d'Aurevilly"
56- 62: "Paul Arène"
63- 84: "La morale et la science"
85- 95: "Contes chinois. *Histoire de la dame à l'éventail blanc*"
96-122: "Chansons populaires de l'ancienne France. 1. Chansons d'amour. II. Le soldat. III. Chansons de labour"
123-131: "Villiers de l'Isle-Adam"
132-142: "Un moine égyptien"
143-152: "Léon Hennique"
153-164: "Le poète de la Bresse, Gabriel Vicaire"
165-178: "Le baron Denon"
179-186: "Maurice Spronck"
187-203: "Une famille de poètes: Barthélemy Tisseur, Jean Tisseur, Clair Tisseur"
204-211: "Rèveries astronomiques"
212-225: "M. Maurice Bouchor et l'histoire de Tobie. – Histoire des deux amants d'Auvergne"
226-235: "Joséphin Péladan"
236-246: "Sur Jeanne d'Arc"
247-256: "Sous les Galeries de l'Odéon"
257-266: "Édouard Rod"
266-277: "J.-H. Rosny"
278-285: "François Coppée"
286-295: "Les idées de Gustave Flaubert"
296-304: "Paul Verlaine"
305-316: "Dialogues des vivants: *La Bête humaine*"
317-328: "Nouveaux dialogues des morts: *Une gageure*"
329-339: "Une journée à Versailles"
340-351: "Auguste Vacquerie"
352-362: "Octave Feuillet"
363-370: "Bouddhisme. *Histoire de la courtisane Vasavadatta et du marchand Oupagoupta*"
371-379: "Les chansons du chat-noir"
393-717: *Quatrième Série*
393-401: "Madame Ackermann"
402-409: "Notre cœur"
417-426: "La jeunesse de M. de Barante"
427-433: "Mysticisme et science"
434-443: "César Borgia"
444-450: "M. James Darmesteter"
451-478: "Contes et chansons populaires. Jean-Francois Bladé, Albert Meyrac"
479-491: "Le P. Didon et son livre sur Jésus-Christ"
492-511: "Cléopâtre"
512-521: "Madame Judith Gautier"
522-531: "M. Jean Moréas"

532-540: "Apologie pour le plagiat. *Le fou et l'obstacle*"
541-550: "Apologie pour le plagiat. Molière et Scarron"
551-561: "Jules Tellier"
562-578: "La rame d'Ulysse. Lettres de M. Eugène Pottier; M. A. Ed. Cuaignet; M. P. Lalanne; M. Cunisset-Carnot; M. P. Clairin; M. Gustave Friteau"
579-591: "Blaise Pascal et M. Joseph Bertrand"
592-599: "M. Maurice Barrès. *Le Jardin de Bérénice*"
600-607: "Théodore de Banville"
607-617: "M. Gaston Boissier"
618-630: "L'empereur Julien"
631-640: "Gyp: *Une passionnette*"
641-652: "J.-J. Weiss'
653-660: "Madame de la Fayette et M. le comte d'Haussonville"
661-667: "Un poète breton: M. Charles de Goffic"
668-677: "Albert Glatigny"
678-684: "M. Marcel Schwob"
685-703: "Madame de la Sablière, d'après des documents inédits"
704-717: "Mithridate"

Tome VIII.
3-304: *La Rôtisserie de la Reine Pédauque*
309-511: *Les Opinions de M. Jérôme Coignard*

Tome IX.
5-390: *Le Lys rouge*
395-535: *Le Jardin d'Epicure*

Tome X.
5-260: *Le Puits de Sainte Claire:*
5- 12: "Prologue"
15- 40: "Saint Satyre"
43- 56: "Les Guido Cavalcanti"
59- 65: "Lucifer"
69- 73: "Les Pains noirs"
77-106: "Le Joyeux Buffalmacco"
109-113: "La Dame de Vérone"
117-211: "L'Humaine Tragédie"
215-222: "Le Mystère du Sang"
225-233: "La Caution"
237-247: "Histoire de Doña Maria d'Avalos et de Don Fabricio, duc d'Andria"
251-260: "Bonaparte à San Miniato"
263-516: *Pierre Nozière*

Tome XI.
5-222: *L'Orme du Mail*
225-453: *Le Mannequin d'Osier*

Tome XII.
3-277: *L'Anneau d'améthyste*

281-551: *M. Bergeret à Paris*

Tome XIII.
3-115: *Clio:*
3- 23: "Le Chanteur de Kymé"
25- 69: "Komm l'Atrébate"
71- 85: "Farinata degli Uberti ou la Guerre civile"
87- 94: "Le Roi Boit"
95-115: "La Muiron"
119-353: *Histoire comique*
359-557: *Sur la Pierre blanche:*
377-505: "Gallion"
507-557: "Par la Porte de corne ou par la porte d'ivoire"

Tome XIV.
9-229: *Crainquebille, Putois, Riquet et plusieurs autres récits profitables:*
9- 52: "Crainquebille"
53- 76: "Putois"
77- 84: "Riquet"
85- 92: "Pensées de Riquet"
93-102: "La Cravate"
103-114: "Les Grandes Manoeuvres à Montil"
115-124: "Émile"
125-136: "Adrienne Buquet"
137-152: "La Pierre gravée"
153-158: "La Signora Chiara"
159-168: "Les Juges intègres"
169-178: "Le Christ de l'océan"
179-190: "Jean Marteau"
191-198: "La Loi est morte mais le juge est vivant"
199-210: "Monsieur Thomas"
211-220: "Vol Domestique"
221-229: "Edmée ou la Charité bien placée"
239-304: *Crainquebille* (pièce)
313-484: *Le Mannequin d'Osier* (pièce)
491-539: *Au Petit Bonheur*

Tome XV.
3-598: *Vie de Jeanne d'Arc,* I

Tome XVI.
3-464: *Vie de Jeanne d'Arc,* II

Tome XVII.
5-265: *Rabelais*
269- 95: *Auguste Comte*
299-325: *Pierre Laffitte*

Tome XVIII.
3-420: *L'Ile des Pingouins*
433-481: *La Comédie de Celui qui épousa une femme muette*

Tome XIX.
5-121: *Les Contes de Jacques Tournebroche:*
5- 16: "Le Gab d'Olivier"
19- 38: "Le Miracle de la Pie"
41- 59: "Frère Joconde"
63- 66: "La Picarde, la Poitevine, la Tourangelle, la Lyonnaise et la Parisienne"
69- 82: "La Leçon bien apprise"
85- 88: "De une horrible Paincture"
91- 99: "Les Etrennes de Mademoiselle de Doucine"
103-121: "Mademoiselle Roxane"
127-343: *Les Sept Femmes de la Barbe-Bleue et autres contes merveilleux*
127-163: "Les Sept Femmes de la Barbe-Bleue, d'après des documents authentiques"
167-213: "Le Miracle du grand Saint Nicolas"
217-241: "Histoire de la Duchesse de Cicogne et de M. de Boulingrin"
245-343: "La Chemise"

Tome XX.
3-316: *Les Dieux ont soif*

Tome XXI.
7-335: *Le Génie latin:*
7- 16: "Daphnis et Chloé"
17- 36: "La Reine de Navarre"
37- 69: "Paul Scarron"
71-102: "Remarques sur la Langue de la Fontaine"
103-141: "Molière"
143-169: "Jean Racine"
171-181: "Alain-René Le Sage"
183-208: "Les Aventures de l'Abbé Prévost"
209-243: "Bernardin de Saint-Pierre"
245-270: "Chateaubriand"
271-274: "Xavier de Maistre"
275-286: "Benjamin Constant"
287-310: "Sainte-Beuve Poète"
311-335: "Albert Glatigny"
339-370: *Les Poèmes du Souvenir*

Tome XXII.
3-322: *La Révolte des anges*

Tome XXIII.
5-281: *Le Petit Pierre*
285-564: *La Vie en fleur*

Tome XXIV.
5-367: *Pages d'Histoire et de littérature.* I
5- 27: "Madame de la Sablière, notice"
31- 46: "Le Marquis de Sade, notice"
49- 58: "Jocko, notice"

61-122: "Histoire d'Henriette d'Angleterre, étude"
125-143: "La Princesse de Clèves, préface"
147-150: "Le Palais de Fontainebleau, préface"
153-158: "Le Café Procope"
161-163: "Vieux Péchés, préface"
167-184: "Le Faust de Goethe, lettre préface"
187-195: "Le Dernier Abbé, préface"
199-221: "Promenades félibréennes"
225-248: "Hérodias, préface"
251-255: "l'Année littéraire, préface"
259-264: "Un Hollandais à Paris en 1891, préface"
267-333: "l'Elvire de Lamartine"
337-348: "Le Roi Candaule, préface"
351-352: "Le Chemin de Paradis, épigramme"
355-359: "Jeunes Madames, préface"
363-367: "Lettre de Sicile sur l'Oaristys"

Tome XXV.
5-413: *Pages d'Histoire et de littérature,* II:
5- 8: "Dîner de Molière, discours"
11- 18: "Le monument de Marceline Desbordes-Valmore, discours"
21- 31: "Lorenzaccio, étude"
35- 39: "Mentis, préface"
43- 45: "Les Plaisirs et les Jours, préface"
49- 60: "Alphonse Daudet, étude"
63- 66: "Histoire du chien de Brisquet, préface"
75- 81: "Pallas Athéna, étude"
85- 89: "Les Arts et les Artistes, préface"
93- 97: "Le Tombeau de Molière, hommage"
101-117: "P.-P. Prud'hon, étude"
121-128: "Petits Châteaux de Bohème, préface"
131-132: "Petite Histoire parlementaire, préface"
135-141: "La Reine Cléopâtre, préface"
145-148: "Pensées philosophiques, préface"
151-158: "Les Heures latines, préface"
162-182: "Stendhal, étude"
185-188: "Les Mémoires d'un rat, préface"
191-193: "La Garçonne, préface"
197-206: "Le Livre de la pitié et de la mort, préface"
209-219: "Sages et Poètes d'Asie, préface"
223-251: "Marguerite"
255-282: "Le Comte Morin"
285-293: "Pâques ou la Délivrance"
297-305: "Monsieur Patru"
309-311: "La Terre"
315-332: "Le Miracle de l'Avare"
335-343: "L'Escalade"
347-353: "Dialogue aux Enfers"
357-359: "La Terre et l'homme"
363-391: "Discours de Réception à l'Académie française"

393-413: "Une des plus grandes découvertes du siècle"

Tome XXVI.
La Vie littéraire, cinquième série (Paris, Calmann-Lévy, 1949):
1- 9: "La critique et l'École normale"
10- 20: "M. Édouard Drumont et la question juive"
21- 35: "Lohengrin à Paris"
36- 55: "Taine et Napoléon"
56- 63: "Les débuts de Victorien Sardou"
64- 70: "Essai philosophique sur le logement"
71- 77: "Souvenirs sur Champfleury"
78- 86: "Pierre Loti: *Le Roman d'un enfant*"
87- 93: "A propos de *Thermidor*"
94-102: "L'Argent"
103-117: "Enquête sur l'évolution littéraire"
118-125: "Paul Verlaine: *Mes hôpitaux*"
126-135: "Elvire"
136-143: "Littérature socialiste"
144-155: "Le Missel des femmes"
156-165: "Un prédicateur populaire: Olivier Maillard"
166-176: "La Vie littéraire en 1846: Charles Monselet"
177-184: "Catherine Théot"
185-194: "La Fête de l'être suprème"
195-203: "Lamennais"
204-230: "Un nouvel évangile: Jésus à Paris"
231-237: "La statue de Baudelaire"
238-243: "Ernest Renan"
244-252: "Robert de Montesquiou: *Les Chauves-souris*"
253-259: "Marcel Schwob: *Le Roi au masque d'or*"
260-269: "Rémy de Gourmont: *Le Latin mystique*"
270-278: "Stéphane Mallarmé: *Vers et prose*"
279-285: "Maurice Barrès: *L'Ennemi des lois*"
286-291: "Forain"
292-301: "José-Maria de Hérédia: *Les Trophées*"
302-306: "Hippolyte Taine"
307-312: "Jean Lahor: L'Illusion"
313-319: "Paul Hervieu: *Peints par eux-mêmes*"
320-330: "M. Jules Soury"
331-337: "Réponse à M. Jules de Sohet"
338-342: "Note relative à *l'Enquete sur l'évolution littéraire* de Jules Huret"

B. WORKS CONCERNING ANATOLE FRANCE

I. *Books*

Ahlstrom, Alvida, *Le Moyen Age dans l'Œuvre d'Anatole France* (Paris, Editions Les Belles Lettres, 1930). Thèse de doctorat, Strasbourg.

Antoniu, Annette, *Anatole France critique littéraire* (Paris, Boivin, 1929).

Axelrad, Jacob, *Anatole France, a Life Without Illusion (1844-1924)* (New York, Harper, 1924).

Ayrolles, Abbé Jean-Baptiste Joseph, *La Prétendue Vie de Jeanne d'Arc de M. Anatole France, monument de cynicisme sectaire* (Lyon, Vitte, 1910).

Bainville, Jacques, *Au Seuil du Siècle* ("Les Dieux ont soif." "Les Vieux attendrissements de M. Anatole France.") (Paris, Capitolc, 1927).

Bancquart, Marie-Claire, *Anatole France polémiste* (Paris, Nizet, 1962).

Bédé, Albert et Jean LeBail, *Anatole France vu par la critique d'aujourd'hui* (Paris, Editions Les Belles Lettres [Études françaises 5e cahier], 1925).

Blanck, Robert, *Anatole France als Stilkünstler in seinen Romanen, = Arbeiten zur Romanischen Philologie,* Nr. 7 (Münster, 1934).

Boillot, Felix François, *L'Humour d'Anatole France* (Paris, Les Presses Universitaires de France, 1933).

Borély, Marthe, *La Femme et l'Amour dans l'œuvre d'Anatole France* (Paris, Crès, 1917).

Brandes, Georg, *Anatole France* (Berlin, Bard, Marquardt, 1928).

Bresky, Dushan, "The Art of Anatole France", unpublished doctoral thesis (on multilith), University of Washington, Seattle, May 1962.

Brousson, Jean-Jacques, *Anatole France en pantoufles* (Paris, Crès, 1924).

Cadieux, Doris Jean, "Anatole France's Ideas of Women", unpublished thesis submitted for the degree of M.A., University of Washington, 1941.

Calmette, Pierre, *La grande passion d'Anatole France* (Paris, Seheur, 1929).

Carias, Léon, *Anatole France* (Paris, Editions Rieder, 1931).

Cerf, Barry, *Anatole France. The Degeneration of a Great Artist* (New York, Lincoln, MacVeagh, 1926).

Chevalier, Haakon M., *The Ironic Temper. Anatole France and His Time* (New York, Oxford University Press, 1932).

Clerc, Charly, *Le Génie du Paganisme* (Paris, Payot, 1926).

Clouard, Henri, *Histoire de la littérature française du symbolisme à nos jours – 1885 à 1914* (Paris, Editions Albin Michel, 1947).

Cor, Raphael, *Anatole France et la pensée contemporaine* (Paris, E. Pelletan, 1909).

Corday, Michel, *Anatole France d'après ses confidences et ses souvenirs* (Paris, Flammarion, 1927).

Dargan, Edwin Preston, *Anatole France,* publication in cooperation with MLAA Oxford University Press, 1937).

Des Hons, Gab., *Anatole France et Racine, ou la clé de l'art francien* (Paris, Armand Colin, 1927).

Desonay, Fernand, *Le Rêve hellénique chez les poètes parnassiens* (Paris, Champion, 1928).

Durant, Will, *The Adventures in Genius* (New York, Simon and Schuster, 1931).

Faguet, Emile, *Propos littéraires,* Vols. I and III (Paris, Lecène et Oudin, 1902).

Gaffiot, Maurice, *Les Théories sociales d'Anatole France* (Alger, E. Grandet, 1923).

George, W. L., *Anatole France* (London, Nisbet, 1915).

Giraud, Victor, *Anatole France* (Paris, Desclée de Brouwer, 1935).

Gsell, Paul, *Anatole France and His Circle,* translated by Frederic Lees (London, John Lane, 1922).

Guerard, Albert Léon, *Five Masters of French Romance. Anatole France, Loti, Bourget, Barrès, Romain Rolland* (London, Unwinn, 1916).
Harry, Myriam, *Trois ombres, Huysmans, Lemaître, Anatole France* (Paris, Flammarion, 1932).
Jefferson, Carter, *Anatole France: The Politics of Skepticism* (New Brunswick, N. J., Rutgers University Press, 1965).
Johannet, René, *Anatole France, est-il un grand écrivain?* (Paris, Plon, 1925).
Kuehne, O. R., *A Study of the Thaïs Legend* (Philadelphia, University of Pennsylvania, 1922).
Lanson, Gustave *L'Art de la prose* (Paris, Librairie des Annales politiques et littéraires, 1908).
Le Brun, Roger, *Anatole France* (Paris, Sansot, 1904).
Le Goff, Marcel, *Anatole France à la Béchellerie* (Paris, Delteil, 1924).
Lemaître, Jules, *Les Contemporains. Études et portraits littéraires,* (Paris, Lecène et Oudin, Vol. I, 1902; Vol. III, 1905).
—, *Litterary Impressions,* translated by A. W. Evans (London, Daniel O'Connor, 1921).
Levaillant, Jean, *Essai sur l'évolution intellectuelle d'Anatole France, Les aventures du scepticisme* (Paris, Colin, 1965).
Marvaud, Jean, *Anatole France, écrivain français* (Paris, Lefebvre, 1962).
Masson, G.-A., *Anatole France: Son œuvre* (Paris, Nouvelle Revue Critique, 1923).
Maurras, Ch., *Anatole France politique et poète* (Paris, Plon, 1934).
May, James Lewis, *Anatole France. The Man and His Work* (London, John Lane, 1924).
Michaut, G., *Anatole France* (Paris, Tongemoing, 1913).
Nousanne, Henri de, *Anatole France philosophe sceptique?* (Paris, Peyronnet, 1924).
Pouquet, Mme. Jeanne, *Le Salon de Madame Armand Caillavet* (Paris, Hachette, 1926).
Roujon, J., *La Vie et les opinions d'Anatole France* (Paris, Plon, 1925).
Sareil, Jean, *Anatole France et Voltaire* (Paris: Minard; Genève: Droz, 1961).
Schlumbohm, Dietrich, *Der Aufstand der Engel, Anatole France und seine Literarischen Vorläufer* (Hamburg, Romanisches Seminar der Universität Hamburg, 1966).
Shanks, Lewis Piaget, *Anatole France* (Chicago, The Open Court Publishing Company, 1919).
Suffel, Jacques, *Anatole France* (Paris, Le Seuil, 1954).
Stewart, Herbert Leslie, *Anatole France the Parisian* (New York, Dodd, Mead Co., 1927).
Truc, Gonzaque, *Anatole France, l'artiste et le penseur* (Paris, Garnier, 1924).
Valéry, Paul, *Discours de réception à l'Académie française* (Paris, Gallimard, 1927).
Walton, Loring Baker, *Anatole France and the Greek World* (Durham, N.C., Duke University Press, 1950).
Whitridge, Arnold, *Critical Ventures in Modern French Literature* (New York, Scribner, 1924).
Woolsey, Pierce Edgar, "Greek and Latin Influence in the Work of Anatole France", unpublished doctoral dissertation, Cornell University, Ithaca, N.Y., 1932.

II. *Articles*

Becker, A., "La Prose rythmée dans 'La Révolte des anges', *Mercure de France,* May 16, 1914, pp. 320-325.

Billy, André, "Anatole France devant la critique contemporaine", *Revue de Paris* Vol. LII, No. 3, (1945), pp. 6-8.

Bresky, Dushan, "Rhythm and Rhyme in France's Prose", *Proceedings of the 14th Annual Meeting of the Pacific Northwest Conference on Foreign Languages,* April 18-20, 1963.

—, "Le Verdict à demi injuste", *Actes abrégés* (Vancouver, June 1965). *Proceedings of the annual meeting of the A.P.F.U.C.*

Cain, Julien, "Le Drame amoureux du 'Lys rouge' fut inspiré à France par son amie . . . " *Le Figaro Littéraire,* September 20, 1958, p. 3.

Carias, Léon, "Quelques sources d'Anatole France", *La Grande Revue,* December 25, 1912, pp. 725-737.

Clouard, H., "La Sagesse d'Anatole France", *La Revue critique des idées et des livres,* August 10, 1912, pp. 257-271.

Crawford, J. P. Wickesham, "Anatole France", *Pennsylvania University Lectures,* 1914-1915, pp. 99-125.

Dargan, Edwin Preston, "Anatole France and the Imp of the Perverse", *The Dial,* February 8, 1919.

Delakas, Daniel I., "Thomas Wolfe and Anatole France: A Study of Some Unpublished Experiments'", *Comparative Literature,* Vol. IX (1957), pp. 33-50.

Duhamel, Georges, "Anatale France, gardien du language", *Revue de Paris,* June 1945, pp. 1-5.

Fournier, Charles, "Anatole France l'humaniste", *Monde Nouveau,* October 15, 1924, pp. 1-5.

Gottschalk, Walter, "Anatole France der Dichter und sein Werk", *Zeitschrift für die französische Sprache und Literatur,* Vol. 50 (1927).

Gregh, Fernand, "Le Style", *Les Annales politiques et littéraires,* July – December 1924, p. 421.

Guehenno, J., "Anatole France ou le dernier sage", *Grande Revue,* April 14, 1924, pp. 198-219.

Hariel-Hoche, Claude, "Anatole France, le payen", *Monde Nouveau,* October 15, 1924.

Havens, George R., "Anatole France and the French Revolution", *American Society Legion of Honor Magazine,* Vol. XXVI, pp. 229-239.

Holbrook, W. C., "A Note on the Technique of Anatole France", *Modern Language Notes,* (1932), Vol. 47.

Huse, H. R., "Art and beauty", *Quarterly Review of Literature,* I, No. 1, (Autumn, 1943), pp. 49-53.

Lanson, Gustave, "La Vie et l'œuvre", *Les Annales Politiques* et littéraires, Vol. 83, (July – December 1924), p. 420.

Lalo, Charles, "Anatole France et l'esthétique", *Le Lys Rouge,* No. 40 (1948).

Levaillant, Jean, "Aspects de la création littéraire chez Anatole France", *Revue de l'histoire littéraire de la France,* October-December 1955, pp. 469-91.

Mongrédien, Georges, "L'Œuvre poétique d'Anatole France", *Revue mondiale,* May 15, 1921, pp. 179-187.

P., G. Anonymous article entitled "Opinions allemandes sur Anatole France", *La Revue rhénane,* November 1924, pp. 74-77 contains a French résumé of the following essays by E. R. Curtius (*Kölnische Zeitung,* October 13, 1924) Fritz Schohnöfer (*Frankfurter Zeitung,* October 15, 1924).

Peyre, Henri, Book review: "Sareil, Jean, *Anatole France et Voltaire, The French Review,* Vol. XXXV, No. 3, (January, 1962), pp. 334-36.

Poizat, A., "Anatole France, poète et critique", *La Muse française,* Vol. III, (April 10, 1924), pp. 370-82.

Rat, Maurice, "Grammairiens et amateurs de beau langage; Anatole France", *Vie et langage,* No. 123, (June 1962).

Ryland, Hobart, "Anatole France, Le Marquis de Sade, et Courtilz de Sandras", *Kentucky Foreign Language Quarterly,* Vol. IV, pp. 200-04.

Schaffer, Aaron, "Anatole France and Poetry", *Publications of the Modern Languages Association of America,* March, 1932, pp. 262-82.

Stapfer, Paul, "L'Art et la matière chez Anatole France", *Bibliothèque Universelle et Revue Suisse,* Vol. XXIII, pp. 225-252, 565-94.

The Times Literary Supplement, (Sept. 29, 1966), No. 3, p. 370. "Olympus Redivivus? Anatole France's reputation", anonymous article.

Triebel, L. A., "Anatole France: the dreamer", *Contemporary Review,* No. 1000 (April, 1949), pp. 220-25.

Walton, Loring B., "A Manuscript Fragment of Thaïs: its stylistic and other Revelations",*Publications of the Modern Languages Association of America,* Vol. LXXI, No. 5.

Will, J. S., "Anatole France and his critics", *University of Toronto Quarterly,* Vol. X (July, 1941), pp. 435-449.

Woolbridge, B. M., "Sylvestre Bonnard and Philetas", *Modern Language Notes,* Vol. XXXVII (1922), pp. 56-58.

—, "The Original Inspiration of 'Le Procurateur de Judée' ",*Modern Languages Notes,* Vol. XL (1925) pp. 483-485.

Zully, Flloyd. Jr., "Anatole France and Dante", *Modern Languages Notes,* Vol. LXIX, No. 6, (June, 1954), p. 420.

C. WORKS ON AESTHETICS USED OR CONSIDERED IN THIS STUDY; GENERAL WORKS

Beardsley, Monroe C., *Aesthetics Problems in the Philosophy of Criticism* (New York, Harcourt, Brace [c] 1958).

Beck, M., "Cognative Character of Aesthetic Enjoyment", *Journal of Aesthetics,* Vol. 3 (1945), pp. 55-61.

Bergson, Henri, *Laughter, an Essay on the Meaning of Comic* (London, Macmillan, 1913).

Boileau, Nicolas, *Le Lutrin, L'Art Poétique* (Paris, Larousse, 1934).

Brandin, Louis M. and Hartog, W. G., *A Book of French Prosody* (London, Blackie, 1904).

Briggs, Thomas H., *Poetry and its Enjoyment* (New York, Bureau of Publications Teachers' College Columbia University [c], 1957).

Burke, Edmund, *A Philosophical Enquiry into the Origin of our Ideas of the*

Sublime and Beautiful (London, J. T. Boulton, [c] 1958).

Burke, Kenneth, *The Philosophy of Literary Form* (Louisiana, State University Press, 1941).

Camus, Albert, *La Peste.* (Paris, Gallimard, 1947).

Cressot, Marcel, *Le style et ses techniques; précis d'analyse stylistique,* 3e éd. Paris, Presses Universitaires de France, 1956).

Cuisenier, André, *L'Art de Jules Romains, Jules Romains et l'unanimisme* (Paris, Flammarion, [c] 1948).

Daudet, Léon, *Mes Idées esthétiques* (Paris, Fayard, [c] 1939).

Dějiny československé literatury, Josef Hrabák, ed., 3 Vols. (Praha, 1959).

Dondo, Mathurin M., *Vers libre, a logical development of French verse* (Paris, Champion, 1922).

Drew, Elizabeth, *Discovering Poetry* (New York, W. W. Norton [c] 1933).

Eastman, Max, *Enjoyment of Poetry with Anthology for Enjoyment of Poetry* (New York, Scribner, 1954).

—, *The Sense of Humor* (New York, Scribner, 1922).

Egri, Lajos, *The Art of Dramatic Writing* (New York, Simon and Schuster, 1946).

Gandon, Yves, *Le Démon du style* (Paris, Plon, 1938).

Gmelin, Hermann, *Das Prinzip der Imitatio in den romanischen Literaturen der Renaissance,* = *Romanische Forschungen,* Vol. XLVI, published as a separate work. (Erlengen, 1932).

Goethe, J. W., *Goethes Werke,* Vol. III (Hamburg, Christian Wegner, 1949).

Gourmont, Rémy de, *Esthétique de la langue française* (Paris, Mercure de France, 1923).

Grammont, Maurice, *Petit Traité de versification française,* 16e ed. (Paris, Colin, 1958).

Gregory, I., *The Nature of Laughter* (New York, Harcourt, 1924).

Greig, J. Y. T., *The Psychology of Laughter and Comedy* (London, Allen and Unwinn, 1923).

Gutman, René-Albert, *Introduction à la lecture des poètes français* (Paris, Renée LaCoste, 1961).

Homer, *Homeri Opera.* Ed. D. B. Monro and T. W. Allen (Oxford, Clarendon Press, 1951).

Hytier, Jean, *Le plaisir poétique, étude de psychologie* (Paris, Presses Universitaires de France, 1926).

—, *Les techniques modernes du vers français* (Paris, Presses Universitaires de France, 1926).

Krafft, Jacques G., *Essai sur l'esthétique de la prose* (Paris, Vrin, 1952).

Leacock, Stephen Butler, *Humour: – its theory and technique with examples and samples* (London, John Lane, 1935).

Suppl. XIII ([Leipzig], 1904).

Mann, Thomas, *Gesammelte Werke.* "Doktor Faustus", (Oldenburg, S. Fisher Verlag, [c.] 1960).

Marshall, Henry Rutgers, *The Beautiful* (London, Macmillan, 1924).

A Modern Book of Esthetics, an anthology ed. by Melvin Rader (New York, Holt, 1953).

Monro, D. H., *Argument of Laughter* (Melbourne, Melbourne University Press, 1951).

Morier, Henri, *Dictionnaire de Poétique et de Rhétorique* (Paris, Presses Universitaires de France, 1961).

Munro, Thomas. *Toward Science in Aesthetics* (New York, Liberal Arts Press, 1956).

Nahm, Milton Charles, *Aesthetic Experience and Its Presuppositions* (New York, London, Harper, 1946).

Nowottny, Winifred, *The Language Poets Use* (London, The Athlone Press University of London, 1962).

Rader, Melvin, "The Root Values of Art", *Journal of Philosophy,* Vol. 38 (1941), pp. 324-332.

Randall, John Herman Jr., *The Making of the Modern Mind* (Boston Houghton, Mifflin, [c.] 1940).

Rudler, Gustave, *Les techniques de la Critique et de l'Histoire Littéraires* (London, Oxford University Press, 1923).

Santayana, George, *The Sense of Beauty Being the Outlines of Aesthetic Theory* (New York, The Modern Library, [c.] 1955).

Sayce, Richard A., *Style in French prose: a method of analysis* (Oxford, Clarendon Press, 1953).

Sedgewick, G. G., *Of Irony Especially in Drama* (Toronto, The University of Toronto Press, 1935).

Smith, S. Stephenson, *The Craft of the Critic* (New York, Crowell, 1931).

Sparshott, F. E., *The Structure of Aesthetics* (Toronto, University of Toronto Press, 1963 .

The Oxford Book of Latin Verse, from the earliest fragments to the end of the 5th century A.D., chosen by H. W. Garrod (Oxford, Clarendon Press, 1912).

Thompson, J. A. R., *The Dry Mock, A Study of Irony in Drama* (Berkeley and Los Angeles, University of California Press, 1948).

Tourneur, Z., *Une Vie avec Blaise Pascal* (Paris, Vrin, 1943).

Wellek, René and Warren, Austin, *Theory of Literature* (New York, Harcourt Brave, 1949).

—, *A history of modern criticism: 1750-1950,* Vol. IV: *The late nineteenth century* (New Haven, Yale University Press, 1965).

Zielinski, Tadeusz. "Der Constructive Rhythmus in Cicero's Reden", *Philologus,* Suppl. XIII (Leipzig, 1904).

INDEX *

*This index includes names of authors, scholars, historical or literary characters, subjects and the titles of those works by A. F. discussed. References to literary heroes include an abbreviated title of the corresponding work. Major critical studies discussed are indexed only under the name of the pertaining critics in abbreviated form. For details consult also footnotes or the bibliography.